Community Policing

Can It Work?

WESLEY G. SKOGAN

NORTHWESTERN UNIVERSITY

WADSWORTH
CENGAGE Learning™

Australia • Brazil • Japan • Korea • Mexico • Singapore • Spain • United Kingdom • United States

WADSWORTH
CENGAGE Learning

Community Policing: Can It Work
Wesley G. Skogan

Criminal Justice Editor: Sabra Horne

Editorial Assistant: Paul Massicotte

Marketing Manager: Dory Schaeffer

Marketing Assistant: Neena Chandra

Project Manager, Editorial Production: Emily Smith

Print/Media Buyer: Doreen Suruki

Permissions Editor: Kiely Sexton

Production Service: Shepherd, Inc.

Copy Editor: Barb Baugh

Compositor: Shepherd, Inc.

Cover Designer: Yvo Riezebos

Cover Image: DigitalVision/ Getty Images

For product information and technology assistance, contact us at **Cengage Learning Customer & Sales Support, 1-800-354-9706**

For permission to use material from this text or product, submit all requests online at **www.cengage.com/permissions**
Further permissions questions can be emailed to **permissionrequest@cengage.com**

Library of Congress Control Number: 2003102661

ISBN-13: 978-0-534-62505-4

ISBN-10: 0-534-62505-3

Wadsworth
10 Davis Drive
Belmont, CA 94002
USA

Cengage Learning is a leading provider of customized learning solutions with office locations around the globe, including Singapore, the United Kingdom, Australia, Mexico, Brazil, and Japan. Locate your local office at **international.cengage.com/region**

Cengage Learning products are represented in Canada by Nelson Education, Ltd.

To learn more about Wadsworth, visit **www.cengage.com/wadsworth**

Purchase any of our products at your local college store or at our preferred online store **www.ichapters.com**

Printed in the United States of America
1 2 3 4 5   14 13 12 11 10

FD253

Community Policing

Can It Work?

WESLEY G. SKOGAN

NORTHWESTERN UNIVERSITY

Contents

FROM THE SERIES EDITOR vii

FOREWORD ix

PREFACE xii

ABOUT THE AUTHORS xiv

INTRODUCTION, BY WESLEY G. SKOGAN AND JEFFREY ROTH xvii

PART I

Are Police Changing? 1

1 *Trends in Community Policing* 3
Jeffrey A. Roth, Jan Roehl, and Calvin C. Johnson

2 *Community Policing and Police Organizations* 30
Jack R. Greene

PART II

Will the Public Get Involved?   55

3   *Representing the Community in Community Policing*   57
    Wesley G. Skogan

PART III

Will Police Officers Buy In?   77

4   *Can Police Adapt? Tracking the Effects of Organizational Reform
    over Six Years*   79
    Dennis P. Rosenbaum and Deanna L. Wilkinson

5   *Working the Street: Does Community Policing Matter?*   109
    William Terrill and Stephen D. Mastrofski

6   *Diving into Quicksand: Program Implementation and Police Subcultures*   136
    Richard L. Wood, Mariah Davis, and Amelia Rouse

PART IV

Can It Work?   163

7   *Community Policing and Problem Solving*   165
    Nick Tilley

8   *Why Don't Problems Get Solved?*   185
    John E. Eck

9   *Community Policing and the Quality of Life*   207
    Michael D. Reisig and Roger B. Parks

INDEX   228

From the Series Editor

This book is an outstanding addition to the Wadsworth Professionalism in Policing Series. It is easily the most thorough assessment of community policing to date, with contributions by all of the leading experts on the subject.

Community policing has been the most important innovation in American policing since the emergence of the professionalization movement one hundred years ago. Many important questions remain about this development. Have police departments in fact made real organizational changes reflecting community policing principles? Does community policing actually work, in terms of better police services and improved quality of life for neighborhood residents?

The answers to these questions are not easy. The special virtue of this collection of essays is that they explore the issues involved with the proper attention to their complexity. Chapter One examines the adoption of community policing from a broad national perspective. Chapters Two and Three address the question of the "community" in community policing. Several other chapters explore the impact of community policing on police officers. The final three chapters examine the effectiveness of community policing in terms of problem-solving and the quality of life at the neighborhood level.

The authors represented in this collection include scholars who have been most deeply involved in community policing research over the years. Because of the quality of their contributions, this volume will become the standard for assessments of community policing for many years to come.

Professor Samuel Walker
Department of Criminal Justice
University of Nebraska at Omaha

Foreword

I n the summer of 1984, ten police officers took to the streets of the Sunset Park neighborhood of Brooklyn, New York. They had volunteered to be part of at the Community Patrol Officer Project, an experiment launched by the New York City Police Department, working with the Vera Institute of Justice. Their precinct had been divided into ten beats, one for each officer. Each of them was now responsible for a small piece of Brooklyn.

Their assignment seemed simple: talk to the people who lived in these neighborhoods to learn about the community's problems. For the next several weeks, they walked up and down the streets, knocking on doors, introducing themselves to residents, announcing the new initiative, learning about problems, offering to help. Not everything went as planned. The local precinct started getting worried phone calls. "There's someone at the door impersonating a police officer."

This vignette illustrates the distance that had grown between the police and the community. Riding in radio cars, answering one call for service after another, dependent on the 911 system for their assignments, evaluated by how quickly they moved from call to call, limited in their communications with ordinary citizens, the police no longer made house calls, no longer asked how things were going, no longer sought the active partnership of the community they served. "Real" police would not knock on your door to ask about crime problems.

The concept of community policing was embraced by reformers as an antidote to these failings of the modern police. Many big ideas march behind the banner of community policing. The police will solve problems, not just respond to calls for service. The police will develop constructive new partnerships with the community, not serve as occupying forces. The police will be more effective at reducing and preventing crime. The morale of the police will improve as they see the fruits of their labor. Police organizations will become more decentralized, hierarchical structures will be flattened, and specialists imprisoned in outdated chains of command will be replaced by generalists more responsive to a changing world. The police will help organize communities so they can help themselves. Public trust in the police will increase as stereotypes dissolve and understanding is enhanced.

Community policing has promised so much. Now is a good time to step back and see what it has delivered. A solid body of research can now provide empirical foundations for answers to the tough questions. Much of it was funded by the National Institute of Justice and the Community Oriented Policing Services Office of the Clinton Administration, a time when I served as Director of National Institute of Justice.

Not surprising, the record is mixed, as the chapters in this volume attest. But we need to remind ourselves that community policing is more than a passing political slogan or operational fad. These ideas build on a long tradition of research and innovation.

The policing world had been experiencing the tremors of change for several years before these ten officers took to the streets of Brooklyn. In 1974, the Police Foundation released the findings of the Kansas City Preventive Patrol Experiment, which challenged the fundamentals of random patrol policing. Herman Goldstein's 1977 article on problem-oriented policing suggests that the unit of work, for the police, should be a problem, not a criminal event, thereby challenging the image of the police as crime fighters. The Newark Foot Patrol Experiment of the 1970s suggested that levels of fear could be reduced by placing officers on foot, a heresy in the era of motorized patrol. The Kennedy School of Government had just begun its Executive Session on Community Policing, a multiyear initiative to pool the wisdom of innovative police executives and the insights from research into a new concept of the police function.

So, in the longer view, the question is not whether community policing "works" in some mechanical sense, but whether the police function has evolved. Can the police return to the policing style of the 1970s? Will the public allow the police to remain unresponsive to citizens' demands and expectations? No, I think we can agree that the police have changed, the public's expectations of the police have changed, and the core concepts of community policing have become embedded in the discourse of local governance. The community policing movement has made a profound difference in the evolution of American policing.

But the barriers to these fundamental reforms are daunting. The culture of police organizations is highly resistant to change. The demands of the 911 system cannot easily be managed to allow more time for problem solving. Old habits and old stereotypes die hard. And the expectations for community policing have always been higher than any reform effort could deliver.

Yet the stakes are high, so any significant progress is encouraging. In a democratic society, the police play a critical role in providing for the safety of communities and enforcing the law. If, through the community policing movement, public trust in the police can be enhanced, crime and fear can be reduced, and respect for the rule of law can be strengthened, then the decades spent testing new ideas and recommitting to old ideals will have been good investments.

Jeremy Travis

Preface

Since the mid-1980s, there has been a vigorous debate over the role of the police in America's communities, one that has continued into the twenty-first century. New philosophies of policing are being debated in city halls, in newspaper offices, and at public policy conferences. Proponents of zero tolerance, problem solving, intelligence-driven policing, and geo-based accountability trade barbs, while they all jockey to take credit for the astonishing drop in crime taking place around them. From outside the room can be heard the voices of critics demanding an end to police brutality, racial profiling, and the criminalization of "driving while Black." None of them can point to convincing evidence—or, at least, to evidence that convinces those in other camps—that theirs is the right path. What they all have in common is a conviction that the dominant mode of policing at the beginning of the 1980s (disparaged, ironically, as the "professional" model) did not have as much value as *its* proponents proclaimed.

Nationally, community policing is certainly the most widely recognized of these new, replacement models. The concept is so widely known and popular with the public and city councils that it is hard to find a police chief that does not claim that his or her department is on board because they have adopted this or that community-friendly program. Beginning in 1995, the federal government spent almost $9 billion hiring officers who would be charged with doing more community policing, and many departments got bigger as a result. But in 2000, the government commissioned the National Research Council to review evidence of the effectiveness of community policing, and the committee charged with doing so (I was its chairman) found precious little to say about the topic.

This book is the result of a conference that was organized to address this problem. Sponsored by the Searle Family Fund, the meeting was held in Chicago. There the authors of the chapters presented the first drafts of their work and debated the conclusions. The subtitle of the book—Can It Work?— grew out of the ambivalence of the group, for the evidence was clearly mixed. The chapters use an impressive array of surveys, case studies, field observations, and statistical data to address various aspects of the "can it work?" question. The introductory chapter presents a little police history, to set community policing in context. Then, two chapters address evidence of the extent to which community policing has actually been adopted around the country. Another chapter examines the role of the community in community policing, and several chapters address its impact on police officers. Two chapters review the many obstacles to solving the community's problems, one with skepticism and one with ambivalence, and the final chapter concludes that community policing can work after all. But the reader should also pay attention to *how* the various authors address these questions, for they point the way for future research that *will* resolve this issue.

ACKNOWLEDGMENTS

This book is an outgrowth of a conference held at Northwestern University that was sponsored by the Searle Family Fund. One priority for the fund is its "reinventing government" initiative, and it recognizes that policing is today one of the most innovative arms of local government. The authors all wish to thank the Searle Family Fund for its generous support of the meeting and the work that lay behind the production of this volume. In addition to the chapter authors, Alexander Weiss of Northwestern University and Chip Coldren of the University of Illinois at Chicago reviewed the draft chapters and joined in the discussion. Deputy Superintendent Barbara McDonald of the Chicago Police Department added her reflections on the real world of police management.

Both the conference and the production of the book manuscript were coordinated by Lynn Steiner of Northwestern University's Institute for Policy Research, who is project director of the institute's community policing evaluation efforts.

Wesley G. Skogan

About the Authors

Mariah Davis

Mariah Davis was the lead graduate student researcher for the Albuquerque Police Department—University of New Mexico Research Partnership from 1997–2000. She now is a sworn officer serving in the Albuquerque Police Department.

John Eck

John Eck is a criminologist in the Division of Criminal Justice at the University of Cincinnati. He has written extensively on problem-oriented policing, crime patterns, drug markets, and criminal investigations.

Jack Greene

Jack Greene is dean of the College of Criminal Justice at Northeastern University. His research focuses on police organizations and the delivery of police services. He has also written broadly on the implementation of community and problem-oriented policing.

Calvin C. Johnson

Calvin C. Johnson is a criminologist and a member of the staff of the Jerry Lee Center of Criminology at the University of Pennsylvania. He has also served as Director of Research and Evaluation at the Court Services and Offender Supervision Agency for the District of Columbia (CSOSA), and as a research associate at the Urban Institute, Washington, D.C. While at the Urban Institute, he was the senior statistical analyst for their national evaluation of community policing and then conducted an evaluation of organizational restructuring and adoption of community policing by the Washington, D.C. Police Department.

Stephen Mastrofski

Stephen Mastrofski is a political scientist who heads the Administration of Justice Program at George Mason University. With Roger Parks, he directed the National Institute of Justice–funded Project on Policing Neighborhoods, a massive observational study of community policing in two cities.

Roger Parks

Roger Parks is a political scientist in the School of Public and Environmental Affairs at Indiana University. With Steve Mastrofski, he directed the Project on Policing Neighborhoods, an observational study of community policing in two cities.

Michael Reisig

Michael Reisig is a political scientist in the School of Criminal Justice at Michigan State University. His research on policing and corrections has appeared frequently in major journals.

Jan Roehl

Jan Roehl is an applied social psychologist and president of the Justice Research Center. She is currently studying risk assessment in intimate partner violence, efforts to integrate community mediation and community policing, and data-driven, partnership-based approaches for reducing violent crime.

Dennis Rosenbaum

Dennis Rosenbaum is a psychologist in the Departments of Criminal Justice and Psychology at the University of Illinois at Chicago. He is director of his university's Criminal Justice Research Center.

Jeffrey A. Roth

Jeffrey A. Roth is a criminologist and associate director for research of the Jerry Lee Center of Criminology at the University of Pennsylvania. While director of Crime Control Policy Studies at the Urban Institute in Washington, D.C., he conducted a national evaluation of the federal government's community policing policies.

Amelia Rouse

Amelia Rouse is the deputy director of the Institute for Public Policy at the University of New Mexico. Her research focuses on the role of public opinion in federal, state, and local decision-making processes, especially policing, risk perception, education, workers' compensation, transportation, and health care.

Wesley Skogan

Wesley Skogan is a political scientist and faculty associate of the Institute for Policy Research at Northwestern University. He directs an evaluation of Chicago's community policing initiative. He chairs the National Academy of Sciences Panel on Police Policies and Practices.

William Terrill

William Terrill is a policing specialist in the Administration of Justice Program at George Mason University.

Nick Tilley

Nick Tilley is a sociologist at Nottingham-Trent University and a long-time consultant to the British Home Office on police matters. Most of his recent research relates to crime prevention and problem-oriented policing. One of the British policing profession's leading yearly awards is named in his honor.

Jeremy Travis

Jeremy Travis is a senior fellow at the Urban Institute and former director of the National Institute of Justice. He served as Deputy Commissioner for Legal Maters in the New York City Police Department, was Chief Counsel to the House Subcommittee on Criminal Justice, and Special Advisor to the Mayor of New York City. He was a recipient of the American Society of Criminology's August Vollmer Award for his contributions to criminal justice

Deanna Wilkinson

Deanna Wilkinson is a criminologist in the Department of Criminal Justice at Temple University.

Richard Wood

Richard Wood is a sociologist at the University of New Mexico. His research focuses on cultural dynamics in police departments, urban community organizations, and police-community relations.

Introduction

BY WESLEY G. SKOGAN AND
JEFFREY A. ROTH

Community policing is the most important development in policing in the past quarter century. Across the country, police chiefs report that they are moving toward this new model of policing, which supplements traditional crime fighting with a problem-solving and prevention-oriented approach that emphasizes the role of the public in helping set police priorities. What they say they are doing when they do community policing varies a great deal, however. In some places it is in the hands of special neighborhood officers, whereas in other places agencies try to transform the entire organization. Departments point to bike patrols, drug awareness programs in schools, home security inspections, and expanded roles for foot patrol officers as evidence that they have gotten involved. In some cities residents participate in aggressive neighborhood watch patrols as part of their city's program, though in many more places public involvement is limited to being asked to call 911 quickly when they see something suspicious. Agencies have also mounted sophisticated public relations campaigns to sell their programs, and they compete hotly for national awards for innovation. Assistant chiefs get promoted, and chiefs move to more visible cities, because they are said to have made a success out of community policing.

This book takes a critical look behind the resulting "hype" to see if anything is actually happening. Because they are experienced police researchers, the authors started with a suspicion: if almost everyone claims that they are doing something that is as difficult to implement as a serious community policing program, that claim deserves a second look. As they report in their chapters, the authors range from mildly optimistic to decidedly pessimistic about what they have seen.

Where did community policing come from? Into the 1980s, American policing was dominated by the professional model of policing. The professional model emphasized responding rapidly when victims called the police, plus a technically skilled follow-up effort by detectives to find "whodunit" and arrest them. Police focused on each case as it came to them via 911. After responding officers filled out a report (it turns out they usually did not catch anyone themselves), detectives were called in to sift through clues and try to finish the job. When they were not answering calls, the bulk of the force spent their time driving around on "preventive patrol," keeping visible because that was believed to deter crime. By staying mobile, they were available to be sent anywhere headquarters needed them to respond to calls. Police tried to focus on serious victimizing crime. There was a great deal of controversy over their efforts to keep the streets clear of apparent drunks, loiterers, prostitutes, drug dealers, and variously disorderly persons, because some believed that such efforts overstepped the boundaries of the Constitution. It was also apparent that discretionary application of the law to control disorder too often followed racial lines.

Community policing represents an alternative vision of the role of police in society. It challenges almost every "professional" police practice described earlier. Proponents think police should deal with batches of related problems after thinking about them systematically, rather than just driving quickly to the scene of each call and taking a report. They are dubious that detectives add much value to crime fighting and think that more police resources should be devoted to teams of uniformed officers who deal with all of the problems that arise in particular areas. Rather than drive around keeping visible, proponents think those officers should be walking on foot, talking with residents, attending neighborhood meetings, and using the computers in their cars to keep abreast of crime trends in their small assigned beats. Most of all, they believe police should take responsibility for a neighborhood rather than just drive anywhere the computer at the 911 center decides to send them. Proponents also think that police must tackle head-on some of the difficult social disorder issues of our time, and that they should take the lead in coordinating action on the physical decay that blights the face of too many American neighborhoods.

The essays presented here examine this debate over the role of the police in the community. This introductory chapter sets the emergence of community policing in historical and conceptual context. First, we review some of the precursors to community policing, to highlight what each contributed to the evolution of this new model of policing. Then we describe the end product, or at least its current configuration. We present an extended definition of community policing and some cursory evidence of its popularity. Next, we show how the chapters address the "can it work?" question that is part of the title of this book. The first set of chapters examine trends in the adoption of community policing, to see whether anything fundamental is indeed changing. Another addresses the role of the public in securing neighborhood safety, and several chapters address the reaction of police officers, which is often negative, to their involvement in community policing. The final section looks at the effectiveness of community policing in addressing neighborhood problems.

THE ROOTS OF COMMUNITY POLICING

Community policing was eventually constructed out of critiques of the professional model, but the way forward was illuminated by a series of interim experiments in policing. During the 1970s and early 1980s, grassroots attempts to improve on the professional model sprung up here and there around the country. There was no master plan behind them, and there was no thought-out theory about why the innovations might supercede the day's dominant model for policing. Instead, cities around the country tried new things they thought might work. In retrospect, it is possible to give these pilot tests labels: team policing, community outreach, community crime prevention, problem-oriented policing, and fear reduction (Moore, 1992). Though each had its limitations and visibly failed in some places, collectively they broadened society's view of what policing might entail. They changed the nature of police executives' conversations about where policing was heading at the end of the twentieth century, and they led the federal government to get more heavily involved in fostering police innovation.

TEAM POLICING

Police departments in New York City, Cincinnati, and Los Angeles were among the first to try fostering turf-based responsibility among police by forming teams of officers dedicated to particular areas of the city. This would not have been a new idea before about 1910, because at that time most police walked their beat and dealt with whatever they came across, but by the mid-1960s their work was parceled out by radio and they drove wherever the dispatcher sent them. In Los Angeles, team policing worked like this: The patrol force was divided into "X cars" that could be dispatched throughout the city and "basic cars" that were to remain in particular neighborhoods. "Senior lead officers" were assigned to each basic car and given higher pay in recognition of their key role in establishing and maintaining liaison with the community. The city was divided into seventy patrol areas, each policed by three to five basic cars and commanded by a lieutenant. Each lieutenant directed not only the X and basic cars, but all of the special units working in the area (gangs, drug squads, and the like), and had twenty-four-hour accountability for conditions there. Because of this neighborhood-level focus, Mark Moore (1992: 133) describes team policing as "the first modern model of what [was] becoming community policing."

Moore reports that evaluations of team policing in several locations found that the model was popular with the public and sometimes improved neighborhood conditions, including crime rates. However, even successful examples of team policing eventually fell by the wayside. The reasons were varied but included resource constraints (officers in basic cars could not easily be sent from place to place), opposition by higher ups in the chain of command (who could be uncomfortable with delegating responsibility to mere patrol officers), and incompatibility with an organizational culture committed to the professional model. Despite the virtual demise of full-blown team policing in most jurisdictions, several of its vestiges—dispatching rules that keep beat officers in their beats, a team approach to decisions in the field, and pushing decision-making responsibility down to the beat level—are prominent in descriptions of community policing today.

Community Outreach

Special units dedicated to improving community relations date back at least to the 1950s, when "Officer Friendly" visited schools, made speeches, and spoke to citizens in other forums, as a means of gaining the support of community residents. In the wake of urban riots in the 1960s, these units often evolved into community liaison offices. They became more involved in organizing and sustaining public meetings, and in forming advisory committees that gave visible roles to community activists. Meetings and advisory councils then, as now, offered "megaphones for the department [and] . . . antennae tuned into neighborhood concerns" (Moore, 1992: 135). In some places, community relations units became valuable "eyes and ears" for departments attempting to monitor community tensions and coopt potentially dissident leaders. At their best, community relations units opened up two-way channels for communication between police and the community. One shortcoming of the professional model of policing is that it encouraged police to think they would be most effective if they could ignore public opinion and politics, and by the end of the 1950s many lived in insular worlds indeed. In a 1990 conversation with Moore, Herman Goldstein describes community relations units as among the first innovations that alerted chiefs to the potential value of community outreach. They may also have helped to create a congenial climate for building police-community partnerships with action agendas, but the idea that the public could be involved in neighborhood security projects awaited the emergence of another innovation, the community crime prevention movement of the 1970s.

Community Crime Prevention

The community crime prevention movement emphasized collaboration between the police and community organizations. It was built on the observation that, in a democratic society, police cannot effectively deal with crime on their own. At the end of the 1960s, it was widely believed that rising crime could be traced to community disorganization, and it reflected a decline in the factors that had shaped people's behavior in the past: jobs, churches, schools, families, and traditional values. The solution seemed to be organization—getting neighborhood residents involved in voluntary, collective efforts to fight crime on their own. This could include marking their property to deter burglars, forming neighborhood watch groups and resident patrols, "hardening" local businesses against shoplifting and robbery, cleaning up crime-prone spaces open to the public, and challenging the loitering and public drinking that bred simple assaults and petty crimes. Neighborhood groups could battle physical dilapidation by conducting clean-up and fix-up campaigns and by pressuring city bureaucracies for better service. They could involve youths in supervised recreation programs. When playing these roles in securing community safety, residents brought to the table resources and expertise not available to the police (Skogan, 1988).

Community-based anticrime programs were extremely popular during the 1970s. In a national survey conducted in 1981, 12 percent of the adult population claimed membership in a neighborhood group that was involved in crime prevention (cf. Skogan, 1988). When cities began to run out of money in the 1980s, residents' voluntary contributions to neighborhood safety were appreciated. Community crime prevention projects were also the first precursor of community policing to be systematically evaluated, using modern research methods. A large collection of evaluations (e.g., Rosenbaum, 1986) demonstrates that communities can have useful and legitimate roles to play in crime prevention, roles that go well beyond being the "eyes and ears of the police." The community anticrime movement also played an important role in establishing *prevention* as an important, and measurable, goal. In a period in which police were still mostly reactive, coming to the scene only after something bad had happened, communities were instinctively proactive. They did not want bad things to happen in the first place. Community-based prevention remains an active enterprise to this day. Now it is more commonly called "situational" prevention, and it encompasses both resident and police strategies, along with an emphasis on building design, neighborhood layout, and "designing out" crime in the manufacture of products such as automobiles.

Problem-Oriented Policing

In a seminal article, Herman Goldstein (1979) proposes an alternative to the "one crime at a time" approach that characterized professional policing. Goldstein raises the point that clusters of calls—often from the same address—might have a common cause. He reasoned that if police came to understand crime clusters—he dubbed them "problems"—they could reduce the volume of future calls by resolving their common cause. In this model, policing would become problem oriented rather than response oriented. Subsequent research on 911 calls indicates that they were indeed heavily clustered. For example, a study in Minneapolis found that more than 50 percent of calls came from just 3.3 percent of the city's addresses (Sherman, 1989). Goldstein also calls for police to "think outside the box" when it came to solving problems. First, he wants them to analyze problems: to learn more about victims as well as offenders and to consider carefully why they came together where they did. Then he wants them to craft responses that went beyond the traditional solution of arresting someone in the hope that somewhere further down the criminal justice pipeline they would see the error in their ways. Solutions to problems might, for example, require enlisting the help of other city service agencies, or using the civil courts or the health department, or turning to residents to help them "take back the night." Today, well-organized departments identify and promote "best practices" that draw on what their officers have done. Finally (and this was also a new idea), Goldstein wants police to assess how well they did. Did it work? *What* worked, exactly? Did the project fail because we had the wrong idea, or did we have a good idea but fail to implement it?

Problem-oriented policing and community policing are overlapping concepts, but each has a distinctive thrust. Problem-solving projects can be organized without many of the features that accompany community policing. In Chapter 8 of this book, John Eck points out that community policing is differentiated from problem solving by its emphasis on broad roles for the public in identifying, prioritizing, and solving problems. As Eck points out, involving the community is a tactic to be adopted if it is appropriate for the problem at hand, not an end in itself. Problem solving can be conducted without community input, but then it is likely to remain focused on conventionally defined crime that is identified by intensive analysis of police data. Community policing programs can address a wider scope of problems, they have wider problem-solving goals (including "involve the community"), and they use a broader range of tools to address them. They are likely to address teen truancy and problem buildings as well as burglary and theft from autos; officers may use housing or health codes in addition to the criminal code; neighborhood residents and city agencies may focus on cleaning up graffiti, and call that "community policing" too. Beyond that, seeking and using residents' input in identifying problems and setting priorities increase the likelihood that policing projects will address problems of concern to the community and that police tactics will be respectful of neighborhood residents. Somewhere down this path, problem-oriented policing becomes community policing.

Fear Reduction

The final piece of the pre-community policing puzzle is the fear-reduction projects of the 1970s and early 1980s. Reducing communities' fear of crime emerged during the 1980s as a policing problem in its own right, for several reasons. First, observers recognized fear of retaliation as one of several barriers to citizen participation in community crime prevention and problem-solving activities (Grinc, 1994). Second, the finding that fear of crime was not completely determined by the level of victimization (Skogan, 1988) implied that reducing fear would require something different from programs that focused narrowly on crime.

Third, police practitioners and researchers identified two promising strategies for reducing fear: visible police foot patrols and policing disorder. An early spark for fear-reduction initiatives came from successful experiments with foot patrols in Flint, Michigan, and Newark, New Jersey. Although the foot patrols did not reduce property or violent crime, they did reduce citizens' fears; the Flint experiment was so popular that voters passed a tax to continue the program, and calls for service declined (Pate, 1986; Trojanowicz, 1992). Later, federally sponsored experiments in Newark and Houston, Texas, demonstrated that police could reduce fear using tactics such as opening neighborhood substations, going door to door to learn about neighborhood problems, and encouraging citizens to form new neighborhood organizations (Skogan, 1990; Pate et al., 1986).

The second fear-reduction strategy, policing disorder, is an implication of what is sometimes known as the broken windows theory, after the title of a 1982 *Atlantic Monthly* article by James Q. Wilson and George Kelling. They argue that, left uncorrected, signs of physical decay (the metaphorical broken window) and social disorder (e.g., public drinking, groups of loiterers) communicate the message that "anything goes" in the neighborhood. In turn, frightened law-abiding people avoid the area, leaving it to the disorderly and the criminal. Families move out, and no one particularly wants to move in, so property values fall. Buildings deteriorate and begin to fall vacant. Squatters move in, and crack houses open for business.

In some cities the broken windows metaphor has become the rationale for joint police-community efforts to repair signs of physical decay. In Chicago, for example, community policing includes neighborhood clean-ups and graffiti paint-overs by residents, focused trash removal and street repairs by city agencies, and a new police focus on health and building code enforcement. Residents also get involved in controlling social disorder by challenging prostitutes and public drinkers, taking measures to close bad businesses, challenging the liquor licenses of establishments that foster trouble making, and retaking control of parks after dark (Skogan and Hartnett, 1997).

Other cities turned more exclusively to the police to solve their disorder problems by arresting people. Kelling and Coles (1996) describe two examples from New York City, both involving proactive policing. One target was "fare-beaters" who avoided paying to ride the subway by jumping turnstiles instead of inserting tokens. The other was "squeegee men" who, unasked, "washed" the windows of cars stuck in traffic and then intimidated drivers into giving them money. Arresting them became known as "quality-of-life policing." Plummeting crime and fear in New York City seemed to validate this strategy and played an important role in the cheer that arose at the end of the 1990s that "New York Is Back." But much to Kelling's (1999) regret, many observers now describe the New York Police Department's proactive order maintenance strategy as "turning police loose" in ways that led to well-known abuses of their authority. Kelling himself remarks that some New York Police Department adherents to "tough" policing have misconstrued successful assertive policing as license for combative or military policing. New York's model also did not feature any community input into identifying problems or setting police priorities, ignoring the concept of partnership that figures so prominently in the community policing paradigm.

COMMUNITY POLICING
IN THE 1990S AND BEYOND

This brings us to the 1990s, the era of community policing. Community policing advocates picked up the lessons of the past that we have documented and blended them together while adding a few new ingredients. What does the resulting dish look like? What police departments actually *do* when they do community policing turns out to be highly varied. Two of our authors, John Eck and Dennis Rosenbaum (1994) describe community as a "plastic" concept because the range and complexity of programs associated with it are large and continually evolving. When asked if they practice community policing, agencies point to a long list of activities as evidence that they are doing so. These range from bike and foot patrols to storefront offices and citizen advisory committees. At root, however, community policing is not defined by a list of particular activities but rather by strategic organizational adaptation to a changing environment. Police departments practicing community policing adopt some mix of three new, interrelated organizational stances.

One feature of many community policing programs is *decentralization*. Community policing often leads departments to assign officers to fixed geographical areas and to keep them there during their day. Usually they attempt to push authority and responsibility further down their agency's organizational hierarchy to encourage decision making that responds rapidly and effectively to local conditions. Decentralization is supposed to facilitate the development of localized solutions to neighborhood problems. It is intended to encourage communication between officers and neighborhood residents and to promote community-oriented projects. Often there are moves to flatten the structure of departments by compressing the rank structure to shed layers of bureaucracy and to speed communication and decision making within the organization.

The second common feature of departments adopting this new model of policing is *community engagement*. Community policing encourages agencies to develop partnerships with community groups to facilitate "listening" to the community and constructive information sharing. To this end, departments hold community meetings and form advisory committees, survey the public, and create informative Web sites. Wesley Skogan's Chapter 3 in this book describes how these work in Chicago. In some places police share information with residents through educational programs or by enrolling them in citizen police academies that give them in-depth knowledge of law enforcement. Engagement usually extends to involving the public in some way in efforts to enhance community safety. Residents are asked to assist the police by reporting crimes promptly when they occur and by cooperating as witnesses. Community policing often promises to strengthen the capacity of communities to fight and prevent crime on their own. Residents sometimes get involved in the coordinated or collaborative projects when they participate in crime prevention projects or walk in officially sanctioned neighborhood patrol groups. Even where these are old ideas, moving them to center stage as part of a larger strategic plan showcases the commitment of police departments to resident involvement. Other partnerships involve other government organizations that have some direct responsibility for neighborhood quality of life. These agencies can include those responsible for health, housing, and even street lighting.

Third, community policing usually involves *problem solving*. As we note earlier, problem solving is an analytic method for developing crime prevention strategies. As a police strategy, problem solving represents a departure from the traditional approach to policing, which too often was reduced to driving fast to crime scenes to fill out reports of what happened. Community policing problem solving stresses involving the public in identifying and prioritizing a *broad range* of neighborhood problems. One of the consequences of opening themselves up to the public is that police inevitably get involved in more problems and in less traditional problems than they did in the past. At community meetings residents complain about bad buildings, noise, rats in the alley, and people fixing their cars at the curb, not just about burglary. If police reply "that's not our responsibility" and try to move on, no one will come to the next meeting. Of course, the police are not very good at solving all of the problems of stressed neighborhoods, so they need to form partnerships with other agencies of government and see to it that they get the work done. Finally, in many circumstances community policing can involve the public in solving problems as well. Neighborhood residents can paint over graffiti, walk their dogs in areas frequented by prostitutes, hold prayer vigils in the midst of street drug markets, and join court watch groups that bring pressure on judges and prosecutors.

What does all this mean in actual practice? As we note at the outset, police departments everywhere claim that they are doing community policing because it is so popular with the public that no city wants to seem to be out of step with the times. They all have that list of activities to point to when they are asked if they practice community policing. Although this new interest by the public in law enforcement policy is certainly a good thing, the apparent popularity of community policing is also a reason for caution. Translating the fundamental principles of community policing into actual practice is difficult. Abstract concepts need to be turned into lists of practical, day-to-day activities and then enshrined in enforceable orders for officers in the field. The troops out there have to actually go along with those orders, and the emphasis should always be on the "para" in these "para-military" organizations. It can also be surprisingly difficult to get the community involved in community policing and—more predictably—to get other city bureaucracies to take ownership of problems raised in police-community meetings.

Even when all the intended parties seem to be "getting on board," legitimate questions remain. When discretion becomes decentralized to officers on the beat, which uses of discretion get rewarded and which get ignored or penalized? When communities become engaged, are residents mostly listening, talking, exchanging information, coordinating activities, or implementing a shared agenda when they meet with police? When a problem gets solved, who nominated the problem, who participated in planning and executing the response, who assessed the effectiveness of the response, and who checked to make sure the problem stayed solved?

There is evidence that police departments around the country have actually changed how they are organized. A study by the federal government (Hickman and Reeves, 2001) reports that elements of community policing are common, especially among those serving communities of more than 50,000 people. By 1999, almost two-thirds of local police departments reported they had officers serving in full-time community policing roles. Departments employing about 80 percent of the nation's police officers had adopted some form of geographical responsibility for patrol officers, and about half of all officers worked for agencies attempting to do problem solving in a systematic way. Most Americans lived in places where police had formalized problem-solving partnerships with other agencies and groups. Virtually everyone (96 percent) lived in places where police reported meeting regularly with neighborhood residents. More evidence about the spread of community policing is reported in Chapter 1 of this book.

Some of this expansion in community-oriented policing has been financed by the federal government. In 1994, Congress approved the Violent Crime Control and Law Enforcement Act, which included an allotment of $9 billion to hire as many as 100,000 new police officers. The Act specified that one of the roles of these new officers should be "to foster problem solving and interaction with communities by police officers." Title I created a national Office of Community Oriented Policing Services in the Justice Department to coordinate spending these funds. The office also provided training in community policing, paid for new computers and other technological assistance for departments, and assisted them in setting up community policing programs. However, federal support for community policing certainly will be on the wane. The 1994 Act had at least one of its intended effects: major police groups endorsed the presidential candidate who sponsored it. Now crime is down, a new team is in the White House, and federal largess toward local law enforcement is being redirected to post-September 11 concerns. An important test of the staying power of community policing will come when cities have to pay all of its costs.

THIS BOOK

This book reports on new studies of community policing and its close ally, problem-oriented policing. The chapters were completed after the authors met to thrash out their ideas, yet they are still not in total agreement about the status of community policing. This was probably inevitable. The questions the group had to address were hard ones, and there were usually limited data with which to answer them. Some of the chapters in this book are national in scope, whereas others draw on studies of individual cities because they are the best evidence available. The book is organized around those four fundamental questions: Are police changing? Will the public get involved? Will police officers buy in? Can it work?

Are Police Changing?

This is an important question because changing police departments is very hard. Dorothy Guyot (1991) describes the task of changing police as akin to "bending granite." Although there is a lot of talk about innovation in policing, the field is littered with the casualties of failed efforts to make change.

How do we know if police are changing? One way is to conduct on-site analyses of community policing programs, and another is to send questionnaires to large numbers of departments asking what they are doing. The authors of the first chapter in this section ("Trends in the Adoption of Community Policing") do both. Jeffrey Roth, Jan Roehl, and Calvin Johnson look at four key issues: the formation of police-community partnerships, the adoption of a problem-solving orientation toward police work, police roles in crime prevention, and the extent of organizational change to support those three objectives. Each subsection of this chapter combines the findings of agency survey data with "reports from the field" that are based on dozens of site visits. Their survey-based data suggest that in the wake of the 1994 Act, large agencies jumped into wholesale adoption of a whole battery of signature community policing practices, but later took a more cautious and selective approach. Perhaps because traditional policing is inherently community policing in smaller towns, small agencies reported adopting community policing practices more cautiously and still have not adopted them as widely as the large agencies. They may not be able to support specialist community officers when they have a total of only five. The authors' on-site assessments reveal that reported adoption of a community policing practice could have several meanings: that the chief had merely incorporated the practice into the departmental vision, or pinned the practice label on some idiosyncratic local tactic, or had indeed incorporated the practice into agency routines.

The second chapter, Jack Greene's "Community Policing and Organization Change," discusses the obstacles to implementing a serious community policing program. These require wholesale changes in the ways agencies are organized and services are delivered. He argues that political and institutional realities work against any substantial shift away from a "crime fighting" stance by police departments. Proponents of community policing call for changes in how departments are organized, formal ways to form deeper links between police and the community, and changes in the "core technology" of policing—how services are actually delivered. He does not see much evidence that police agencies have reorganized themselves root and branch to accommodate any of these demands, and he draws on organizational theory to explain why. He concludes that many departments have adopted the rhetoric of community policing, but mostly they are still organized to do traditional "professional" policing. There is some evidence that police organizations have become more open to input from their environment (the public, interest groups, other government agencies), which is a key aspect of community policing. A crucial test of community policing will be whether this input actually changes how they prioritize problems and craft their operational strategies, an issue revisited in the next chapter.

Will the Public Get Involved?

The claim that community residents should be deeply involved in efforts to secure community safety is a key rhetorical point in any discussion of community policing. However, it can also be surprisingly difficult to get community residents interested in cooperating with police, especially in poor and disenfranchised neighborhoods. They may not have a history of getting along, and police may be perceived as arrogant and brutal rather than as potential partners. Residents can rightly be skeptical of claims about community policing, and that it will be different this time. They may also have difficulty getting organized by themselves. Civic participation is difficult to sustain in high-crime areas, where fear stifles community life. Residents easily view each other with suspicion rather than with neighborliness, and this undermines their capacity to forge collective responses to local problems. Because they fear retaliation by drug dealers and neighborhood toughs, programs requiring public meetings or organized cooperation may be less successful. As a result, high-crime areas often lack the organizational infrastructure needed to get things done.

Chapter 3, "Representing the Community in Community Policing" by Wesley Skogan, examines whether expectations about community involvement are realistic. Can and will residents step forward and get involved, especially in fear-ridden, high-crime neighborhoods? Will those who do represent the views of the entire community, or only their parochial concerns? Certainly, friends of the police may get involved, but how about those who are critical of their actions? The chapter also directly addresses the challenge posed by Greene in the previous section when it examines the impact of resident involvement on the operation of a community policing program in Chicago. There, the vehicle for grassroots consultation and collaboration between police and residents is neighborhood meetings that are held monthly in all parts of the city. About 6,000 residents and 1,800 officers attend each month. These meetings are intended to be forums for exchanging information and for identifying, prioritizing, and analyzing local problems. They also provide occasions for police and residents to get acquainted, and a vehicle for residents to organize their own problem-solving efforts. The study finds that, in Chicago, beat meetings did a good job of translating residents' priorities into action. There was a strong relationship between residents' priorities and the delivery of city services. However, there was a strong middle-class bias in participation, and the meetings did a better job at representing previously established stakeholders in the community than at integrating marginalized groups with fewer mechanisms for voicing their concerns.

Will Police Officers Buy In?

Police have a remarkable ability to wait out efforts to reform them. Important aspects of police culture mitigate against change. Police resist the intrusion of civilians (who "can't really understand") into their business. They fear that community troublemakers will take over programs and that people will seek to use police for their private purposes or for personal revenge. When police dislike changes proposed from within, they snort that the top brass are "out of touch with the street." They scoff at performing tasks that smack of "social work" or the "wave and smile" policing they associate with community relations programs. Things are not always better among their bosses. The sergeants who immediately supervise them may have only a dim understanding of community policing, which they never practiced. The habits of the old hierarchical management structure are also hard to break. The lieutenants another layer above often resist surrendering their authority to decentralized teams. The labyrinthine reviews and rereviews of decisions provide lieutenants and captains with something to do, and many who have risen to the top under the old

rules find the fluidity of tasks and relationships required by community policing evidence of its faddish character. Another significant issue is that larger
departments have a great deal of difficulty in determining whether community
policing is taking place. Police are good at tracking how many calls they answer
and whether they are making enough arrests and handing out enough tickets.
By and large, they have to trust the professionalism and commitment of their
officers when it comes to dealing with the law-abiding public.

The three chapters in this section of the book address these organizational
change issues. In Chapter 4, Dennis Rosenbaum and Deanna Wilkinson ask,
"Can Police Adapt?" They describe two midsized cities that attempted to adopt
serious community policing programs. The programs called for participatory
management, extensive training, area-based decentralization of police operations, and the creation of special community policing units. As part of their evaluation, the authors track the attitudes of the officers in these cities over a six-
year span. This gives them a unique opportunity to address questions about
organizational change. They find that the best strategy for adopting community
policing may be the "special unit" approach—vesting it in the hands of skilled
and largely volunteer officers—rather than pursuing wholesale, departmentwide
change. The work of most officers doing routine patrol did not change, as
Greene predicts in his chapter, and neither did their hearts and minds.

Chapter 5, "Working the Street: Does Community Policing Matter?" by
William Terrill and Stephen Mastrofski, examines community policing in two
cities: St. Petersburg, Florida, and Indianapolis, Indiana. As the Rodney King
episode of 1991 reminds us, everyone must be concerned about abuses of
police power. Although use of force is inevitable, good policing is associated
with economy in the use of physical and verbal coercion. Reformers hope that
community policing will contribute to less coercive policing. They argue that
community-oriented officers will be less alienated from the citizens they serve,
more committed to developing deep and positive relations with the public, and
more knowledgeable about the people with whom they interact. Others are
more skeptical, fearing that police use of force is too firmly rooted in situational and neighborhood factors to be much affected by new philosophies of
policing. During their study, Terrill and Mastrofski observe how police in the
field interacted with 3,500 suspects. They look at how police treatment of citizens was affected by community policing factors, including department philosophy, officer assignment, officer training, and attitudes about community
policing. They find sobering results. The departments differed in the use of
force, but community policing assignments, training, and even attitudes were
not systematically related to the extent to which officers used coercion.

All of the authors in this section would agree that community policing
involves a war for the hearts and minds of police officers, who distrust
attempts to stuff "social work" down their throats and are dubious about
untried social experiments. In Chapter 6, "Diving into Quicksand: Program
Implementation and Police Subcultures," Richard Wood, Mariah Davis, and
Amelia Rouse examine opposition to community policing among influential
coalitions of officers, ranging from hard-headed "paramilitary" types to "get

ahead" careerists, rule-bound bureaucrats, and expert craftsmen. Wood spent four years tracking changes in the elements of police culture in a large Southwestern city. The chapter traces the evolution of what was once a relatively unified, "traditional" police culture, one that was dominated by a code of silence concerning officer misconduct and resistance to outsiders and change. By the 1990s this department had—like police departments around the country—fragmented into competing factions, reflecting changes in the demography of the city and of police officers themselves. But each of these emergent subcultures had its own, often negative, reaction to community policing, and they undermined the attempt of department and city leaders to implement change. Wood notes that police administrators intent on innovation need to find ways to harness the interests of the various subcultures in their agency and make clever use of divisions among them.

Can It Work?

Community policing and its precursors emerged because of dissatisfaction with important elements of the professional model of policing. Among the sources of discontent was evidence that key elements of the model—including rapid response, the specialization of detective work, and the deterrent effects of both visible patrol and arresting people—were not having much effect on the crime rate. The big-city riots of the 1960s and 1970s were also a reminder that the professional model was not meeting the needs of significant parts of the population, who were increasingly disaffected from the criminal justice system. However, there is to date embarrassingly little evidence that the alternatives to the professional model work much better. Note that the absence of evidence is not evidence of an absence of effectiveness. Studies in scattered cities point to successes on the community policing front, and case studies describing successful problem-solving projects abound. But other studies disagree about broader and more durable effects of a community- and problem-oriented policing, and the jury is still out about both of these movements.

Three chapters of this book address the "can it work?" question. In Chapter 7, Nick Tilley examines the concepts of community and problem solving policing. He argues that although we cannot do community policing without adopting problem solving, problem solving can function as an autonomous police function. The chapter challenges conventional notions by outlining how the concept of community must expand to include nongeographical virtual communities as sites for problem solving. College students provide a good example of a common-interest group that is scattered geographically and typically are not "of" the community where they live yet suffer common crime problems. The chapter describes why the potential of community policing to anticipate, identify, make sense of, and respond to problems has not been fully realized. Using the ideas of effectiveness, efficiency, and equity advanced elsewhere by two of our authors (John Eck and Dennis Rosenbaum), Tilley dissects the limits of community policing and problem solving, using examples from Great Britain and the United States. He argues that both models of policing have fallen far short of their promise, and the rhetoric of their supporters. Community policing has been slow to deliver measurable results, and problem solving turns out to be a lot easier in theory than in practice. He proposes decoupling the two and pushing harder on the police-centered problem-solving side of the equation.

Because he also thinks police are just mediocre at it, John Eck in Chapter 8, "Why Don't Problems Get Solved?" digs more deeply into the problems associated with neighborhood problem solving. Many of the reasons are internal to police agencies: they don't know how to do it, how to manage it, or how to encourage more of it. They don't like change (a recurring theme in this book), and they think they are just too busy to try new things. More sophisticated practitioners lament that "the technology" is not there; that is, we don't know what works in policing generally, and in problem solving in particular. Calling for "the return of the problem solver," Eck recommends a new regimen for police. He argues that academics and researchers need to pay more attention to the nature of problems themselves. There needs to be more research on problems ranging from bored youths to bad liquor stores that yields insights into their causes and tells us why they are concentrated in some places but not others. There needs to be more careful evaluation of what works and what does not in countering problems, and how police can figure out which are the most effective strategies. Because problem solving is vital to any healthy community policing program, more effort needs to be focused on making it effective.

Does community policing work, in the eyes of the public? Are neighborhoods better off because of this new movement? This is a common and important question, yet one for which there have been few answers. Most sociological research on crime and quality-of-life problems has focused on their association with race and class, not on what can be done about them. The final chapter, "Community Policing and the Quality of Neighborhood Life" by Michael Reisig and Roger Parks, traces the impact of community policing in two large cities. It is based on surveys of police officers and neighborhood residents, and official homicide numbers. It shows how community policing activities such as foot and bike patrol, greater police-citizen collaboration, and more intensive motor patrol are associated with enhanced quality of life and lower rates of crime.

OUR CONCLUSION

Well, can community policing work? Taken as a whole, the chapters of this book raise the possibility that community policing can be adopted, that it may increase the legitimacy of the police in the eyes of the public, and that it may help them more effectively target problems that are of priority concern to the community. The agency surveys that are described in Chapter 1 document that programmatic elements of community policing—community partnerships, problem solving, prevention, and policing strategies planned in the neighborhoods—swept the country during the 1990s. The counterpoint, presented in the very next chapter, is that this rhetoric seems not to have reshaped most agencies at their core. However, it is remains that the public expects the police to continue to provide the professional service to which they have become accustomed. A significant fraction of every police department will continue to be involved in responding to the public's calls, directing traffic and arresting speeders, and providing support during emergencies of all kinds. It is not clear that it is feasible to jettison the organizational structure that enables that work to be done efficiently. Skogan (Chapter 3) demonstrates that in at least one large multicultural city, the rhetoric of community policing is backed by enough reality to encourage thousands of residents to turn out every month, voting with their time and energy for the success of the program in their neighborhoods. Reisig and Parks (Chapter 9) find evidence that the adoption of community policing tactics reduced disorder and homicide in two cities.

The difficulty is that the rhetoric that surrounds community policing may discourage some officers from buying in to the concept. After all, it echoes back to the days when community-oriented policing began and ended with an occasional visit from the chief to deliver a speech at a community center. Today, community policing officers can still earn jeers from their colleagues because they are not doing "real police work" and instead are "empty holster guys." However, the national evaluation of the spread of community policing that is described in Chapter 1 cited the Las Vegas, Nevada, police department as an example of how skillful leadership of a problem-solving unit—by a sergeant known as a "cop's cop"—lit a spark of problem-focused, sometimes aggressive, community policing that is reshaping that department and the neighborhoods it polices. It is at least plausible that Terrill and Mastrofski's conclusion (Chapter 5) that the extent of community policing is unrelated to a department's use of force reflects something other than a failure of community policing to reduce use of force; perhaps tacit (or, even better, explicit and structured) permission to continue using appropriate levels of force helped innovative policing in those two cities flourish by making it more acceptable to respected veterans who already command the respect of their fellow officers.

If valid, this scenario would exemplify the "clever use of divisions" that Wood, Davis, and Rouse (Chapter 6) believe is helpful in turning a department toward community policing. In turn, a less adversarial reorientation of a department may free its community policing staff to teach, and its officers to learn, the "better use" of problem solving and other community policing tools that Eck (Chapter 8) finds missing in the typical department. It may even encourage middle managers to follow Tilley's (Chapter 7) suggestion to become more creative in defining communities, developing outreach strategies, and developing responses to their problems.

More fundamental, if community policing is to succeed, we believe that it has to be a city's program and not just the police department's program. Community policing is not cheap; it is labor extensive and thus expensive. When money is tight and resources are hard to come by, it may be at risk. But if its supporters can build broad public and political support for it, the budget for community policing may survive. Political support, and deep support from the community, can also help internally. It can be a tool for overcoming resistance to community policing within a department, if necessary. If it is a good program it will be good politics, and in the end public servants must do what their leaders tell them. Building political capital with the community can pay dividends when instances of brutality or corruption occur, because the promise that it will not happen again will have some credibility. Finally, this will help police departments get other municipal agencies to work with them on problem-solving projects. When those agencies think that community policing is the police department's program, they will not be very enthusiastic about bending their priorities and spending their money on those projects. To work, community policing has to be the city's program.

CITATIONS

Clarke, Ronald V. 1997. "Introduction." in Ronald V. Clarke (Ed.), *Situational Crime Prevention,* 2nd edition. New York: Harrow and Heston, 3–38.

Eck, John E. and Dennis P. Rosenbaum. 1994. "The New Police Order: Effectiveness, Equity and Efficiency in Community Policing." In Dennis P. Rosenbaum (Ed.), *The Challenge of Community Policing: Testing the Promises.* Thousand Oaks, CA: Sage, 3–26.

Goldstein, Herman. 1979. "Improving Policing: A Problem Oriented Approach." *Crime and Delinquency,* 25: 236–258.

Goldstein, Herman. 1990. *Problem-Oriented Policing.* New York: McGraw-Hill.

Greene, Jack R. 2000. "Community Policing in America: Changing the Nature, Structure and Function of the Police." In *Criminal Justice 2000,* Volume 3. Washington, DC: National Institute of Justice, U.S. Department of Justice, 299–370.

Grinc, Randolph M. 1994. " 'Angles in Marble': Problems in Stimulating Community Involvement in Community Policing." *Crime & Delinquency,* 40: 437–468.

Guyot, Dorothy. 1991. *Policing as Though People Matter.* Philadelphia: Temple University Press.

Hickman, Matthew J. and Brian A. Reeves, 2001. *Local Police Departments 1999.* Washington, DC: Bureau of Justice Statistics, U.S. Department of Justice.

Kelling, George L. 1999. " 'Broken Windows' " and Police Discretion. Washington, DC: National Institute of Justice.

Kelling, George and Catherine Coles. 1996. *Fixing Broken Windows: Restoring Order and Reducing Crime in Our Communities.* New York: Free Press.

Moore, Mark H. 1992. "Problem Solving and Community Policing." In Michael Tonry and Norval Morris (Eds.), *Modern Policing.* Chicago: University of Chicago Press, 99–158.

Moore Mark H. and Robert C. Trojanowicz. 1988. "Corporate Strategies for Policing." *Perspectives on Policing,* No. 6 (November). Washington, DC: National Institute of Justice, U.S. Department of Justice.

Pate, Antony M. 1986. "Experimenting with Foot Patrol: The Newark Experience." In Dennis Rosenbaum (Ed.), *Community Crime Prevention.* Newbury Park, CA: Sage, 137–156.

Pate, Antony M., Mary Ann Wycoff, Wesley G. Skogan, and Lawrence W. Sherman. 1986. *Reducing Fear of Crime in Houston and Newark: A Summary Report.* Washington, DC: Police Foundation.

Rosenbaum, Dennis P. (Ed.) 1986. *Community Crime Prevention: Does It Work?* Beverley Hills, CA: Sage.

Sherman, Lawrence W. 1989. "Repeat Calls for Service: Policing the 'Hot Spots.' " In Dennis Kenney (Ed.), *Police and Policing: Contemporary Issues.* New York: Praeger, 150–164.

Skogan, Wesley G. 1988. "Community Organizations and Crime." In Michael Tonry and Norval Morris (Eds.), *Crime and Justice: An Annual Review.* Chicago: University of Chicago Press, 39–78.

Skogan, Wesley G. 1990. *Disorder and Decline: Crime and the Spiral of Decay in American Cities.* New York: Free Press.

Skogan, Wesley G. and Susan M. Hartnett. 1997. *Community Policing, Chicago Style.* New York: Oxford University Press.

Trojanowicz, Robert. 1992. "Building Support for Community Policing." *Law Enforcement Bulletin,* 61: 5.

Wilson, James Q. and George Kelling. 1982. "Broken Windows." *The Atlantic Monthly,* March: 29–38.

PART I

Are Police Changing?

1

Trends in the Adoption
of Community Policing[1]

JEFFREY A. ROTH, JAN ROEHL, AND CALVIN C. JOHNSON

Title I of the 1994 Violent Crime Control and Law Enforcement Act (the Crime Act), which was titled the "Public Safety Partnership and Community Policing Act," had four objectives. Of these, the first and most visible was widely interpreted as "putting 100,000 cops on the beat." However, many observers, including some who were deeply involved in advocating passage of Title I and planning its implementation, placed at least as high a priority on its second objective, "to foster problem solving and interaction with communities by police officers," that is, to encourage and accelerate transitions to community policing by police agencies throughout the country.

Title I became the statutory basis for creating the Office of Community Oriented Policing Services—the COPS Office—and authorizing it to spend $9 billion on grants to state, local, and other public law enforcement agencies and on supporting functions. These functions included training and technical assistance in community policing through the Community Policing Consortium; forging partnerships among police, researchers, and community residents through a network of regional community policing institutes; and encouraging compliance with grant requirements, including the requirement to implement community policing.

Therefore, measuring the success of the COPS program (as we call it) in achieving its community policing objective was one key question for the national evaluation of its efforts. Early findings on that question from a multiwave national survey and site-assessment observations are reported elsewhere (Roth, 2000; Roth and Ryan, 2000) for 1995–98. This paper draws on an update survey conducted in the summer of 2000 to describe 1995–98 trends in agencies' implementation of community policing for the entire period, 1995–2000.

[1]The research reported here was supported, with funds transferred from the Office of Community Oriented Policing Services, under an award (95-IJ-CX-0073) to the Urban Institute by the National Institute of Justice, Office of Justice Programs, U.S. Department of Justice. Findings and conclusions reported here are those of the authors and do not necessarily reflect the official position or policies of the U.S. Department of Justice. The authors' views should not be attributed to the Urban Institute, the University of Pennsylvania, their trustees, or their funders.

WHAT IS COMMUNITY POLICING?

As debate began over the 1994 Crime Act, anyone advocating community policing as a break with the dominant professional policing model could point to a variety of objectives, strategies, and tactics. Reasonable people could (and still do) argue over which of the objectives and strategies discussed in the Introduction to this book were essential to real community policing.

However, as evaluators we did not have to settle those arguments. Our goal was to measure progress toward the objectives set by the first COPS Office director. Guided by the agency director (Brann, 1995) we assessed the extent to which police agencies adopted (a) tactics for partnership building, (b) problem oriented policing, and (c) crime prevention, plus (d) organizational mechanisms they set up to support these three goals.

We used two primary measurement devices to develop the information reported in this paper. The first is a sequence of telephone surveys conducted in the fall of 1996 and repeated in the summers of 1998 and 2000 with a probability sample of municipal and county law enforcement agencies. The sample was stratified to overrepresent large agencies serving jurisdictions with populations of 50,000 or more and to underrepresent small agencies serving jurisdictions with smaller populations. One module of the survey was a tactics checklist that asked respondents about the implementation status of each of the four objectives described above. In the 1996 Wave 1 survey, we asked about implementation status before 1995 (the first full year of the COPS program) and at the point of data collection, September–October 1996. These status reports were updated in Wave 3 and Wave 4 surveys conducted in the summers of 1998 and 2000. The responses to our survey are best regarded as official agency statements because each respondent was either the chief executive or someone designated by the chief to speak on behalf of the agency.

There are important questions about the validity of survey responses as a description of agencies' actual policing practices. The authors of the chapters in this book debated them hotly. First, the person filling out the form may not know the true state of affairs or share the researcher's vocabulary for describing it. For example, we believe that the decrease in problem solving reported by some small agencies for 1995–98 may indicate that those agencies' understanding of problem solving became more accurate, not that they abandoned problem-oriented policing during the period. Second, Maguire and Mastrofski's (2000) criticism applies in this case, that our survey items were not designed to measure the depth or extent of an activity. For example, a response that an agency holds regular community meetings could refer to one annual presentation to a community audience, monthly working meetings with community representatives in every patrol area, or nearly anything in between. Third, the responses may be intended to present an ideal to which the chief aspires, or a standard with which the chief believes the agency should comply to retain COPS funding, achieve accreditation, or satisfy some other requirement. Indeed, site teams that visited thirty agencies as part of the national evaluation of COPS discovered that many reported com-

Table 1.1 Mean Percent of Community Policing Tactics Implemented, by Objective, Agency Size, and Year

Objective/Agency Size (# Tactics)	MEAN PERCENTAGE OF TACTICS IMPLEMENTED		
	Pre-1995	1998	2000
Partnership Building (8 Tactics)			
Large Agencies	57.9	80.2***	80.1
Small Agencies	28.0	33.4***	42.7###
Problem Solving (11 Tactics)			
Large Agencies	55.4	85.5***	86.5
Small Agencies	43.1	43.9	59.7###
Prevention (11 Tactics)			
Large Agencies	58.0	77.4***	76.9
Small Agencies	38.6	38.6	49.5###
Supportive Organizational Changes (10 Tactics)			
Large Agencies	41.7	67.4***	66.0
Small Agencies	24.7	31.4***	45.2###

Note: Significance level of the 1995–98 change in percentage of community policing practices in use is as follows:

***p-value < .01   **p-value < .05   *p-value < .10

Significance level of the 1998–2000 change in percentage of community policing practices in use is as follows:

###p-value < .01   ##p-value < .05   #p-value < .10

munity policing practices—especially those related to partnership building, problem solving, and organizational change—turned out to have wide ranges of meanings in actual practice (Roehl et al., 2000). The high cost of site visits, of course, precluded visiting a statistically meaningful sample of agencies as part of the national evaluation.

Despite these shortcomings, the survey data used in this report have two important advantages for describing 1995–2000 trends in community policing practices. The data pertain to a national probability sample of agencies. And, for all chiefs who claim that their agencies are doing community policing, even inaccurate responses seem likely to describe what they believe community policing should mean in their jurisdictions. Therefore, at a minimum the data are useful for describing trends in police chiefs' definitions of community policing.

Table 1.1 summarizes the survey findings. For each of the four objectives, the average percentages of community policing practices reportedly in use by large agencies increased by statistically significant amounts between the pre-1995 period and 1998, the first four years of the COPS program. Between 1998 and 2000, large agencies' adoption of community policing practices ground to a halt; none of the four change measures changed by to a statistically significant extent.

On average, small agencies were using smaller percentages of all four sets of tactics in 1995. Between 1995 and 1998, the small agencies showed statistically significant increases in their use of tactics for only two of the objectives— partnership building and supportive organizational changes. For both, the increases were smaller than for the large agencies. Although large agencies' adoption of community policing tactics stagnated between 1998 and 2000, the small agencies increased their use of tactics for all four objectives by statistically significant amounts. Nonetheless, their use of tactics for all four objectives still lagged well behind that of large agencies in 2000.

Our second task was to conduct observations and interviews in thirty COPS grantee agencies, twenty-six of which were local or county police or sheriffs' departments serving jurisdictions larger than 50,000 population. The site visits were intended in part to validate the survey data by measuring the ground truth underlying the survey responses and to provide more qualitative data from which to draw deeper insights and useful examples of how each tactic was being interpreted. At least one visit was made to each site by a team of at least one police researcher and one practitioner; about half were visited twice. Depending on agency size, the duration of visits ranged from two to five days, and the team size ranged between two and five members. Because the site visits were made during 1997 and 1998, conditions on site may well have changed by 2000.

In this age when the community policing vocabulary is well known and Federal funding rewards agencies for implementing community policing, one might expect it to be difficult, in our limited time on site, to separate the rhetoric of community policing from the reality of what the agencies actually do. Indeed, it often was. However, the enormous variation we detected across sites in the operational meaning of even signature community policing tactics provides reassurance about the validity of our site reports. For detailed information on the thirty sites visited, see Roth (2000) and the site reports.

The next four sections describe trends between 1995 and 2000 in the nature of community policing that agencies are delivering. The descriptions are organized around the four community policing objectives articulated by the COPS Office: partnership building, problem solving, prevention, and organizational practices in support of those objectives.

THE SPREAD OF PARTNERSHIP BUILDING

At the crux of partnerships involving law enforcement agencies is the belief that reducing crime and disorder require the coordinated, concentrated effort of individuals and organizations affected by and concerned with the problems. As crime has multiple causes, the presumption is that solutions must be equally multifaceted and cannot be reached by the police acting alone.

Today, the rhetoric of partnerships is at the center not only of community policing but of many Federally funded strategies recounted in Roehl et al. (2000) to attack crime, drug abuse, and other community problems. Among law enforcement agencies, there are many variations in the nature of partnerships: the partnership-building tactics employed, the participants, and the extent of collaboration. We first present survey data on recent growth in police partnership-building activities, then use reports from the field to explore the nature of working partnerships in different law enforcement agencies. The latter discussion relies heavily on findings reported by Roehl et al.

Partnership Building: Survey Findings

In the three survey waves, we measured agencies' community partnership-building activities using a list of eight tactics. These tactics were drawn from accounts of early community relations activities and community policing demonstrations. Added together to form an index, in 1995 they had moderate internal consistency. (Internal consistency is the extent to which an agency adopting one tactic is likely to adopt another.) These tactics were generally, but not strongly, likely to be adopted together as a package; therefore, a count of how many of them were adopted is a good measure of the general concept of partnership-building activities. To measure tactic-specific implementation status in large agencies around the time the COPS program was launched, we computed the percentage of all large local and county agencies claiming pre-1995 use of each tactic. To measure 1998 and 2000 implementation status, we added the pre-1995 figure to the percentage of agencies responding that they adopted the tactic since the previous reference point.

For large agencies, Figure 1.1 shows a pattern of early adoption followed by near stagnation between 1995 and 2000. Between 1995 and 1998, the growth in use of all eight tactics was statistically significant. Between 1998 and 2000, in contrast, only the percentages of agencies conducting citizen police academies and carrying out crime prevention projects with businesses continued to grow slowly. The percentages of agencies working side by side with citizens—to prevent crime, to remove signs of disorder, and to clean up neighborhoods—actually declined by statistically insignificant amounts. The declines are consistent with comments heard in a few sites that such efforts often had only temporary effects, offered no basis for developing long-term collaborative strategies, and jeopardized community police officers' morale.

For small agencies, an index of Wave 1 survey data on the pre-1995 implementation status of all eight tactics also had a moderate consistency. The Wave 4 survey provided the responses from which we calculated tactic-specific implementation status for small agencies in 1998 and 2000. To measure the 1998 tactic-specific implementation, we computed the percentage of all small municipal and county agencies claiming pre-1998 implementation of each tactic. To measure the 2000 tactic-specific implementation status, we added the pre-1998 figure to the percentage of agencies responding that they started using the tactic between 1998 and 2000.

The tactic-specific percentages in Figure 1.1 show that in 1998, small agencies were using all tactics except neighborhood cleanups at significantly greater percentages than in 1995. The largest net gains between 1995 and 1998 were on the implementation of resident surveys (+12 percentage points) and regular community meetings (+11 percentage points). All other partnership-building tactics experienced net gains between 3 and 5 percentage points.

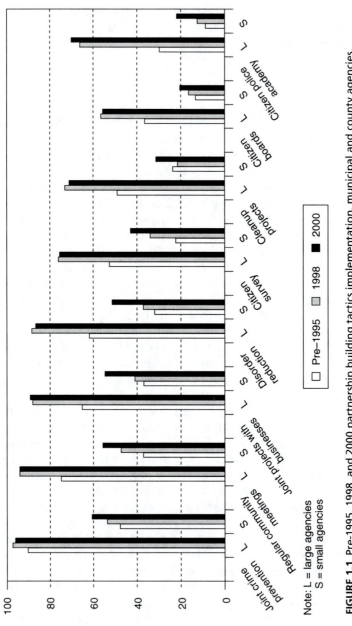

FIGURE 1.1 Pre-1995, 1998, and 2000 partnership building tactics implementation, municipal and county agencies.

Small agencies continued to adopt all eight partnership-building tactics between 1998 and 2000. The greatest net gains (10 percentage points or more) were made on projects with residents to remove signs of disorder, joint projects with businesses, cleanup projects, and citizen police academies. Nevertheless, between 1998 and 2000 the adoption rate accelerated over the 1995–98 period for all tactics except regular community meetings and citizen surveys.

Partnerships: Reports from the Field

The partnerships we found on site visits fall into two general categories. The first is *problem solving partnerships,* which are formed with other service providers, enabling the police to work in concert with others to identify, analyze, and solve problems, often using collective resources (staff, equipment, etc.). Local city and county agencies are arguably the most common and coequal partners in problem-solving responses, particularly tactics involving civil-abatement processes, cleanups and revitalization, and environmental changes. Typical local partners include the departments responsible for code enforcement, housing, zoning, public works, social services, and parks and recreation. Problem-solving partnerships may also include elected officials, school officials, business representatives, and private organizations. They may or may not include community representatives who provide input as to how resources should be allocated and used to solve multiple problems.

Examples of problem-solving partnerships abound in the COPS-funded sites that we visited. Some were formal, such as the Oakland Police Department's Beat Health Unit, in which the police and inspectors from code enforcement, sewers and sidewalks, and vector control (the agency that controls rodent and roach problems) work together to abate crime, drug, and disorder problems. Other problem-solving partnerships change members and tactics, depending on the problem at hand.

One trend of note is physically locating the problem-solving partners under one roof. In Miami, mini city halls are located in each of the twelve neighborhoods served by Neighborhood Enhancement Teams (NETs). In addition to the community policing officers and civilian staff, the mini city halls are staffed by zoning inspectors, sanitation inspectors, and other city and community workers. We observed similar structures, with variation in the colocated agencies, in Huntington Beach, California, and Cobb County, Georgia. In Nashville, Tennessee, centers in Enterprise Zones house community police officers, social services (Family and Children's Services, welfare representatives, and job-training programs), and small businesses (e.g., hair braiding, nail salon, and thrift store).

The second common type of partnership observed on site is *community partnerships* that include the police and neighborhood residents, community groups, and businesses. They have multiple purposes and may at times be equivalent to problem-solving partnerships at the neighborhood level. The level of community partnership activities varied widely, from mere *information sharing,* to *coordination* (i.e., planning and executing joint activities involving all part-ners), to occasional *collaboration* (i.e., adoption by all partners of a joint agenda).

Community partnerships in the sites visited include those at the neighbor-hood level and those that represent the full jurisdiction (city or county). At the neighborhood level, the partnership may be informal, with community police officers regularly attending meetings of neighborhood organizations to exchange information, identify and prioritize problems, develop solutions, and so on. These neighborhood-level community partnerships may also be more formal, such as Oakland's Neighborhood Crime Prevention Councils, New Bedford's (Massachusetts) Neighborhood Councils, San Bernardino County's (California) Station Advisory Boards, Los Angeles's Citizen Police Advisory Boards, and Fort Worth's advisory committees in Neighborhood Policing Offices.

Many of the visited agencies had created advisory committees composed of community representatives that typically report to the chief law enforce-ment executive, concern themselves with public safety matters that cover the entire jurisdiction, and address agencywide issues. These include Austin's Chief's Forum, Pocatello's Citizens Advisory Board, Mascoutah's Police Advi-sory Committee, and Oakland's Community Policing Advisory Board.

The key word in most of these community partnerships is "advisory." Although police departments are opening up to community input and influence, most police executives remain reluctant to give the community real authority and responsibilities. The underlying reasons for this are many and complex. Legal issues, such as accountability requirements on the chief as outlined in local laws or administrative regulations, must be considered. Some resistance probably reflects beliefs that trained and experienced police officers know best about certain issues, coupled with an abiding sense of responsibility to ensure that police resources are used efficiently, ethically, and legally. It is not uncommon for citizens upset about a crime problem to demand a police response that is, in a word, illegal.

One indicator of collaboration between police and communities may be the extent to which partnerships have evolved from formal jurisdiction-level affiliations to commonplace beat-level interactions between citizens and police at the level of one to one or small groups. For example, between the first and second site visits to the San Diego School Police, the concept and practice of partnerships moved beyond formal partnership agreements to routine projects involving individual officers, parents, and school staff members.

PROBLEM SOLVING

Problem solving is the most well-known and widely accepted component of community policing and has been far more clearly specified than partnership building. Problem solving has evolved from the much broader concept of problem-oriented policing, first developed and introduced to the police field by Herman Goldstein in an article titled "Improving the Police: A Problem

Oriented Approach" (1979), which was later expanded into a book (Goldstein, 1990). As the field's awareness of problem-oriented policing occurred simultaneously with the advent of community policing, much early debate focused on which should be the dominant form of policing (Capowich and Roehl, 1994). Although for many, the concept of problem has evolved from Goldstein's emphasis on widespread substantive problems (e.g., commercial robberies downtown) to a common focus on repeat calls to a specific location, problem solving—the centerpiece of problem-oriented policing—is widely considered an essential element of community policing (Cordner, 1998).

Many law enforcement agencies find problem solving a practical and palatable first step in their transition to community policing. Although some problem solving, such as boarding up abandoned property, continues to be criticized as not real police work, problem solving can also be sold to the troops as working smarter to end the need to respond endlessly to the same location. However, perhaps to avoid appearing soft on crime, traditional enforcement tactics such as undercover drug buys, surveillance, saturation patrols, and arrest are increasingly being included in the arsenal of problem-solving tactics.

Problem Solving: Survey Findings

We measured agencies' problem-solving activities using a list of eleven tactics. Most of the tactics were worded to describe components of Goldstein's paradigm without using the key terminology of that approach (e.g., the SARA model of problem solving—scanning, analysis, response, and assess). Other tactics were selected to tap community involvement in problem solving and to measure adoption of applicable new technology (i.e., geographic-based information systems) or organizational arrangements (i.e., police or probation teams). For both large and small agencies, these tactics had a moderately higher interitem reliability than the items used to measure community partnership building.

For large agencies, Figure 1.2 shows that problem-solving activities in our list proliferated considerably between 1995 and 1998. During that period, our sample reported adopting an average of 3.3 new problem-solving tactics, so that by 1998 their use had become nearly universal. On average, they were using 9.4 tactics, or 85.5 percent of the 11 in our list by 1998.

Because problem solving was so widespread by 1998, it is not surprising that the adoption rate slowed dramatically thereafter, so that by 2000 the mean number of tactics implemented had climbed by only 0.1, to 9.5. However, there were increases of about 6 percentage points in the fractions of agencies adopting the two practices that were not already nearly universal: analyzing crime problems with Geographic Information System (GIS) software and working with probation officers on problem-solving projects.

The nature of problem solving also reportedly took on more of a community cast. Since 1998, analyzing problems with the community has been the most widely reported tactic, and about 90 percent of large agencies reported using residents' input to identify problems and to measure the impact of responses to the problems.

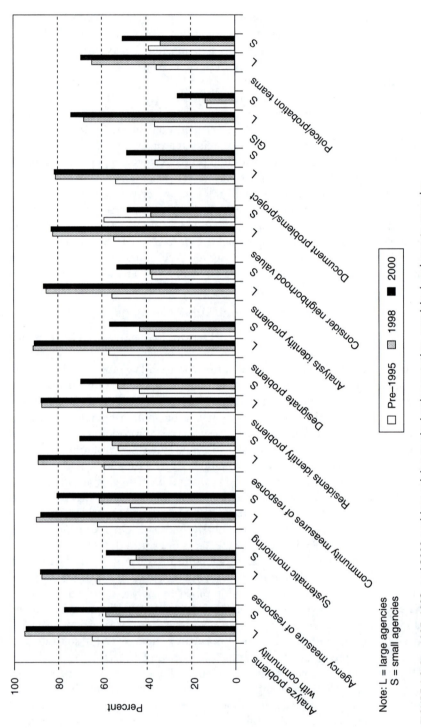

FIGURE 1.2 Pre-1995, 1998, and 2000 problem-solving tactics implementation, municipal and county agencies.

For small agencies, four of the eleven tactics were reportedly less widely used in 1998 than in 1995: considering neighborhood values in planning responses, using agency data to measure response effect, analyzing problems with probation officers, and documenting problems and projects in writing. These losses were offset by increases in the percentages reporting use of all the other problem–solving tactics except analyzing crime data.

Small agencies continued to adopt all eleven problem–solving tactics between 1998 and 2000. By 2000, all but one of the problem–solving tactics was reportedly in use by 50 percent to 80 percent of the small agencies. Use of the exception, analyzing crime problems using GIS software, more than doubled between 1995 and 1998, to 27 percent of all small municipal and county police agencies.

Problem Solving: Reports from the Field

Although Goldstein's writings and subsequent versions disseminated by the Police Executive Research Forum (Eck and Spelman, 1987) provide a clear prototype for problem solving, our site teams found astonishing variety in local interpretations of the term. We grouped the interpretations we observed in thirty sites into five categories, only one of which closely resembles Goldstein's prototype. We also found individual departments that demonstrated multiple versions of problem solving. The five versions we observed were:

1. Problem solving that fits the established model, supported by documentation and incorporation of problem solving into training and strategic planning functions. At least fifteen of the sites visited demonstrated advanced use of this model. Included are departments such as San Diego, which has long been recognized as a leader in problem-oriented policing; Fort Worth, where neighborhood police officers concentrate on beat-specific problem-solving and prevention efforts; and Los Angeles, where senior lead officers dedicated to beats were placing a strong emphasis on formal problem solving at the time of our first visit.

    Many sites considered enforcement a primary problem-solving tool, even though the elemental principle of problem solving—focusing on resolving the underlying causes of problems—is predicated on the belief that enforcement tactics have been or will be unsuccessful in resolving the problem in the long term. Arrest was repeatedly cited during site visits as a common tool pulled from the problem-solving toolbox. This interpretation is exemplified by the Buffalo Police Department, where the three elements of problem solving were described as strict enforcement, high visibility, and increased communication. In North Charleston, South Carolina, problem solving was conducted by police teams with no community participation, and team responses were characterized as tactical (i.e., enforcement oriented).

2. Problem solving as purely a matter of local definition, which does not comport with any of the common definitions. Cobb County's inclusion

of off-duty work and a new county radio system is one example. In another jurisdiction the problem-solving response to a repeat burglary problem in a specific neighborhood was to drive around looking for the suspects' car.

3. Problem solving as primarily an area-based crime attack strategy under the rubric of zero tolerance or some other local definition. Austin's Crime NET, Fresno's CRASH and Goldstar components, Huntington Beach's Directed Enforcement actions and task forces, Milwaukee's Knock and Talk and Quality of Life policing, Newark's Crime Enforcement Zones, the joint actions of North Charleston's SPEED Team, and to a lesser degree Racine's Special Assignment shift all fit this definition.

4. Problem solving that is all but invisible to the observer seeking documentation or hard evidence but is said to be incorporated into the approach of generalist or split-force officers; Flint, Fort Worth, New Bedford, Maricopa County, and reportedly the Enterprise Zone community policing initiatives in Nashville fit this model.

5. Problem solving as long-range prevention activities, interspersed with small tactical efforts that meet the standard definitions; Sandy City, New Bedford's school-based activities, and Cobb County's COPE seem to fit this model. These types are described more fully in Roehl et al. (2000).

Our teams occasionally observed two or more types of problem solving in a single agency, because problem solving evolved between site visits, multiple types coexisted simultaneously, or both. At the time of our visit to the Des Moines Police Department, its Neighborhood Area Resource Coordinator (NARC) unit was blending undercover drug market operations with rudimentary problem solving; simultaneously, a lone officer and the River Bend Community Association were adding to their extraordinary track record of successes achieved with problem solving fitting the established Type 1 definition.

The Las Vegas Metropolitan Police Department was at the early stages of preventive problem solving (Type 5) during our first site visit, with prevention activities being planned under a multiagency Partnership Against Violence and its Effects (PAVE) and effective, if informal, problem-oriented policing projects being done by a new Utility Squad, whose sergeant had renamed it the Problem Solving Unit. By the second visit, PAVE was long forgotten. However, the agency had clearly evolved to Type 1, with Problem Solving Units in all districts, a model formalized in departmental orders, an in-service training program in problem-solving, and problem-solving training for officers and residents from all districts being conducted by the COPS-funded Western Community Policing Center.

The extent of formal problem-solving training ranged from none to minimal in most agencies; even the San Diego Police Department, a long-established leader in problem solving, only added the SARA model to its field-training checklist in 1997. However, some departments had gone to great lengths to teach problem solving on the job, through supervision and documentation. The Austin Police Department had created a deputy chief of staff position to coordinate community policing and problem solving, and sworn staff at lower ranks had explicit supervision responsibility for problem-solving in Flint, Lakeland, Miami, New Bedford, Oakland, and Racine. Formal documentation requirements for problem-solving projects were far from universal; documentation seemed most complete in San Diego, Fresno, Huntington Beach (California), Los Angeles, Oak Park (where each project is governed and documented by a police community contract), San Bernardino County, Austin, and Sandy City.

Community participation in problem solving seems to evolve in one of three ways. Agencies such as Oak Park, Fort Worth, the San Diego School Police, and Pocatello had set up formal structures for collaborative efforts by the time of our site visits; San Diego and Las Vegas were in the process of doing so. In other jurisdictions, commercial interests stimulated projects, sometimes carried out as off-duty details at shopping malls or amusement parks. In still others, strong and effective community participation had evolved through individuals or their relationships: a community activist and police lieutenant related by marriage in Des Moines; an energetic public housing director and security director in New Bedford; and extraordinarily committed community activists, rental property managers, and small business owners elsewhere.

CRIME PREVENTION

The roots of modern-day prevention in law enforcement agencies may be traced to the community crime prevention efforts of the 1970s and 1980s, many of which were funded by the Law Enforcement Assistance Administration (now BJA) and evaluated by the National Institute of Law Enforcement and Criminal Justice (now NIJ) (Rosenbaum, 1986). These strategies—neighborhood and block watches (Cirel et al., 1977); citizen patrols (Yin, Vogel, and Chaiken, 1977); surveillance and reporting of suspicious behavior to police (Bickman, Lavrakas, and Green, 1977); and environmental design changes, commonly referred to as Crime Prevention through Environmental Design, or CPTED (Fowler et al., 1979; Fowler and Mangione, 1982; Crowe, 1991)—evolved into the community-based antidrug efforts of the 1990s (Roehl et al., 1995). The central tactics of these early efforts can be readily seen in the prevention practices of today.

Another theoretical rationale for one specific community crime prevention strategy is the broken windows or incivilities hypothesis raised by Wilson and Kelling (1982). Broken windows theory underpins community policing varieties that emphasize quality-of-life issues; emerging zero-tolerance strategies are often erroneously attributed to the broken windows hypothesis, as well (Kelling, 1999).

Prevention has, in many ways, been the gateway to community policing, as many of the earliest collaborative interactions with the public have been for prevention. Police have traditionally worked with local children both formally and informally through groups such as the Boys and Girls Clubs, Police Athletic Leagues, and agency-specific activities such as fairs, summer camps, and so on. Law enforcement agencies have long had crime prevention officers and "Officer Friendlies," who provide traditional services such as lectures and brochures on individual safety, security checks on homes and businesses, property marking with engraving pens, and children's photo ID programs.

We found that the prevention side of community policing, as defined by the COPS grantees visited, is highly programmatic. When asked about their prevention efforts under community policing, police representatives nearly always cited discrete programs (e.g., DARE and Neighborhood Watch) and techniques (e.g., preventive patrol and alternatives for youth). They did not articulate any philosophy of prevention, the logical product of collaboration with communities and problem solving focused on underlying causes.

Prevention: Survey Findings

We measured agencies' prevention activities using a list of eleven tactics. Primary prevention tactics were generally drawn from the literature on community crime prevention or were selected as successors of that strategy. Secondary prevention tactics were generally more recently-developed approaches to resolving crime or disorder problems in troubled neighborhoods. Tertiary prevention programs were generally those prominent in the victims' movement or represented other methods of repairing harm done by crime.

The percentage of large agencies using every preventive tactic on our list grew significantly between 1995 and 1998. In contrast, Figure 1.3 shows that between 1998 and 2000, only participation in cooperative antitruancy programs with schools expanded, and that only from 74 percent to 78 percent of agencies. Participation in victim assistance programs dropped a little, from 83 percent of agencies to 78 percent. There were also smaller nonsignificant decreases in drug education programs in schools (from 96 percent to 93 percent), in late-night recreation programs (from 26 percent to 24 percent), and in battered women's programs (from 82 percent to 79 percent).

In all three years the most common primary prevention programs were drug education programs in schools such as DARE and police/youth programs such as Boys and Girls Clubs. The fastest growing tactic in this group was varying preventive patrol styles, such as bike and foot patrol, which are widely considered signature community policing tactics. The most common secondary prevention programs were code enforcement and confidential hotlines. Along with code enforcement, the fastest growing secondary prevention programs were mediation and cooperative truancy reduction programs with schools. The most commonly adopted tertiary prevention program between 1995 and 1998 was graffiti removal, but the most commonly used were victim assistance and battered women's programs.

Figure 1.3 shows that in 1998, small agencies were using seven of the eleven tactics in lower percentages than in 1995. The decreases were small but statistically significant for drug education programs in schools, mediation to resolve disputes and conflicts, code enforcement to combat disorder, cooperative programs with schools to reduce truancy, confidential hotlines for reporting drugs

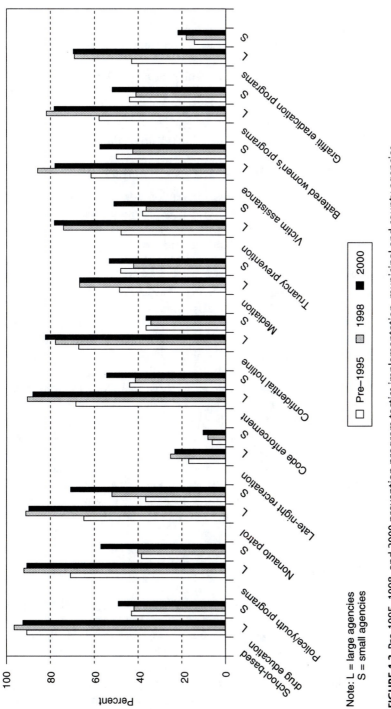

Note: L = large agencies
S = small agencies

FIGURE 1.3 Pre-1995, 1998, and 2000 prevention program tactics implementation, municipal and county agencies.

and guns on the street, and victim assistance programs. There were substantial increases in the use of varying styles of preventive patrol (e.g., bike and foot), police/youth programs, graffiti-eradication programs, and late-night recreation programs.

By 2000, the small agencies made significant increases in their usage rates for prevention programs, including those for which use had dropped during the preceding three years. Consequently, ten of the eleven tactics were in significantly wider use in 2000 than in 1995, and the exception, confidential drug and gun hotlines, had returned to its 1995 level after a drop in 1998.

Prevention Programs: Notes from the Field

In most of the departments we visited, prevention was an explicit community policing goal but was rarely the first priority. Prevention programs tended to include fairly standard DARE, neighborhood watch, Boys and Girls Clubs, and Police Athletic League activities. However, the activities of some Neighborhood Watch programs are evolving into fairly sophisticated surveillance and problem solving. Some youth programs, such as Nashville's Enterprise Zones, involve the police in bringing the resources and services of multiple agencies to bear on youth and families with special needs.

For adults, several departments were providing education on how to avoid victimization, providing crime prevention information via the Internet, and organizing telephone trees to alert neighboring businesses of crimes. The San Diego Police Department operates an active and innovative sexual assault prevention program in collaboration with male–female teams from the community. Several departments offer training to rental property managers in tenant screening, CPTED, and crime- and drug-free property management. In Milwaukee, officers work closely with property managers who blacklist undesirable tenants in an effort either to displace them to other areas or to secure agreements to change behavior. Our site teams observed several successful examples of code enforcement, drug and gun hotlines (when operated by a trusted community-based institution rather than the police), CPTED, and safety planning and cell phones for domestic violence victims to prevent repeat victimization.

SUPPORTIVE ORGANIZATIONAL CHANGE

Shifting from reactive response to proactive problem solving, developing partnerships with the community and non–law enforcement agencies, and expanding prevention initiatives generate pressures for organizational changes in police agencies. As one urban police department says in opening its community policing training sessions, "Good community policing isn't new to the best officers. But the organizational support you'll start getting for it is."

Organizational change is difficult in any organization, and the conventional wisdom of the past is that law enforcement agencies are particularly resistant to change. A common assumption accepted by many police practitioners and observers is that departments will "most likely require 10 or more years for full implementation" (Roberg, 1994). Yet in many of the COPS-funded agencies we examined, at least temporary organizational changes in support of community policing reportedly occurred with astonishing speed.

In some departments, turnover at the chief's level and other top command positions has spurred rapid changes in direction, philosophy, and structure. In others, departmental leaders have worked to restate the organization's mission, followed by changes in policy and operation designed to achieve new goals. This is not to say that change has been easy or that all officers have readily accepted and followed the new philosophy. Skolnick and Bayley (1986) may be right in concluding that innovation may require "urging retirement on members of the old guard." Indeed, during the national evaluation of COPS, when one lieutenant was asked about a site visitor's sense that his department's enthusiasm for community policing seemed high in the field but nonexistent around headquarters, he responded, "I've been with the department for 12 years. I get [community policing], and everyone who came in with my class or later gets it. By the time we're in charge, we'll be doing community policing from top to bottom. And [because officers are eligible for retirement after 20 years] an 8-year transition isn't that long compared to other departments." Nevertheless, most law enforcement agencies we visited deserve credit for their capacity to change when new, seemingly sensible ways of doing business are presented.

Traditionally, organizational change requires several components—setting and clearly communicating new goals and objectives, changing policies and procedures in support of the new goals and objectives, providing training and support to employees to enable them to implement the new procedures, and rewarding employees for making appropriate changes. In addition, community policing is generally thought to require new procedures to create time for interaction with the community, beat integrity to facilitate becoming acquainted with the neighborhood one is policing, and authority to permit officers to exercise greater discretion while on patrol.

Organizational Changes: Survey Findings

We measured changes in agencies' organizational practices using a list of ten items that are more or less commonly used to pursue the objectives listed in the preceding paragraph. Figure 1.4 illustrates that for large agencies, all ten of the organizational practices in our list had become significantly more widespread between 1995 and 1998. Between 1998 and 2000, however, the trend reversed for organizational practices. Providing the community a voice in nominating problems and setting priorities was a little less common in 2000 (60 percent) than in 1998 (67 percent). There were also small, statistically insignificant drops in the percentages of agencies reporting that they participated in multiagency task forces, used alternative response modes to calls, set patrol area boundaries to coincide with community boundaries, used a team approach instead of the chain of command, or took other steps to expand beat officers' discretion. Even after the drops, the percentages of agencies that had

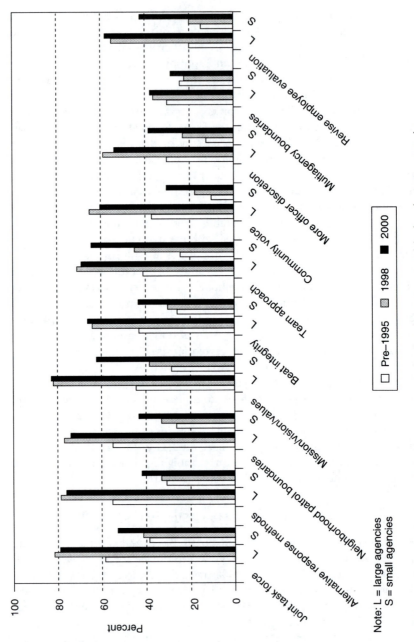

Note: L = large agencies
      S = small agencies

Pre-1995 ☐   1998 ▨   2000 ■

FIGURE 1.4 Pre-1995, 1998, and 2000 supportive organizational changes, municipal and county agencies.

adopted these organizational practices remained upward of 20 percent higher in 2000 than they had been in 1995.

Only one supportive organizational practice continued to spread among large agencies between 1998 and 2000. The percentage of agencies that had revised their personnel-evaluation measures grew very slightly, from 54 percent of agencies in 1998 to 58 percent in 2000. The prevalence of three other practices—revised mission statements, dispatch rules to strengthen beat integrity, and setting beat boundaries to coincide with other agencies' service area boundaries—remained essentially constant.

For small agencies, Figure 1.4 generally reflects a modest pace of change between 1995 and 1998, followed by greater change between 1998 and 2000. During the first reference period, reported use of seven of the ten organizational practices increased by less than 10 percentage points. The exceptions were: coordination of beat boundaries with other agencies' administrative boundaries, which decreased by a small but statistically significant percentage, from 26 percent to 24 percent; increasing reliance on team policing instead of chain of command, which spread from 26 percent to 45 percent of small agencies; and expanded beat officers' discretion, which spread from 13 percent to 25 percent of agencies.

Between 1998 and 2000, reported organizational change accelerated rapidly. The percentage of agencies that reported making a change grew significantly for all ten practices. More important, every 1998–2000 increase exceeded the corresponding 1995–98 increase.

Organizational Changes: Notes from the Field

As our site teams examined what lay behind the official reports of organizational changes, four kinds of changes proved especially interesting. These were the realignment of beat boundaries and assignments to maximize beat integrity, changing performance criteria for officers engaging in community policing, revising mission and/or values statements, and the role of special units.

Realigning Beat Boundaries and Assignments   Generally, beat boundaries are defined using multiple criteria, including physical boundaries (freeways, rivers, etc.), identified neighborhoods, and the number of calls for service. Approximately 22 percent of the surveyed agencies reported realigning their beat boundaries between 1995 and 1998; 35 percent of the agencies visited had adopted a strategy we called "geo-deployment": simultaneously realigning beat boundaries to conform to natural neighborhood boundaries or service areas and deploying patrol or dedicated community police officers to these geographic areas. Among those agencies, the Oakland and San Diego police departments demonstrated two different approaches and made clear that the correct approach depends on local context.

The Oakland Police Department increased the number of beats from thirty-five to fifty-seven, aiming to serve naturally occurring neighborhoods of between 5,000 and 7,000 residents with fully dedicated individual officers. A community police officer is being assigned to each beat, and patrol officers will cover a beat or two depending on need. Like other agencies, Oakland also lengthened the amount of time an officer is assigned to a given beat, to increase the opportunity to get to know, and be known by, citizens.

In contrast, the San Diego Police Department was in the process of collapsing each district from four or more beats, each patrolled by one officer, into two service areas, each patrolled by a team of four or five officers. Simultaneously, patrol resources were being expanded by breaking up special units and deploying new COPS-funded officers. Senior command anticipated that the restructuring would cause some reduction in general familiarity between individual officers and residents. However, the new structure was expected to maintain the beat integrity of the team as a whole while expanding the flexibility to free up an officer from response duty to work on a specific problem-oriented policing project or attend a community meeting, for example, while the rest of the team covered patrol duties for the entire sector (see Maxfield, Langston, and Roth, 1998, for additional details).

Changing Performance Criteria   Approximately 35 percent of both the national sample of agencies and the agencies visited reported changing performance criteria to reward community policing activities. Several reported the changes were informal. This typically referred to supervisors' taking into account the amount of problem solving and community contact conducted by individual officers. Where the changes were formal, personnel evaluation forms have been revised, and the changes have been formally communicated to the rank and file. A fairly dramatic change in performance criteria was implemented by the North Charleston police chief, who instituted a public scoreboard in each precinct, displaying, by month, each officers' sick days, annual leave, military leave, calls dispatched, calls assisted, and self-generated activities (e.g., security checks, problem-solving activities, etc.). The scoreboard, needless to say, has been a hotly contested measure of officer performance.

In a Locally Initiated Research Partnership administered by the National Institute of Justice, the Arlington County (Virginia) Police Department and the Urban Institute found that a rudimentary system consisting of a large MS Word table, created primarily to track each problem-solving project, also had the beneficial effects of an informal performance review system. The system was intended merely to record each action taken on a project, its effect, and the recommendation for follow-up—primarily for transmitting information across shifts and across different days-off schedules. However, because the system was open to all officers in the district and each entry was identified to a specific officer, date, and time, the system encouraged informal competition among officers. Simultaneously, it created a quantitative and qualitative record of each officer's contributions, which was available for formal performance review.

Revising Mission, Vision, or Values Statements   About 37 percent of agencies in the national sample and 30 percent of those visited reported revising mission and/or values statements during 1995–98. In most departments, it appears that these revisions were made by a committee composed of command and rank-and-file officers. About 30 percent also reported developing long-range plans, typically covering the next five years, to implement community policing. In Oakland, the strategic plan was developed by a group of police and community representatives. In Austin, a plan for community policing was developed in 1991, then revised and updated in 1993 and 1996.

Mission and value statements developed by police organizations are intended to communicate their core beliefs and principles that will drive the delivery of services to their communities. In the Fresno County Sheriff's Department, one value statement reads in part to "work collaboratively with neighborhoods to understand the true nature of crime and develop cooperative strategies." In Buffalo, the mission statement includes a commitment to help facilitate input into the police decision-making process, and in Austin, the mission statement includes the language "to protect and serve through community partnerships."

The challenge, of course, is to create a tangible connection between the words of such statements and the actual way the organization behaves within its community. It is possible for mission and value statements to be mere words on paper that are inserted into frames and hung on walls in offices throughout the organization. Under these circumstances, many people in the organization may not know of these statements, and mechanisms are not in place to ensure accountability for units and individuals to perform consistently with them. In a few other organizations, however, even a three-day site visit was long enough to hear a casual reference to the mission statement as a reason for some decision—evidence that officers are aware of it. Roehl et al. (2000: 197–198) describes experiences of three departments—San Diego, Austin, and Oakland—that demonstrate ways to develop such statements and encourage widespread buy-in to the principles it communicates.

Special Units: More Risks Specialized community policing units carry some well-known risks (see, e.g., Sadd and Grinc, 1994). Nevertheless, many believe that when they are successful at least for a time, special units are a helpful way station on the path to organizationwide community policing. Special units serve to steep officers in problem solving and community policing, training them while indoctrinating them in the principles. The best of these officers (such as the senior lead officers in the Los Angeles Police Department) may then return to patrol as field training officers and proselytizers. Special units may also show the value of community policing (in solving and preventing crimes, in improving community relations, etc.) to observers and skeptics within and outside the department. In Sandy City, for example, a problem-solving team investigating reports that people were living in U-Lock-It storage units made the largest drug bust in the city's history after finding four freezers full of cash and marijuana; excess electrical usage was one indicator of the problem uncovered during the assessment phase of the SARA model. The first Las Vegas Metropolitan Police Department Problem Solving

Unit, whose sergeant had negotiated the right to "throw away the stat[istic]s" in having his unit's performance assessed, nevertheless prided itself on "holding its own" in statistical measures, "bailing other units out" of threatening situations, and excelling at "rock 'n roll" policing when needed.

Unfortunately, experience in other cities suggests that the successes of such units may create a climate of doused expectations when the chief tries to extend the principles that worked in the successful unit to the entire department. Former members of the special unit may feel disappointed because they no longer have all the resources they had in the special unit. Nonmembers may now feel the weight of new community policing responsibilities added to their old duties to respond to calls. At the stage of conversion from special unit to generalist community policing, special morale-building work may be needed, even (or perhaps especially) with high performers.

CONCLUSIONS AND NEXT STEPS

The survey findings reported here indicate that at least at the level of announced agency policy, reported use of community policing tactics proliferated between 1995 and 2000 in both large and small agencies. Although community meetings and Neighborhood Watch–type programs remained the mainstays of partnership building, two-way communication opportunities expanded through such programs as resident surveys, citizen advisory boards, and citizen police academies.

With respect to problem solving, more agencies began reporting they were using elements of Goldstein's (1979, 1990) paradigm. They also reported involving community residents more fully in identifying problems and measuring the effects of responses to them, as well as bringing geocoding to bear on these tasks. Yet on site, problem solving turned out to have an astonishing variety of meanings, many of which would be unrecognizable to those immersed in problem-oriented policing.

The use of packaged programs such as DARE, Boys and Girls Clubs, and programs for victim assistance and battered women expanded between 1995 and 2000, and therefore remained the most common approaches to prevention. However, the prevention tool kit expanded during those years, as bike and foot patrols, code enforcement, truancy-prevention partnerships, and confidential hotlines for reporting guns and drugs all proliferated.

Among organizational changes to support community policing activities, the most rapidly growing were those intended to signal change: revised mission statements and new performance review criteria for community police officers. These devices risk being hollow icons, but our site teams saw several examples of their use to reorient behaviors. Also, through the survey and in the field, we observed a variety of procedural innovations intended to give community policing officers more time in their assigned areas, more time to do community policing, and more discretion to deal immediately with conditions they encounter.

There is ample evidence that the police field has accepted the viability of partnership-based problem solving and prevention strategies as relevant and useful to their mission of crime fighting. Initial evidence from various COPS sites suggests a lesser degree of comfort when it comes to developing and appreciating community partnerships. The police have always been inclined to establish partnerships or alliances that enable them to tackle a job with shared resources. Involving other agencies in specific aspects of problem solving has not been a difficult leap for police departments to make. Establishing community partnerships, however, is more difficult, as they must involve sharing some level of power with the community.

Within the scope of the national process evaluation of COPS, we did not address at least three key questions that could be studied using these survey data: why some innovations were adopted more widely than others; how the overall shape of community policing changed between 1995 and 2000 in U.S. law enforcement agencies; and what the relationships were among policing levels, practices, and crime.

Explaining Innovation

The survey data indicate that the community policing practices we examined varied substantially in the extent of their adoption between 1995 and 2000, and the extent of their use as of 2000. Although we did not conduct formal tests, we noticed partial consistency with Weiss's (2000) model of innovation, which explains police agencies' adoption of innovations in terms of *risk mediation* (i.e., minimizing vulnerability to civil lawsuits), *cosmopolitanism* (i.e., participation in elite national policing organizations and activities), and *peer emulation* (i.e., tendency to imitate other agencies). The wide adoption of problem-solving and GIS analyses seem consistent with cosmopolitanism, given the extent to which those technologies are promoted by elite organizations such as the Police Executive Research Forum and the Police Foundation, respectively. The lower prevalence of all community policing practices in small agencies than in large ones suggests that small agencies may need fewer special tactics to overcome social distance between police officers and the communities they police, that some organizational supports involving patrol district boundaries and dispatch rules may be irrelevant in small jurisdictions, or that the vocabulary of community policing practices is not commonly used in small jurisdictions. Additional research using these data could address more systematically the factors and process that influence law enforcement agencies' choices among innovations to adopt.

The Shape of Community Policing

Maguire and Mastrofski (2000) have reported the most sophisticated study to date of how to measure community policing. They began by noting that there is widespread (though not universal) agreement that community policing exists as a viable concept but relatively little agreement on just what that concept is.

They then did a statistical clustering of the lists of community policing tactics gathered in four national studies that surveyed agency practices: Wycoff (1994) and three collections of required reports submitted by applicants or grantees to the COPS Office between 1994 and 1997. Maguire and Mastrofski (2000) found evidence that definitions of community policing were becoming more uniform over time, but concluded with a call for future research involving multiwave surveys of a single representative agency sample, with various improvements in future survey instruments. The data analyzed in this report would provide an opportunity not only to replicate the Maguire and Mastrofski test on a new database but also to conduct the analysis in terms of packages of community policing practices and to disaggregate the analysis by agency size, indicators of community support in 1995, and other relevant characteristics.

Can It Work?

The ultimate test of community policing is, of course, whether local crime levels fall after a police agency adopts new community policing practices. Because a federal program simultaneously offered all jurisdictions identical new incentives to adopt community policing and add new officers, the evaluation data analyzed here are a unique resource for disentangling the simultaneous relationships between crime and law enforcement tactics and strength that have plagued research on that question (Blumstein, Cohen, and Nagin, 1978; Eck and Maguire, 2000).

The national COPS evaluation data could be linked with Uniform Crime Reporting data to examine the use and impact of COPS resources within police agencies and to relate these organizational and practice changes to changes in crime. The exogenous COPS intervention created a new opportunity to identify the causal relationship from policing levels to crime. The full survey database could be used to measure the crime control effectiveness of various technologies, several varieties of community policing, and several specific policing practices. It could be used to examine interactions between officer counts and policing tactics in determining crime rates. By identifying outlier agencies in which specific community policing strategies performed remarkably better or worse than expected, future analyses of these data may lay the groundwork for subsequent qualitative study of contextual factors that mediate the crime impact of changes in policing levels and community policing strategies.

CITATIONS

Bickman, Leonard, Paul J. Lavrakas, and Sandra K Green. 1997. Evaluation Program-Phase I Summary Report, Citizen Crime Reporting Projects. Washington, DC: Law Enforcement Assistance Administration, U.S. Department of Justice.

Blumstein, Alfred, Jacqueline Cohen, and Daniel Nagin. 1978. *Deterrence and Incapacitation: Estimating the Effects of Criminal Sanctions on Crime Rates.* Washington, DC: National Academy of Sciences.

Brann, Joseph E. 1995. *Statement Before the Subcommittee on the Judiciary U.S. House of Representatives Concerning Oversight of the Office of Community Oriented Policing Services.* (Washington, DC)

Capowich, George, and Jan Roehl. 1994. "Problem-Oriented Policing: Actions and Effectiveness in San Diego." In Dennis P. Rosenbaum (Ed.), *The Challenge of Community Policing: Testing the Promises.* Thousand Oaks, Calif.: Sage, 127–146

Cirel, Paul, Paul Evans, David McGillis, and Deborah Whitcomb. 1997. An Exemplary Project: Community Crime Prevention in Seattle, Washington. Washington, DC: National Institute of Law Enforcement and Criminal Justice, U.S. Department of Justice.

Cordner, Gary. 1998. "Problem-Oriented Policing vs. Zero Tolerance." In T. O'Connor Shelley and Anne Grant (Eds.), *Problem-Oriented Policing: Crime-Specific Problems, Critical Issues and Making POP Work.* Washington, DC: Police Executive Research Forum, 39–51.

Crowe, T. D. 1991. *Crime Prevention Through Environmental Design: Applications of Architectural Design and Space Management Concepts.* Boston: Butterworth-Heinemann.

Eck, John E. and Edward R. Maguire. 2000. "Have Changes in Policing Reduced Violent Crime? An Assessment of the Evidence." In Albert Blumstein and Joel Wallman (Eds.), *The Crime Drop in America.* New York: Cambridge University Press, 137–186.

Eck, John E. and William Spelman. 1987. *Solving Problems: Problem-Oriented Policing in Newport News.* Washington, DC: Police Executive Research Forum.

Fowler, Floyd J., Jr. and Thomas W. Mangione. 1982. *Neighborhood Crime, Fear, and Social Control: A Second Look at the Hartford Program (Executive Summary).* Washington, DC: National Institute of Justice, U.S. Department of Justice.

Fowler, Floyd J., Jr., Molly E. McCalla and Thomas W. Mangione. 1979. *Reducing Residential Crime and Fear: The Hartford Neighborhood Crime Prevention Program.* Washington, DC: U.S. Government Printing Office.

Goldstein, Herman. 1979. "Improving Policing: A Problem-Oriented Approach." *Crime and Delinquency,* 25: 236–258.

Goldstein, Herman. 1990. *Problem-Oriented Policing.* New York: McGraw-Hill.

Greenwood, Peter, Jan Chaiken, and Joan Petersilia. 1977. *The Criminal Investigation Process.* Lexington, MA: Heath.

Grinc, Randolph. 1994. " 'Angels in Marble': Problems in Stimulating Community Involvement in Community Policing." *Crime and Delinquency,* 40: 437–468.

Kansas City Police Department. 1980. *Response Time Analysis: Volume II- Part I Crime Analysis.* Washington, DC: U.S. Government Printing Office.

Kelling, G. A. 1999. *"Broken Windows" and Police Discretion* (NCJ 178259). Washington, DC: National Institute of Justice.

Kelling, George A. and Catherine Coles. 1997. *Fixing Broken Windows.* New York: Free Press.

Kelling, George A., Antony Pate, Duane D. Dieckman, and Charles Brown. 1974. *The Kansas City Preventive Patrol Experiment: A Technical Report.* Washington, DC: Police Foundation.

Klockars, Carl B. 1991. "The Rhetoric of Community Policing." In Jack Greene and Stephen D. Mastrofski (Eds.), *Community Policing: Rhetoric or Reality.* New York: Praeger, 239–258.

Lurigio, Arthur J. and Dennis P. Rosenbaum. 1994. "The Impact of Community Policing on Police Personnel: A Review of the Literature." In Dennis P. Rosenbaum (Ed.), *The Challenge of Community Policing: Testing the Promises.* Thousand Oaks, CA: Sage, 147–163.

Maguire, Edward R. and Stephen D. Mastrofski. 2000. "Patterns of Community Policing in the United States." *Police Quarterly* 3 (March): 4–45.

Maxfield, Michael, Elizabeth Langston, and Jeffrey A. Roth. 1998. *Making Time: An Issues Brief from the National COPS*

Evaluation. Washington, DC: The Urban Institute.

Moore, Mark H. 1992. "Problem-Solving and Community Policing." In Michael Tonry and Norval Morris (Eds.), *Crime and Justice: A Review of Research.* Chicago: University of Chicago Press, 99–158.

Moore, Mark H. 1994. "Research Synthesis and Policy Implications." In Dennis P. Rosenbaum (Ed.), *The Challenge of Community Policing.* Thousand Oaks, CA: Sage, 285–299.

Moore, Mark H., David Thacher, Catherine Coles, Philip Sheingold, and Francis Hartmann. 2000. "COPS Grants, Leadership, and Transitions to Community Policing." In Jeffrey A. Roth (Ed.), *National Evaluation of the COPS Program—Title I of the 1994 Crime Act,* Washington, DC: National Institute of Justice, (NCJ 183643), 247–274.

Moore, Mark H. and Robert C. Trojanowicz. 1988. "Corporate Strategies for Policing." *Perspectives on Policing, No. 6.* Washington, DC: National Institute of Justice and Harvard University.

Pate, Antony M., Mary Ann Wycoff, Wesley G. Skogan, and Lawrence W. Sherman. 1986. *Reducing Fear of Crime in Houston and Newark: A Summary Report.* Washington, DC: Police Foundation.

Police Foundation. 1981. *The Newark Foot Patrol Experiment.* Washington, DC: Police Foundation.

President's Commission on Law Enforcement and Administration of Justice. 1967. *The Challenge of Crime in a Free Society.* Washington, DC: U.S. Government Printing Office. Reprinted by Department of Justice, Office of Justice Programs, 1997.

Roberg, Roy R. 1994. "Can Today's Police Organizations Effectively Implement Community Policing?" In Dennis P. Rosenbaum (Ed.), *The Challenge of Community Policing: Testing the Promises.* Thousand Oaks, CA: Sage, 249–257.

Roehl, Jan, Calvin Johnson, Michael Buerger, Stephen Gaffigan, Elizabeth Langston, and Jeffrey A. Roth. 2000. "COPS and the Nature of Policing." In Jeffrey A. Roth (Ed.), *National Evaluation of the COPS Program—Title I of the 1994 Crime Act.* Washington, DC: National Institute of Justice (NCJ 183643), 179–240.

Roehl, Jan, Harold Wong, Charles Andrews, C., Ralph Huitt, and George E. Capowich. 1995. *A National Assessment of Community-Based Anti-Drug Efforts.* Pacific Grove, CA: Institute for Social Analysis.

Rosenbaum, Dennis P. 1986. "The Problem of Crime Control." In Dennis P. Rosenbaum (Ed.), *Community Crime Prevention: Does it Work?* Beverly Hills, CA: Sage, 11–18.

Roth, Jeffrey A. 2000 (Ed.), *National Evaluation of the COPS Program—Title I of the 1994 Crime Act.* Washington, DC: National Institute of Justice.

Roth, Jeffrey A. and Joseph F. Ryan. 2000. *The COPS Program After 4 Years. Research in Brief.* Washington, DC: National Institute of Justice (NCJ 183644).

Sadd, Susan and Randolph Grinc. 1994. "Innovative Neighborhood Oriented Policing: An Evaluation of Community Policing Programs in Eight Cities." In Dennis P. Rosenbaum (Ed.), *The Challenge of Community Policing.* Thousand Oaks, CA: Sage, 27–52.

Skogan, Wesley G. 1987. "The Impact of Victimization on Fear." *Crime and Delinquency, 33:* 135–154.

Skolnick, Jerome H. and David H. Bayley. 1986. *The New Blue Line: Police Innovation in Six American Cities.* New York: Free Press.

Trojanowicz, Robert C. 1982. *An Evaluation of the Neighborhood Foot Patrol Program in Flint, Michigan.* East Lansing: Michigan State University.

Trojanowicz, Robert C. 1994. *Community Policing: A Survey of Police Departments in the United States.* East Lansing:

National Center for Community Policing, Michigan State University.

Weiss, Alexander, 2000. "The Communication of Innovation in American Policing." *Policing: An International Journal of Police Strategies and Management* 20(2): 292–310.

Wilson, James Q. 1989. *Bureaucracy.* New York: Basic Books.

Wilson, James Q. and George L. Kelling. 1982. "Broken Windows: The Police and Neighborhood Safety." *Atlantic Monthly,* March, 29–38.

Wycoff, Mary Ann 1994. *Community Policing Strategies.* Washington, DC: National Institute of Justice.

Yin, Robert K., Mark Vogel, and Jan Chaiken. 1977. *National Evaluation Program–Phase I Summary Report: Citizen Patrol Projects.* Washington, DC: Law Enforcement Assistance Administration, U.S. Department of Justice.

2

Community Policing
and Organization Change

JACK R. GREENE

This chapter examines how American law enforcement has changed in light of nearly fifteen years of discussion devoted to community and problem-oriented policing. Here, "change" refers to whether the police have adopted a more preventive approach to their efforts, whether they are more or less well integrated into their external environments, whether the core technology (how policing is produced) has changed significantly, and whether police are adopting a broader role definition and set of behaviors. These changes should be the most visible with the adoption of community policing.

Today's models of community and problem-oriented policing have emerged from an often-conflicted history of the police. That history coupled with modern pressures for police reform set the stage for this inquiry.

Reform of the American police has deep historical roots, beginning in the late 1800s and continuing to the present. At each juncture of reform the police have been challenged to be less political, more efficient, and more responsive to community problems (see Kelling and Moore, 1988). Most recently, under the rubric of community policing, reformers anticipated that the police should also be more accountable (for a review of community and problem-oriented policing in the United States, see Greene, 2000).

Virtually all reforms of the police in the twentieth century expected to change not only how the police do business, but also how the police were to be organized. Between the turn of the twentieth century and World War II, reformers struggled to wrest control of policing from ward politicians. Their largely successful shift to administrative policing distanced the police from that kind of political interference so that they could control and discipline their officers and provide service more evenhandedly. Such shifts created an environment in which the police adopted much of their current organizational and service-delivery apparatus.

Strict chain of command, emphases on command and control, rapid call-response systems, and the development of a professional ideology all sought to distance the police from political patronage and a service-delivery system that often disadvantaged those out of political favor (Walker, 1977). The reform era in policing (Kelling and Moore, 1988) introduced formalism (rule making), centralization (in decision making), and specialization (work subdivided by process) into modern-day policing. As agencies were also growing in size and complexity—in communications, decision making, and the like—command and control systems were introduced to further structure police organizations and their system of call response. An industrial model of policing emerged—cloaked in the symbolism of military, hierarchical control (Manning, 1977).

The administrative era of policing sought foremost the control of the police organization by those charged with managing these agencies—police chiefs and command officers. Such reforms asserted that professional, not political, norms should guide policing and that adoption of such norms would indeed improve the equity, efficiency, and impact of police services. From the mid-1940s through the mid-1980s, administrative and professional norms were said to have guided police work.

More recently, community and problem-oriented policing have emerged as means for reorganizing the police in the latter decades of the twentieth century. Whereas the police under norms of political policing were criticized for their lack of response to the politically powerless, under norms of community and problem-oriented policing American law enforcement was challenged for being too bureaucratic, insular, and at times defiant of the public.

The administrative era of policing had indeed worked. The police became less overtly political, but in doing so they routinized internal processes, elaborated on management and control systems, and professionally distanced themselves from political processes and, of course, from the public as well. Institutionally, the police became inward looking; in many respects protecting and promoting the organization itself became their primary goal. As Herman Goldstein (1987) describes it, "process goals" eclipsed "outcome goals." And, the police cloaked themselves in several institutional myths (Crank and Langworthy, 1992), presenting themselves as uniformed, selectively organized, and focused on rapidly responding to emergencies, typically those involving crime.

Beginning in the 1950's with the passage of early civil rights legislation, and continuing into the 1980s, the institution of the police came under closer scrutiny and engendered considerable criticism for being inefficient, ineffective, and, most important, unaccountable. Since the 1980s the police in America have been pressured on many fronts to move from administrative to community policing.

Community and problem-oriented policing can be seen as rationales for changing the manner in which police deliver services. The community policing philosophy calls for modifying the structure of police agencies to make them more environmentally responsive, and a broadening of the police role from that of the traditional thief taker to a focus on problem solving and improving community quality of life. Community policing and its derivatives seek to restructure the police, flatten police organizations, despecialize them, increase decisional latitude among police officers and lower level supervisory personnel, and reduce organizational complexity (see Mastrofski, 1998; Mastrofski and Ritti, 2000).

As Goldstein (1987) suggests, in the early stages of this reform movement there were at least three threshold requirements for police agencies to shift from traditional to community and problem-oriented approaches. First, agencies needed to integrate the philosophy, and later the practice of community policing, throughout the organization—avoiding the tendency to make this new approach yet another specialization within police departments. Second, to be successful, community and problem-oriented policing values needed to emerge within police departments to influence strategic and tactical decision making and behavior. This would avoid the sloganism that has accompanied many past police reforms, many of which were more "eyewash and whitewash" than substantive. Third, according to Goldstein, the then-fledgling community and problem-oriented approaches needed to overcome anticipated resistance from the police culture, a culture said to be inward looking and disdainful of change.

The importance of Goldstein's (1987) admonishment lies in the notion that for community and problem-oriented policing to become the new technology of American policing required substantial change within and of police organizations. Such changes are the subject of this chapter.

For policing to shift from traditional to community styles several organizational and service-delivery issues emerge. These issues concern how police organizations are to interact with their wider environments; how they structure work internally; and how they socialize, or resocialize, police officers for newly emerging roles.

If the American police have indeed been successful in making such a transition from traditional to community policing, it should be visible. This transition should be visible in *broadened network relationships* with external agencies and constituents. It should be the result of actual *changes to the formal organization of policing.* Finally, such a transition should be associated with changes in the core technology of police work—or the *way police work is done.* Such a transition from traditional to community-oriented policing should result in changes in the ways police work and police organizations are defined.

Morash and her colleagues speaking to issues of the future of community-policing initiatives suggest the importance of structural and service-delivery changes. As they suggest:

> Community policing is the delivery of police services through a customer-focused approach, utilizing partnerships to maximize community resources in a problem-solving format to prevent crime, reduce the fear of crime, apprehend those involved in criminal activity, and improve a community's quality of life. . . . A customer-based approach requires a transformation in the police organization itself to improve police services. Input from both internal customers (i.e., police employees at all levels) and external customers (i.e., residents, businesses, and visitors) is stressed to strike a balance between legally mandated services and the delivery of police services deemed important to all stakeholders in maintaining or improving a community's quality of life. (Morash et al., 2002: 278)

Put another way, and in the parlance of organizations, police agencies involved in community and problem-oriented approaches should adopt and emphasize an open system approach to organizational design. These organizations should be less formalized, less complex, and more decentralized. They should exhibit a broader range of organizational interventions, have a larger number of boundary-spanning roles and partnerships with other agencies and the community, and have greater police officer attachment to role definitions consistent with community and problem-oriented policing definitions (see Greene, 1998).

One way to understand how far police departments have evolved, faced with more than 100 years of reform, is to turn to concepts and theories derived from the comparative study of organizations (for an excellent review of the measurement issues and applications of comparative organizational analyses to policing, see Maguire and Uchida, 2000). Such an examination results in a better understanding of how police organizations and service delivery are expected to change under norms of community and problem-oriented policing. Whether such changes have occurred, and at what rate, is the focus of this chapter.

POLICE ORGANIZATIONS: TRADITIONAL ROOTS TO COMMUNITY BLOSSOMS

When policing left its political roots it did so by adapting a style of service delivery and a method of organization that borrowed heavily from the military, and from the then-emerging professions. Both emphasized a separation of functions and management from day-to-day politics—the foremost value of progressive reformers (see Fogelson, 1977, particularly, chaps. 2 and 6). The emergent style of policing sought to distance the police from overt political interference while increasing administrative control over the police, concentrating such control in the hands of police chiefs.

As policing began to separate itself from direct political interference in the early 1900s, it turned to models of military and industrial organization. Other than the church, the military was the primary model of large-scale organization before the Industrial Revolution. The military model also had the advantages of similarity in function (social control) to the police, once the police shifted their focus from preventing crime to declaring war on crime (Fogelson, 1977). Moreover, the military had enjoyed a long history of independence from local politics—something reformers sought of American policing. The military enjoyed a form of legitimacy, presented a uniform image, and stressed internal command and control. Such attributes suggested, among other things, a more centralized form of organization, authority tied to rank, and specialization of function. Each of these characteristics furthered the agenda of progressive reformers, establishing the political independence of the police and, hence, their accountability to the general public.

In addition to the attributes associated with the military model, at the turn of the century a management ideology emphasizing a more scientific approach to organizing and supervising work was emerging from the then-growing industrial and public administration sectors. Successful managers and those focused on developing general theories of management all sought to improve organizational efficiency through the skillful use of labor (e.g., see Taylor, 1911; Gulick and Urwick, 1937; Barnard, 1938). Although not translated until the 1940s, the work of Henri Fayol (1949) and Max Weber (1947) also provided a rationale for making organizations more formal, structured, and predictable.

What resulted from this curious intersection of military and industrial organizational thought was a style of police organization, management, and service delivery that emphasized control and efficiency. There are several features of this organizational system. First, it emphasizes separation of organization and environment and the maintenance of organizational boundaries—something that was intentionally blurred in the political era of policing. This, it was hoped, would set boundaries to fend off political incursions into police agency functioning (e.g., who got promoted or assigned to particular duties).

Second, it emphasized centralized command and control, hierarchy of authority, written rules and regulations (formalization), and staff review. This had the effect of wresting power for day-to-day operations from the hands of politicians and placing such control in the hands of appointed police chiefs. Moreover, such processes created the illusion of control over day-to-day policing (Manning, 1977), even though the management of daily contingencies was more likely a supervisory or work group undertaking (Manning, 2002).

Third, as police agencies, most particularly those in big cities, were becoming larger, functional specialization was introduced—partly to gain further control over work flow and decision making and partly to improve efficiencies in operations that were associated with specialization in industry. Much of this specialization centered on separating detective functions from patrol officer functions.

Police agencies emerged from this era of reform as highly formalized and structured bureaucracies that focused considerable energy on matters of internal control and oversight, while fending off the external environment. Much of this structure remains in American policing today.

At the same time the police were adapting many attributes of military and industrial organization, like other public organizations they were also adopting an ideology of professionalism (Wilensky, 1964: 137–158)—an ideology that furthered the separation of the police from their many publics (see, Walker, 1977). The ideology of professionalism afforded the police both increased status (often self-assumed) and a method for claiming independence in decision making and action from their wider environments. The norms of the profession, it was argued, should guide the decisions and actions of the police, just like they did for lawyers, architects, engineers, and teachers. Throughout the 1930s, 1940s, 1950s, and into the 1960s the American police refined and perfected this curious combination of military and professional organization.

In the 1960s the police came under great public criticism. Criticisms of the police bureaucracy under the traditional model suggested that police organizations, because of their authoritarian model of management and rigid structures, alienated most who came into contact with them—police and public alike. Such criticisms suggest that in the mid-1960s and continuing through the 1980s the police were adrift, separated from their constituent (the public), unable to produce safety and order (inefficient), and rife with dissatisfied employees, whose dissatisfaction was displayed as corruption or abuse of authority.

From the perspective of community interactions and relations, distrust of the police, a particularly common theme in American policing in the 1960s, stems from civic beliefs that the police treated people differentially under color of law. Minority communities believed and had considerable evidence of such differential treatment. Such civic concerns continue to the present (e.g., see Harris, 2002). In short, the community had come to be alienated largely because the police organization had distanced it from participation and review, and negative police actions had largely been exposed in minority communities and continue to the present (Kennedy, 1997).

Community and problem-oriented police can largely be viewed as responses to public criticisms of the police beginning in the 1960s (see Greene and Pelfrey, 1997, for a review of this shift in power relationships between the police and the community). As such, community and problem-oriented policing also represent a new rationale for organizational and service-delivery change.

The change dynamics implied of community and problem-oriented policing are many. First, they call for broadening environmental relations, that is, forging local relationships between the police and the public to enhance police acceptance in the community and acceptance of the community. They also suggest the need for decentralizing police operations and decision making to make them more accountable to local publics, including opening the strategic planning process to public comment and input. Next, community and problem-oriented policing strategies call for despecializing police agencies, that is, moving from a specialist organization to one that emphasizes more generalized police roles. Finally, these newest of police reforms call for changing the manners and customs of the American police, that is, the core technology by and through which police services are provided.

In earlier reforms police organizations were modeled as classic bureaucracies. They were authority centric, highly specialized, and complex. They developed complicated internal communications systems and sought ways to buffer themselves from what they perceived to be a hostile external environment. As control-centered bureaucracies (Manning, 1977), police agencies emphasized command and control functions at the upper levels of management while creating elaborate rule and regulation systems to oversee the work of line personnel. Institutionally, they cloaked themselves in images of uniformity and professionalism (Crank and Langworthy, 1992) as a way of maintaining external relations with powerful elites, as well as reinforcing a selective institutional presentation to the public.

Many comment on changing police organizations as the central feature to ensure the long-term survival of community policing (see Sparrow, Moore, and Kennedy, 1990; Moore, 1992; Lurigio and Rosenbaum, 1994; Morash et al., 2002). These changes imply shifts in the underlying philosophy of policing, a broadening of the police domain, and a reorientation of internal police organizational structures.

EVIDENCE OF SHIFTS IN THE
INSTITUTION, STRUCTURE, AND
FUNCTIONS OF AMERICAN POLICING

Given that policing occurs within an organizational and service-delivery context, changes in policing philosophy or style should be detectable on several organizational levels. Four are briefly considered here. First, given the emphasis of community and problem-oriented policing on the interaction between the police organization and its wider environments, changes in the institutional presentation of the police to their wider audience are considered. Second, as community and problem-oriented policing are meant, in part, to simplify police departments, we should be able to detect some shift in organizational complexity, formalism, and the level of centralization in authority and decision making. Third, as these newer styles of police are meant to change the core business of the police, attention can also be focused on the technology of policing or how police work gets done. Finally, community and problem-oriented policing potentially calls for significant role change for the police. How or if the police are making this role change is important to understand as the institution of policing continues to evolve under pressures for reform.

Institutional Shifts Versus Organizational Assessment

Formal organizations (including police departments) are often seen as systems of planned, rational, and controlled activities stemming from myriad social interactions that are purposive and goal oriented. These formal organizations are usually described as structures with their associated inputs, throughput, and outputs. Efficiency and control in social arrangements in the organization are the dominant themes associated with these systems.

Formal organizations can also been viewed within the institutional contexts from which they arise and the institutional myths with which they identify and reinforce. As Meyer and Rowan suggest:

> Institutionalized products, services, techniques, policies, and programs
> function as powerful myths, and many organizations adapt them
> ceremonially. But conformity to institutional rules often conflicts sharply
> with efficiency criteria, and conversely, to coordinate and control activity
> in order to promote efficiency undermines an organization's ceremonial
> conformity and sacrifices its support and legitimacy. (1977: 340)

Police organizations are cloaked in institutional myths (Crank and Langworthy, 1992) that become presentational strategies to the wider environment. The symbolic and cultural components of police organizations have received considerable attention (see Skolnick, 1966; Manning, 1977, 2002; Brown, 1981; Crank, 1994). The conflict in shifting policing as an institution is often associated with the tension between what the police do and what the police present themselves as doing (Manning, 1977).

Part of this struggle is imbedded in the powerful histories associated with policing, particularly in the United States. Of course, most of these histories are local (New York vs. Los Angeles vs. Chicago), attesting to variation in police agency role adoption. Despite these varied local histories, an overarching history of modern-day policing in the United States connects law enforcement with structured and control-centered police organizations (see, Carte and Carte, 1975; Miller, 1976; Fogelson, 1977; Walker, 1977; Monkkonen, 1981). Moreover, this history of the police connects them to ideas of crime suppression and deterrence as the central role for American law enforcement. The rhetoric of crime control has dominated the latter half of the twentieth century in policing circles, and it continues to exert a powerful influence, with the resurgence of zero-tolerance policing (see Bratton, with Knobler, 1998; Silverman, 1999).

To the extent that the larger institution of policing is philosophically and strategically shifting toward community and problem-oriented philosophies, we should be able to observe a broadening of the police service domain to a wider and more inclusive audience, and increased emphasis on crime prevention as opposed to crime suppression.

Changes in the institution of policing, then, are likely to be more reflected in the rhetoric than the reality of policing, the way policing symbolizes itself to external others. In this regard there is some evidence that the institution of policing is shifting, and some that it has not shifted very far from its crime suppression and crime-fighting roots.

Zhao, Thurman, and Lovrich (1995) find that the institution of policing appears to be shifting, albeit slowly, toward the language and symbolism of community policing. In an assessment of 215 police agencies completing a survey conducted by the Division of Government Studies at Washington State University, Zhao, Thurman, and Lovrich conclude that based on self-reported community policing activities, police agencies across America were indeed expanding their organizational domains. That is, these agencies reported significant changes in the technology used, the populations served, and the range of services provided. Many of the programs identified in this analysis sought to implement community policing in culturally diverse communities. As reported by Zhao, Thurman, and Lovrich, the intent of these programs was to improve police and community interaction, as well as community relations.

Analyzing the same data and commenting on institutional change in policing, Zhao (1996) suggests that the motivation for change in policing does not appear to be driven by agency adoption of community and problem-oriented policing values, however. Instead,

> COP innovations are more likely to occur in large cities, where police organizations are more pressured to change. . . . Primary findings support the conclusion that COP innovation is more likely a result of forced change than of a concerted effort at philosophical reform. (Zhao, 1996: 69)

Despite the lack of internal genesis or motivation for change, Zhao (1996: 77–82) finds that many ongoing changes in policing were not superficial, but that they often represented the beginning stages of community-oriented policing implementation. They also find that police agencies were indeed trying to respond to greater, but often conflicting, demands from the environment (see the following discussion). In a follow-up analysis on these issues Zhao, Lovrich and Turman (1999: 74–92) analyze police agency survey data collected in 1993 and again in 1996. They conclude that there has been marked change in programming and training in community policing over this period, but widespread institutionalization of these efforts continue to be uncertain.

More recently, Jeffrey Roth (2000) completed a national evaluation of the COPS Program of the Justice Department. Some of the key findings of the evaluation were presented in Chapter 1. Although their report identified many ongoing changes in police tactics, as well as some structural changes (as discussed later), questions of institutional shift are more difficult to draw from this report. With respect to institutional shifts toward crime prevention, Roth concludes:

> Prevention has, in many ways been the gateway to community
> policing. . . . We found that the prevention side of community policing,
> as defined by the COPS grantees visited, is highly problematic. When
> asked about their prevention efforts under community policing, police
> representatives nearly always cited discrete programs and strategies. They
> did not articulate any philosophy of prevention, the logical end product of
> true collaboration and problem solving focused on underlying causes.
> Prevention in the minds of the vast majority of COPS grantees visited
> refers to specific crime prevention programs, not a more global, diffuse
> model of reducing and ultimately preventing crime through problem
> resolution and active collaboration. (2000: 214–215)

In a more qualitative assessment of ten police agencies as part of the national evaluation of the COPS Program, Moore and colleagues (chap. 7 in Roth, 2000: 247–268) are more positive in their assessment of institutional change. They conclude that having a favorable environment and an organizational history that emphasized and supported innovation, coupled with continuity in management commitment to community and problem-oriented policing, went a long way in shaping a climate for institutional shift. Such antecedents to institutional shift were present in many of the ten sites visited. It is interesting that organizational history with innovation was poor or unfavorable in these same sites, attesting to how police agencies themselves inhibit institutional change. These findings, of course, must be tempered given the sample size ($n = 10$) and the findings from the more empirical assessments in this same volume, which were less optimistic about such institutional shift (Roth, 2000).

In a recent assessment of institutional issues surrounding the adoption of community-based policing, Mastrofski and Ritti (2002: 183–210) conclude that police agencies continue to seek legitimacy from the public even when they are unable to demonstrate performance. The symbolic, rather than the instrumental, goals of the police drive programs that help insure institutional legitimacy.

In sum, evidence for institutional shift in policing is, at best, weak. Although agencies have adapted aspects of the rhetoric of community and problem-oriented policing, crime fighting and crime suppression remain the mainstay of the police. Institutionally, the police still represent themselves as uniformed, selectively organized, and focused on crime. Perhaps the most telling commentary on the state of community policing definition as gleaned from the national evaluation of the COPS Program reveals the continuing institutional struggle in American law enforcement (Roth, 2000: 237):

> Our national survey and site visit results indicate that COPS funding has accelerated the pace and broadened the area covered by the umbrella term "community policing." . . . Certainly, COPS funding has enabled a great number of law enforcement agencies to move ahead in their implementation of community policing as locally defined. Funding conditioned expressly on community policing implementation, coupled with peer pressure to embrace this model of policing, has also led a substantial number of law enforcement agencies to stretch the definition of community policing—to include under its umbrella traditional quick-fix enforcement actions, draconian zero tolerance policies, long established crime prevention programs, and citizen advisory councils that are clearly *only* [authors' emphasis] advisory.

The institutional struggle continues.

Police Organizations and Their Environments

All organizations find themselves immersed in an environment. How they choose to deal with that environment—either shunning it or passively or actively interacting with it—distinguishes between organizations said to be closed systems and those seen as open systems. The idea of open versus closed systems is most visible in the concepts of Max Weber's (1947) bureaucracy, and Alvin Gouldner's (1959) natural system.

For Weber, organizational efficiency—adopting the most rational process for achieving organizational goals—was in large part dependent on separating the organization from its environment, thereby establishing organizational predictability and long-term stability (see Weber, 1947, particularly "Types of Authority and Imperative Coordination," 324–386). Everything within Weber's idea type bureaucracy sought to increase the organization's long-term viability. Goals and objectives were clear, work was subdivided, offices were hierarchically organized, decision making and authority were attached to organizational position, entrance to the organization was based on universalistic standards, and impersonality governed organizational transactions.

To accomplish this, Weber's organizations were distanced from their social and economic environments. For Weber, formal organizations (bureaucracies) as opposed to communal or associational organizations, were likely to be closed, limiting transactions between the environment and the organization (1947: 139–143). Closed systems often see the environment as hampering organizational rationality. They seek to reduce this interference by sealing themselves off from the environment, or at least minimizing environmental interference (for a review, see Thompson, 1967: 1–6).

In contrast to the closed-systems perspective, open- or natural-systems perspectives view organizations as intimately engaged with their environments—much like natural organisms. They import energy from the environment; transform that energy within the organization; and export goods, services, ideologies, and information to the wider environment. Katz and Kahn (1966: 19–26) outline nine distinguishing characteristics of open systems. They include: (1) energy importation from the environment; (2) internal processing or throughput; (3) output; (4) a systems cycle; (5) negative entropy—or the importation of more energy than that used by the organization; (6) information input, feedback, and coding processes; (7) homeostasis or the balancing of internal and external forces toward organizational health; (8) organizational differentiation or the elaboration of roles and functions; and (9) equifinality or the presence of multiple means toward the same organizational end. In the open-systems model, the organization is seen as constantly monitoring its environment and adjusting to environmental threats and opportunities (see Lawrence and Lorsch, 1967).

Much of the literature on organizational analysis focuses on the role of the environment in shaping the goals and objectives of the focal organization (see Perrow, 1979: 200–247). Actively monitoring the environment, the organization assesses uncertainty posed by environmental conditions and adjusts its internal dynamics to address these conditions (Thompson, 1967). At times the organization is passive in a turbulent environment (Maniha and Perrow, 1965); at other times it is the organization that seeks to manipulate the environment for its own purposes (Lawrence and Lorsch, 1967; Perrow, 1967).

The environments surrounding police agencies can be either hostile or friendly, they can be aggressive or passive, and they can be affected by whether the police organization is environmentally dependent or autonomous (Wilson, 1968). In turn, the internal dynamics of the agency can respond to or try to rebuff these environmental pressures. The extent to which rejection of the environment is possible depends on the autonomy-dependence relationship between the focal organization and the environment, the strength and persistence of environmental demand, and the coping mechanisms available within the agency to resist external influence.

In the logic of organization analysis, environments play an important role (see Thompson, 1967). For most organizations there are two levels of environment: the general environment that encompasses the organization as a whole and individual task environments that influence aspects of the organization's functioning. In policing, both the general environment and task environments have been shifting for some time. What is less clear is the police department's adaptation to these changing environments (see Zhao, 1996).

Traditional models of police organization assume either that the environment is passive or that it can be controlled by the organization. As previously indicated, this model of organization is referred to as a closed system. Under the logic of closed systems, the focal organization (in this case a police department) fails to see itself as dependent on the environment, views itself as autonomous in policy and decision making, and stresses its capacity to buffer the organization from the outside world (see Cordner, 1978). Of course, the police do not operate in a vacuum and cannot be divorced from their external environment. Moreover, the environment in which police organizations find themselves today requires a model of organization that emphasizes policing as an open system—this is the central emphasis of community policing.

As part of the community and problem-oriented reform agenda in policing, police organizations are expected to open up to participate with other public and private agencies. Such institutional collaborations anticipate a widening of the organizational set for the police and active engagement of that set. The organization's set refers to the external agencies with whom the focal agency regularly interacts (see Evan, 1966). In policing, it includes other governmental agencies, the private sector, and the community.

Evidence of generalized environmental effects on policing are many. Wilson's (1968) typology of police agencies sees them as greatly influenced by the political culture of the community in which the agencies found themselves. Langworthy (1986), in a study of 152 larger police agencies, provides some empirical support for Wilson's conclusion that community political culture (type of government) influenced police agency style (generally measured relative to arrests for lower level crimes). Slovak (1986) also finds in a study of 42 police agencies that police organizational characteristics and their environments influenced police legalism, although his analysis suggests that the organization, not the environment, account more for any differences in police legalism measured. Crank (1990), in an assessment of 284 Illinois police departments, concludes that organizational factors more influenced variations in arrest statistics for urban departments, whereas environmental factors were more likely to explain variation in arrests in rural departments.

In regard to the impact of the environment on community or problem-oriented policing, the evidence is more mixed. Zhao (1996: 51–70) finds that city size and region were significantly related to community policing innovations, but that the political culture (measured by type of government and how city council members were selected) of cities was not related to these innovations. Zhao does find, however, that changes in police adoption of community-oriented styles were largely associated with externally focused change measured by community social disorganization and external pressures for affirmative action programs. Finally, Zhao concludes that community participation and neighborhood empowerment appear to facilitate community policing innovation in the sample of police agencies studied.

Roth's (2000: 190–199) study of the COPS program casts additional light on the capacity of police agencies to effectively engage the environment. They report that partnership-building activities among surveyed agencies ($n = 267$) increased significantly between the pre-1995 period and 1998. Most notably were agency increases in such tactics as instituting regular community meetings, surveying citizens, and increasing interaction with citizen action and advisory boards. This study, coupled with the work of Skogan and Hartnett (1997), highlights an emergent strategy of the police to engage the community in discussion about crime and public safety, as well as to assess the quality and effectiveness of police actions in the community.

One cautionary note about the openness of police agencies to the environment is in order, however. Roth (2000: 237) also find that, in general:

> Problem-solving partnerships for coordinating the appropriate application of a variety of resources are commonplace in many of the agencies visited. Yet all too often, partnerships are in name only, or simply standard, temporary working arrangements. Partnerships with other law enforcement units and agencies merely to launch short-term crackdowns are not in the spirit of problem solving *or* [authors' emphasis] partnerships. Nor are partnerships in which citizens and business representatives are merely "involved," serving primarily as extra "eyes and ears" as before. True community partnerships, involving sharing power and decision making are rare at this time.

Such conclusions are also consistent with those of Rosenbaum, Lurigio, and Davis (1998), who suggest that the dynamics of community participation in community or problem-oriented policing are not well understood. They indicate that although the police may indeed be able to mobilize communities and businesses after a crisis or dramatic crime, long-term activation and interaction is difficult to sustain and predict.

Despite findings suggesting that police agencies are becoming more open to their environments, several other issues remain. For example, Zhao, Thurman, and Lovrich (1995) find several environmental impediments to adopting community and problem-oriented policing. First, they find that there is persistent community pressure to fight crime. Here the concern is that the community is focused on visible police protection, potentially eroding the desire of the police to shift from crime fighting to prevention. Second, but related, they find that the community constantly pressures the police for immediate results, again potentially undermining longer term strategies to grapple with underlying problems. Finally, they suggest that the level of support from other government agencies has not yet developed to a level where the police can engage other institutions to address crime, fear, and disorder problems.

Organizational Complexity, Formalization, and Centralization of Decision Making

Complexity in organizations refers to the internal structuring of the organization, its division of labor, levels of hierarchy, functional specialization, job ranks, and the like (see Scott, 1992). In general, as organizations increase in size, so too does their complexity. But even small organizations can exhibit complexity. Organizations can differentiate themselves horizontally in the way they subdivide work. They can differentiate themselves vertically by the levels of supervision they create. And they can differentiate themselves spatially by the number of locations where work is performed or supervised. These horizontal, vertical, and spatial dimensions of organizations influence their complexity, as well.

Horizontal and vertical differentiation within organizations generally occurs in conjunction with assumptions about the skills of those performing the work, the task complexity, and the criticality of the work performed. All things being equal, highly skilled professionals who understand the tasks to be performed are likely to reduce the need for horizontal and vertical complexity. Such is the nature of professional organizations. In contrast, unskilled workers involved in complicated tasks are likely to result in an organization with considerable horizontal and vertical complexity. The general model for this type of organization is the assembly line.

A mediating factor in complexity is the criticality of the tasks performed. Thus, even a highly skilled workforce may need work to be divided, as the costs of error may be exceedingly high. The operating room with specialized medical personnel all tasked with individual medical, life-monitoring responsibilities illustrates this condition.

A final element in assessing organizational complexity is related to the spatial dispersion of organizational functions and activities. Spatial dispersion is illustrated by organizations that have field offices, where all or a portion of organizational goals, activities, and tasks are pursued or performed. In fact, horizontal and vertical differentiation can occur within subunits that are spatially distributed.

The general argument among those who study organizations comparatively is that conditions external to the organization, as well as internal processes associated with work flow and the supervision of the work process, influence organizational complexity (see Perrow, 1967; Thompson, 1967; Pfeffer and Salancik, 1978; Aldrich, 1979; Weick, 1979).

Formalization in organizations refers to the degree to which rule making shapes life (see Scott, 1992). Formalization can be seen as on a continuum ranging from organizations that attempt to structure most if not all employee choices and behaviors to those that exert a minimum of rules and regulations, mainly to guide and shape, but not control decisions and actions. The assembly line in which decisions are uniform and the product is constant is an illustration of maximum formalization. In organizations that deal with new and constantly changing information and work routines, formalization is likely to be minimal.

Formalization tends to be associated with the increased centralization of power. That is, in organizations with high levels of formalization (rules, regulations, and policies) authority and power tend to be concentrated at the top of the organization.

In human service organizations, such as the police, in which means and ends are less certain, some degree of decisional latitude is warranted. This suggests that formalization is inversely related to workforce professionalization and to the nature of the problems addressed by the organization—certain or uncertain (see Perrow, 1967, for a discussion).

Centralization refers to the concentration of formal authority—or power within an organization. Formal authority and its distribution within any organization define where (at what organizational level) decisions are made (see Scott, 1992). When decision making occurs largely at the top of the organization, it is said to be centralized; when it occurs at multiple levels and across many functions within an organization, it is said to be decentralized.

The evidence regarding organizational complexity in police agencies in an era emphasizing community and problem-oriented policing is not particularly positive. Generally speaking, in the era of community and problem-oriented poling, police agencies retained much of their complexity and even elaborated on some.

Maguire (1997) analyzes data from five databases including three waves of the Law Enforcement Management and Statistics (LEMAS) series for 1987, 1990, and 1993; data from a Police Foundation survey (Wycoff, 1994) focused on community policing; and a Michigan State University survey (Trojanowicz, 1994) examining community policing practices in a national sample of police agencies. Data from these five sources are aggregated for 236 large municipal police agencies.

Maguire (1997: 567–568) finds that these agencies grew by an average of 6 percent in the number of employees, but did not significantly change task complexity over this period. These same agencies became a bit "squatter," that is, showed some decrease in their internal hierarchies, but actually elaborated on internal specialization. In other words, they became more specialized.

Maguire (1997) find that the degree of formalization—as measured by the level of written policy and procedure—also did not change. On all counts, the 236 agencies identified for this analysis demonstrated little organizational change (with the exception of less hierarchy) over the six years of the analysis—a period of considerable emphasis on community and problem-oriented policing as the preferred model of police management and service delivery.

In a study of ninety Florida law enforcement agencies, Gianakis and Davis (1998) attempt to measure the depth of community policing implementation. They create a measure of community policing implementation that range from rhetorical support for community policing to actual structural changes within the agencies, including decentralization. Their analysis suggests that the range and depth of changes reported were unrelated to agency size or the length of time the agency had been involved with community policing concepts (measured by the date the agency announced community policing adoption).

These results are supported in part by the finding from the national evaluation of the COPS program. For example, Roth (2000: 227–234) found a wide array of changes in organizational supports for community and problem-oriented policing. These include changes in mission, values, and vision statements; increased task force involvement; and team approaches to problem solving. Despite such changes, it is not clear that such changes actually affected the structure and level of specialization of these agencies. A close examination of the data collected suggests that changes in areas related more to the structure of the organization and specialization within these agencies were less likely to be expanded during the period under study (pre-1995 to 1998).

Perhaps the most telling commentary on the state of structural change under the auspices of community and problem-oriented policing is provided in a study conducted by Wycoff (1994). In a national survey of police departments conducted by the Police Foundation in 1993, Wycoff asked respondents whether community policing required major reorganization of police agencies. Although 61 percent of the respondents from large police agencies agreed that "community policing requires major changes of organizational policies, goals or mission statements" (1994: 32), only 34 percent agreed that structural change was necessary, or even called for under norms of community and problem-oriented policing. Such a finding is consistent with the general absence of structural change observed in policing over the era of community and problem-oriented policing reform.

Changing the Nature of Police Work

From the broadest of views, police work has not changed significantly in more than 100 years. At its root, policing is an information-gathering and -processing function seeking to identify community public safety problems and conditions that give rise to crime, disorder, fear, and victimization, and then to respond to those problems and conditions (see Manning, 1988). It began in the old "watch and wards" where the police simply monitored the community for potential disturbances. It has advanced under norms of traditional policing into a much more sophisticated enterprise, but one that still involves watching and responding to crime and social disorder.

The central question in shifting from traditional to community or problem-oriented policing is "does the core technology of police work actually change?" In traditional policing the police responded to incidents, took reports, interviewed witnesses and victims, and investigated accidents. They also submitted reports to their supervisors and to detectives. In some respects the information and work flow of traditional policing follows the logic of the assembly line. That is, under traditional policing the police are largely summoned by the public (Black, 1980), they respond by either apprehending someone at the scene or taking a report, and they submit a report to a supervisor who approves it and forwards it to detectives for investigation. The detective may follow up on the case and may call in other criminal experts to collect or process evidence. Finally the case is cleared (completed) either by arrest or through an exceptional clearance process (e.g., we know who did it but cannot prosecute for any number of reasons).

Under norms of community policing the police are expected to solve problems and contribute to community quality of life. Using modes of community and problem-oriented policing, it is necessary to understand better how the police solve problems, by what means and with what effects. Incorporated within norms of community policing, the police look more like social diagnosticians, not assembly-line workers. They must know the community, assess community troubles, diagnose causes from consequences, and implement any number of treatments that address specifically identified community problems. Community and problem-oriented policing obviously have important implications for the nature of police work as well as for how police officers understand, accept, and adopt new and often more complex roles.

Community and problem-oriented policing is said to be affected by changes in the intelligence by which policing is undertaken, as well as in the objectives of policing itself. That is, policing is said to shift from response-driven calls for service to a system in which the police actively identify problems and community concerns and then proactively institute programs to ameliorate problems in community settings. They do this, in part, by shifting their focus from being a secondary intervention (respond to crisis) to a primary intervention (prevent or ameliorate problems).

For policing to change its character there is the fundamental need to address two important issues. First, police organizations need to be analytic about the causal networks in which they seek to intervene, as well as about the variable impacts of a wide range of police interventions. Second, how police officers interact with their clients, how decision making occurs, and how problems are solved create a need to understand how the police convert information about crime, victimization, and community disorder into decisions and actions that address such problems.

At both the organizational and individual levels, problem solving is said to be reshaping the intelligence of the police. This occurs in a process that involves scanning the environment and defining problems, analyzing the causes and consequences of these problems, designing and implementing appropriate responses, and assessing the impact of interventions (Eck and Spelman, 1987; Goldstein, 1990).

Police organizations have historically collected information on serious and nonserious crime, traffic violations, juvenile offenders, arrestees, and the general conditions associated with crime (see, Dunworth, 2000). Within police departments this information has traditionally been kept in many unrelated information systems, and once collected this information has had little utility for predicting future problems and future police responses. As Dunworth et al. (2000) suggest, police agencies have historically lacked an analytic framework for using this information and the means to collate diverse information sources. As a consequence, the formal and analytic organization of policing has suffered in its attempt to be anything more than reactive to crime and disorder. Specifically, Dunworth et al. (2000: 5–17) suggest that information requirements under norms of community and problem-oriented policing call for the police to better understand: (1) how their community interfaces, (2) how their interorganizational linkages and interactions work, (3) how work groups function within police agencies, (4) what threats and opportunities are posed by the environment, (5) how problems can be defined and addressed, (6) how to ensure area accountability, and (7) how to feed all of this information into a strategic management process within the police agency. Their analysis concludes that given developments in expanding community and problem-oriented policing, most agencies fall considerably short in their ability to capture and use these types of information.

At the individual police officer level, experience has generally substituted for analysis. That is; officers were largely left to their own devices in selecting problems to address and the means to address these problems, if they were addressed at all. With the advent of computerization and its adoption by the police, the capacity to link differing sources of information to better understand discrete problems was greatly enhanced. Despite such an enhancement it is not at all clear that the police systematically exploit multiple information sources in their pursuit of a better understanding of crime, disorder, victimization, fear, and community quality of life. Even current efforts to target locations for police interventions through computer mapping fall considerably short of systematically integrating information to improve police systems responses. Rather, current crime-mapping efforts have often been restricted to displaying serious crime patterns almost exclusively.

In Chapter 5 of this book, John Eck presents a critique of problem solving, suggesting that much of what occurs under the label of problem solving is shallow, unanalytic, and largely ineffective. In practice, the police fail in most of the problem solving steps. During scanning the police often fail to clearly specify the problem they seek to address. Their analysis of problems is quite rudimentary. When it comes to their response, much of what falls under the guise of community and problem oriented policing is really traditional police tactics such as crackdowns, streets sweeps, and the use of arrest, often masked as community and/or problem solving interventions. These tactics may be being applied to poorly defined and analyzed problems. Finally, there is rarely a meaningful assessment of what has been accomplished. Rosenbaum, et. al. (1998: 194–195) provides a similar critique of the capacity of the police to actually solve problems.

In Chapter 1, Roth suggests that the police are now engaged in many more community and problem-oriented programs than they were in the past. Cumulatively, this may suggest some shifts in the core technology of policing. However, in their detailed reports he (Roth, 2000: 206–214) reports mixed messages regarding the shift in the nature of police work on the ground. First, he suggests that there is considerable variation in what is called problem solving. This ranges from definitions that emphasize the SARA model or some variation of it to definitions that relabel traditional police tactics under the guise of community policing. Second, he finds that community policing responsibilities are associated with a split-force (209) function within agencies. This is a bit of a sleight of hand, however, because split force as used suggests that some police officers are charged with community policing activities while others are not—specialization by any other name? Third, Roth finds that training, supervision, and formal documentation for community and problem-oriented policing are generally ill defined or lacking. Such findings do not suggest either considerable investment in, or movement toward, changes in the core technology of police work—that is, how police work is actually done under norms of community and problem-oriented policing.

Zhao, Lourich, and Thurman (1999), in a follow-up study on the value orientations of police officers within a single police agency, find some support for shifts in street-level officer focus. They find a significant and positive relation between officers' ranking of equity and their level of support for building community partnerships. Such value shifts may be the result of shifts in organizational culture and individual value adaptation to this cultural shift. Whether this is leading or following changes in police work is at yet uncertain.

In an assessment of how officers spend their time with the community in Indianapolis, Parks, Mastrofski, and DeJong (1999: 483–518) find that community policing specialists indeed had the ability to spend more time in community interaction. Despite this time availability, these authors find that these community policing specialists chose to spend less face time with the public and more behind-the-scenes time as compared with patrol generalists. Such a finding calls into question whether community policing values and actions permeate the ranks of community policing specialists.

In a recent analysis of patrol identification with community policing in public housing settings, Kane (2000) finds that community-oriented policing assignments help to expand officer identity with and efficacy for the community. Riley (1999), on the other hand, finds that some officers who volunteered for community policing assignments did so for reasons other than community attachment—often for better working schedules or conditions. Moreover, given recent shifts toward zero-tolerance policing, it is not clear whether the police identify with community facilitation and partnerships or with the suppression of social disorder, or both. The mix of these identities has yet to be thoughtfully sorted.

The best that can be said to date is that many police departments across America have adopted a framework for response that includes elements of problem solving. This framework is yet evolving, and with support and cross-communication among police agencies the new technology of policing will continue to emerge. But, as a cautionary note, it is clear that the police imagination remains captured by nineteenth-century ideas about crime and police response, most particularly as zero-tolerance policing has gained popularity among the police and politicians in recent years.

CONCLUSIONS

For nearly twenty years American policing has been in the throes of yet another reform—shifting from traditional to community and problem-oriented policing. This reform has indeed been glacial and not global.

In recent times this reform has captured public and political imagination. It has been led by a few highly visible police agencies such as San Diego and Chicago, and championed by academic researchers and policy analysts. The language and symbolism of policing have indeed changed in the intervening years. In this sense, the efforts of the past twenty years have changed the discourse over what the police should do and, in a smaller way, how they should go about doing it.

After nearly twenty years of experimentation, however, the results for police work and police organizations are mixed. In general, many if not most police agencies have publicly embraced the broad tenets of community policing. In these times it is difficult not to embrace such concepts. They have political capital and for several years they have been key to increasing local access to federal funding. Unfortunately they remain "plastic concepts" (Eck and Rosenbaum, 1994: 3); broad philosophic statements; and a wide array of techniques, orientations, programs, and individual efforts, often loosely tied to philosophy, if tied to it at all.

More specifically, it can be argued that the institutional premise of policing has not shifted as dramatically as anticipated by advocates. The police still cling to an institutional definition that stresses crime control and not prevention. In fairness to the police, part of the dilemma is associated with mixed messages they receive from their many constituents. It appears that the community wants decisive and forceful police action—typically in other neighborhoods—and limited involvement in the affairs of public safety. More than a decade ago, this was a part of Manning's (1989) critique—suggesting the potential for overexpectation in regard to what level of involvement communities actually want in matters of public safety. What is not clear is what level of community participation the police should anticipate, under what circumstances, and with what reinforcements.

Related to the preceding discussion, it is not clear that the police can or desire to broaden their organizational set. The relations they have with other agencies are typically characterized as episodic. It is equally unclear what capacities or willingness resides in other agencies to actually work with the police. In a few sites, such as Boston and Chicago, it is clear that some interagency relations do exist.

In all practicality, and as best evidence suggests, the police have modestly incorporated communities and external others into discussions about public safety, if not into actual policy and decision making. Today the police collect considerable information from the community; how that information shapes police decision making is less clear at present. Moreover, there remains considerable distance between the preachment and practice in the openness of police organizations to engage either their general or task environment. A limited and police-controlled participation model appears to be the dominant response to environmental pressures for interaction. This controlled participation model, nonetheless, has opened access for communities and others to engage the police—a practice that was reserved to political elites in prior eras.

By all available evidence, police organizations (their structures, division of labor, and the like) have not been radically or even significantly altered in the era of community and problem-oriented policing. Police agencies have generally grown in size and complexity, and have shown some evidence of a reduction in hierarchy, but they also show continued and, indeed, broadened specialization. Even under norms of community and problem-oriented policing, many agencies appear to use a split-force model, reinforcing organizational specialization (see Roth, 2000). Furthermore, existing evidence (Maguire, 1997) suggests that organizational gains to policing stemming from civilianizing the workforce showed no net change between 1987 and 1993. On most fronts, and with limited information, the structure of police organizations appears relatively unscathed in the wake of community and problem-oriented policing.

Finally, although there is considerable anecdotal evidence of an emerging new style of policing, aggregate analyses of problem-solving and community outreach efforts are less conclusive. What the police actually do to engage the community and to solve community problems remains illusive.

Despite our inability to measure change in policing as an institution, organizational structure, or set of core technologies, at present, communities appear to be safer, have more confidence in their police, and are less fearful. This of course varies considerably by which community is queried.

The legacy of institutional and organizational reform stemming from community and problem-oriented policing is uncertain at present. It may be that the police have effectively repackaged their efforts with a community and problem-oriented label. It may also be that community and problem-oriented advocates need to continue to press for institutional, organizational, and service-delivery reform.

One final comment is necessary. Much of the evidence of shifts in policing from traditional to community and problem-oriented policing has been built on self-reported data from police agencies themselves. Subsequent analyses must be careful of the potential that agencies may actually overreport community and problem-oriented policing actions and interventions for reasons of social desirability. As we base our discussions about change in policing on these studies, we should be cognizant of the source of these data and build in appropriate controls to ensure the accuracy and reliability of the data used in these analyses (see Maguire, 1997, and Maguire and Uchida, 2000, for a discussion).

CITATIONS

Aldrich, Henry. 1979. *Organizations and Environments.* New York: Prentice Hall.

Barnard, Chester I. 1938. *The Functions of the Executive.* Cambridge, MA: Harvard University Press.

Black, Donald. 1980. *The Manners and Customs of the Police.* New York: Academic Press.

Bratton, William. J., with Paul Knobler. 1998. *Turnaround: How America's Top Cop Reversed the Crime Epidemic.* New York: Random House.

Brown, Michael. 1981. *Working the Street.* New York: Sage.

Carte, Gene E. and Elaine E. Carte. 1975. *Police Reform in the United States: The Era of August Vollmer, 1905–1932.* Berkeley: University of California Press.

Clark, Ronald V. 1998. "Defining Police Strategies: Problem-Solving, Problem-Oriented Policing, and Community-Oriented Policing." In Tara O'Connor Shelley and Anne C. Grant (Eds.), *Problem-Oriented Policing: Crime-Specific Problems, Critical Issues and Making POP Work.* Washington, DC: Police Executive Research Forum, 315–330.

Cordner, Gary W. 1978. Open and Closed Models in Police Organizations: Traditions, Dilemmas, and Practical Considerations. *Journal of Police Science and Administration,* 6: 22–34.

Crank, John P. 1990. "The Influence of Environmental and Organizational Factors on Police Style in Urban and Rural Environments." *Journal of Research in Crime and Delinquency,* 27: 166–189.

Crank, John. P. 1994. "State Theory, Myths of Policing, and Responses to Crime." *Law and Society Review,* 28: 325–351.

Crank, John P. and Robert Langworthy. 1992. "An Institutional Perspective on Policing. *Journal of Criminal Law and Criminology,* 83: 338–363.

Dunworth, Terrence. 2000. "Criminal Justice and the IT Revolution." In *Criminal Justice 2000,* Volume 3. Washington DC: National Institute of Justice, 371–426.

Dunworth, Terrence, Gary Cordner, Jack R. Greene, Tim Bynum, Scott Decker, Thomas Rich, Sean Ward, and Vincent Webb. 2000. *Police Department Information Systems Technology Enhancement Project.* Washington DC: Office of Community Oriented Police Services, U.S. Department of Justice.

Eck, John E. and Dennis P. Rosenbaum. 1994. "The New Police Order: Effectiveness, Equity and Efficiency in Community Policing." In Dennis P. Rosenbaum (ed.), *The Challenge of Community Policing: Testing the Promises.* Thousand Oaks, CA: Sage, 3–26.

Eck, John E. and William Spelman. 1987. *Problem Solving: Problem-Oriented Policing in Newport News.* Washington, DC: Police Executive Research Forum.

Evan, William M. 1966. "The Organization-Set. In James D. Thompson (Ed.), *Approaches to Organizational Design.* Pittsburgh, PA: University of Pittsburgh Press.

Fayol, Henri. 1949. *General and Industrial Management.* London: Sir Isaac Pitman.

Fogelson, Robert. 1977. *Big-City Police.* Cambridge, MA: Harvard University Press.

Gianakis, Gerasimos and Gill J. Davis. 1998. "Reinventing or Repackaging Public Services? The Case of Community-Oriented Policing."

Public Administration Review, 58: 485–498.

Goldstein, Herman. 1977. *Policing a Free Society.* Cambridge, MA: Ballinger.

Goldstein, Herman. 1987. "Toward Community-Oriented Policing: Potential, Basic Requirements, and Threshold Questions." *Crime & Delinquency,* 33: 6–30.

Goldstein, Herman. 1990. *Problem Oriented Policing.* New York: McGraw-Hill.

Gouldner, Alvin. 1959. "Organizational Analysis." In Robert. K. Merton, Leonard Broom, and Leonard S. Cottrell Jr. (Eds.), *Sociology Today.* New York: Basic Books, 405–406.

Greene, Jack R. 1998. "Evaluating Planned Change Strategies in Modern Law Enforcement: Implementing Community-Based Policing." In Jean-Paul Brodeur (Ed.), *How to Recognize Good Policing: Problems and Issues.* Thousand Oaks, CA: Sage, 141–160.

Greene, Jack R. 2000. "Community Policing in America: Changing the Nature, Structure and Function of the Police." In *Criminal Justice 2000,* Vol. 2. Washington, DC: National Institute of Justice, U.S. Department of Justice, 299–370.

Greene, Jack R. and William V. Pelfrey. 1997. "Shifting the Balance of Power Between Police and Community: Responsibility for Crime Control." In Roger G. Dunham and Geoffrey P. Alpert (Eds.), *Critical Issues in Policing: Contemporary Readings,* 3rd edition. Prospect Heights, IL: Waveland Press, 278–296.

Gulick, Luther and L. F. Urwick. (Eds.). 1937. *Papers on the Science of Administration.* New York: Institute of Public Administration, Columbia University.

Harris, David J. 2002. *Profiles in Injustice: Why Racial Profiling Cannot Work.* New York: New Press.

Kane, Robert J. 2000. "Permanent Beat Assignment in Association with Community Policing: Assessing the Impact of Officers' Field Activity." *Justice Quarterly,* 17: 259–280.

Katz, Daniel and Richard I. Kahn. 1966. *The Social Psychology of Organizations.* New York: Wiley.

Kelling, George L. and Mark Moore. 1988. "From Political to Reform to Community: The Evolving Strategy of Police. In Jack R. Greene and Stephen Mastrofski (Eds.), *Community Policing Rhetoric or Reality?* New York: Praeger, 3–26.

Kennedy, Randall. 1997. *Race, Crime and the Law.* New York: Pantheon.

Langworthy, Robert H. 1986. *The Structure of Police Organizations.* New York: Praeger.

Lawrence, Paul R. and Jay W. Lorsch. 1967. *Organization and Environment: Managing Differentiation and Integration.* Cambridge, MA: Harvard Graduate School of Business.

Lurigio, Arthur J. and Dennis P. Rosenbaum. 1994. "The Impact of Community Policing on Police Personnel: A Review of the Literature." In Dennis P. Rosenbaum (Ed.), *The Challenge of Community Policing: Testing the Promises.* Thousand Oaks, CA: Sage, 147–163.

Maguire, Edward R. 1997. "Structural Change in Large Municipal Police Organizations During the Community-Policing Era." *Justice Quarterly,* 14:547–576.

Maguire, Edward R. and Craig D. Uchida. 2000. "Measurement and Explanation in the Comparative Study of American Police Organizations." In *Criminal Justice 2000,* Vol 4. Washington, DC: National Institute of Justice, U.S. Department of Justice.

Maniha, John and Charles Perrow. 1965. "The Reluctant Organization and the Aggressive Environment." *Administrative Science Quarterly,* 10:238–257.

Manning, Peter K. 1977. *Police Work: The Social Organization of Policing.* Cambridge, MA: MIT Press.

Manning, Peter K. 1988. *Symbolic Communication: Signifying Calls and the Police Response.* Cambridge, MA: MIT Press.

Manning, Peter K. 1989. "Community Policing." In Roger G. Dunham and Geoffrey P. Alpert (Eds.), *Critical Issues in Policing: Contemporary Readings,* 3rd edition. Prospect Heights, IL: Waveland Press, 27–45.

Manning, Peter K. 2002. *Managing Contingencies: Drama and the Police.* Chicago: University of Chicago Press.

Mastrofski, Stephen D. 1998. "Community Policing and Police Organization Structure." In Jean-Paul Brodeur (Ed.), *How to Recognize Good Policing: Problems and Issues.* Thousand Oaks, CA: Sage, 161–192.

Mastrofski, Stephen D. and Richard R. Ritti. 2002. "Making Sense of Community Policing." *Police Practice and Research,* 1: 183–210.

Meyer, John W. and Brian Rowan. 1977. "Institutionalized Organizations: Formal Structure as Myth and Ceremony." *American Journal of Sociology,* 83: 340–363.

Miller, Wilber R. 1976. *Cops and Bobbies: Police Authority in New York and London, 1830–1870.* Chicago: University of Chicago Press.

Monkkonen, Eric H. 1981. *Police in Urban America: 1860–1920.* Cambridge, MA: Harvard University Press.

Moore, Mark. 1992. "Problem Solving and Community Policing." In Michael Tonry and Norval Morris (Eds.), *Crime and Justice: A Review of Research,* Volume 15. Chicago: University of Chicago Press, 99–158.

Morash, Merry, J. Kevin Ford, Jane P. White, and Jerome G. Boles III. 2002. "Directing the Future of Community-Policing Initiatives." In Merry Morash and J. Kevin Ford (Eds.), *The Move to Community Policing: Making Change Happen.* Thousand Oaks, CA: Sage, 277–288.

Parks, Roger B., Stephen D. Mastrofski, and Christine DeJong. 1999. "How Officers Spend Their Time with the Community." *Justice Quarterly,* 16: 483–518.

Perrow, Charles. 1967. "A Framework for Comparative Organizational Analysis." *American Sociological Review,* 32: 194–208.

Perrow, Charles. 1979. *Complex Organizations: A Critical Essay.* Glenview, IL: Scott, Foresman.

Pfeffer, Jeff and G. Salancik. 1978. *The External Control of Organizations: A Resource Dependence Perspective.* New York: Harper & Row.

Riley, John. 1999. "Community Policing: Utilizing the Knowledge of Organizational Personnel." *Policing: An International Journal of Police Strategies and Management,* 22: 618–632.

Rosenbaum, Dennis P., Lurigio, Arthur J., and Davis, Robert C. 1998. The *Prevention of Crime: Social and Situational Strategies.* Belmont, CA: Wadsworth.

Roth, Jeff A. (Ed.) 2000. *National Evaluation of the COPS Program—Title 1 of the 1994 Crime Act.* Washington, DC: National Institute of Justice, U.S. Department of Justice.

Scott, William R. 1992. *Organizations: Rational, Natural and Open Systems,* 3rd edition. Englewood Cliffs, NJ: Prentice Hall.

Silverman, Ira B. 1999. *NYPD Battles Crime: Innovative Strategies in Policing.* Boston: Northeastern University Press.

Skogan, Wesley G. and Susan M. Hartnett. 1997. *Community Policing, Chicago Style.* New York: Oxford University Press.

Skolnick, Jerome. 1966. *Justice Without Trial: Law Enforcement in a Democratic Society.* New York: Wiley.

Slovak, Jeffrey. S. 1986. *Styles of Urban Policing: Organization, Environment and Police Styles in Selected American Cities.* New York: New York University Press.

Sparrow, Malcom K., Mark Moore, and David Kennedy. 1990. *Beyond 911.* New York: Basic Books.

Taylor, Fredrick. 1911. *Principles of Scientific Management.* New York: Harper & Row.

Thompson, James D. 1967. *Organizations in Action.* New York: McGraw-Hill.

Trojanowicz, Robert. 1994. "The Future of Community Policing." In Dennis Rosenbaum (Ed.), *The Challenge of Community Policing: Testing the Promises.* Thousand Oaks, CA: Sage, 186–213.

Walker, Samuel. 1977. *A Critical History of Police Reform: The Emergence of Professionalism.* Lexington, MA: Lexington Books.

Weber, Max. 1947. *The Theory of Social and Economic Organization.* New York: Free Press.

Weick, Karl. 1979. *The Social Psychology of Organizing,* 2nd edition. Reading, MA: Addison-Wesley.

Wilensky, Howard. 1964. "The Professionalization of Everyone?" *American Journal of Sociology,* 137: 158.

Wilson, James Q. 1968. *Varieties of Police Behavior.* Cambridge, MA: Harvard University Press.

Wycoff, Mary Ann. 1994. "Community Policing Strategies." Unpublished report. Washington, DC: Police Foundation.

Zhao, Jihong. 1996. *Why Police Organizations Change: A Study of Community-Oriented Policing.* Washington, DC: Police Executive Research Forum.

Zhao, Jihong, Nicholas Lovrich, and Quint Thurman. 1999. "The Status of Community Policing in American Cities." *Policing: An International Journal of Police Strategies and Management,* 22: 74–92.

Zhao, Jihong, He Ni, and Nicholas Lovrich. 1999. "Value Change Among Police Officers at a Time of Organizational Reform: A Follow-up Study Using Rokeach Values." *Policing: An International Journal of Police Strategies and Management,* 22: 152–170.

Zhao, Jihong, Quint Thurman, and Nicholas Lovrich. 1995. "Community Oriented Policing Across the U.S.: Facilitators and Impediments to Implementation." *American Journal of Police,* 14: 11–28.

PART II

∞

Will the Public
Get Involved?

3

Representing the Community
in Community Policing[1]

WESLEY G. SKOGAN

This chapter examines the role that resident involvement plays in community policing. Although definitions vary, resident involvement (along with organizational decentralization and the adoption of a problem-solving orientation by police) is among the core components of most community policing programs. Forms of involvement vary considerably. In some places police try to *educate* residents by involving them in informational programs or enrolling them in citizen police academies that give them in-depth knowledge of law enforcement. Residents are often asked to *assist the police*, usually by being their "eyes and ears" and reporting crimes promptly when they occur. Residents sometimes get involved in the *coproduction of safety* when they partner with the police in crime prevention projects or walk in officially sanctioned neighborhood patrol groups. Finally, residents may be called on to *represent the community* by serving on advisory boards or decision-making committees. Even where these are old ideas, pushing them to center stage as part of a larger strategic plan showcases the apparent commitment of police departments to resident involvement.

The issue is whether these are real and effective venues for resident involvement. Police can hope to gain even if they are not, by accruing some publicity, popularity, and political support via the press conference where these programs are announced. One reason—perhaps the major one—cities adopt community policing is to solve their legitimacy problems and buy peace in poor and disenfranchised neighborhoods. But cities also have a history of not following through very well on promises made in these communities, especially if they are at all difficult, costly, or politically risky. So, rather than taking claims about resident involvement in community policing at face value, analysts need to ask hard questions about them: Who is the community? Who gets involved? Does their involvement make any difference? Whose interests are served by the program?

This chapter examines one form of resident involvement in community policing: representational. It examines the role citizens play in identifying and

[1]The collection of data for this chapter was supported by Grant No. 94-IJ-CX-0046 by the National Institute of Justice, Office of Justice Programs, U.S. Department of Justice. Points of view in this document are those of the authors and do not necessarily represent the official position or policies of the U.S. Department of Justice.

prioritizing neighborhood problems and monitoring the activities of police in Chicago. The chapter first examines the structure of the program and then the issues of who gets involved, what they represent, how effectively they monitor police activity, and the impact of their involvement on neighborhood conditions.

THE ROLE OF THE COMMUNITY
IN CHICAGO

Chicago's community policing initiative features a number of organizational strategies, and resident involvement is built into virtually every aspect of the program. The department adopted a decentralized turf orientation by reorganizing patrol work around small geographical areas, the city's 279 police beats. The dispatching process was adjusted to keep officers on their assigned beats while answering calls, and priority was given to calls for which beat officers' knowledge of local conditions could make a difference. Officers assigned to beat teams are expected to engage in identifying and addressing a broad range of neighborhood problems in partnership with neighborhood residents and organizations, and to attend community meetings. Tactical teams, youth officers, and detectives are also expected to work more closely in support of beat officers, and to exchange information with them and the community more readily.

The department also adopted its own problem-solving model. Officers are to move beyond responding in traditional fashion to individual calls and to adopt, instead, a proactive, prevention-oriented stance toward a wide range of neighborhood problems. An important feature of Chicago's program is that these do not have to be crime problems, and an administrative mechanism was developed that enables beat officers to easily trigger a broad range of city services in response to resident complaints and to support problem-solving projects. Because residents are to play an important role in identifying, prioritizing, and even dealing on their own with local problems, they as well as police were trained in how to implement the model. Between 1995 and 1997, most patrol officers and about 12,000 civilians were taught to analyze how offenders and victims collide at particular locations to create crime hot spots. Both police and residents were also given new tools for solving problems, ranging from computerized crime analysis to the support of an interagency inspections task force.

The vehicle for all grassroots consultation and collaboration between police and residents is neighborhood meetings that are held in almost all of the city's 279 police beats, almost every month. During 1998, an average of 250 beat meetings were held each month and about 5,800 people attended. An average of seven police officers attend each meeting, including the beat's sergeant, beat officers who are on duty, and a few beat team members from other shifts. The latter are paid overtime, at a yearly cost of more than $1 million. The meetings frequently feature presentations by police from special units or detectives, and those who attend include representatives of city service agencies, aldermanic staff, school personnel, local business owners and landlords, and activists representing area community groups. These meetings are perhaps the most important link among residents, police, and many of these agencies and community leaders. Beat meetings are intended to be forums for exchanging information and for identifying, prioritizing, and analyzing local problems. They also provide occasions for police and residents to get acquainted, and a vehicle for residents to organize their own problem-solving efforts. (For further information about the program, see Skogan and Hartnett, 1997.)

The structure of Chicago's community policing program resolves the question of "who is the community" by defining it as the residents of a specific administrative unit of the city, along with assorted building owners, business operators, and others who have a stake in the area. Their representation depends on who shows up for a meeting. This resolution was the result of a political struggle between police and politicians on one side, and a fragmented collection of community organizations on the other, that was played out during the early years of the program. The organizations "outside" wanted "inside." They demanded that the meetings be organized and led by local groups, who would control the agenda and invite police to participate on their terms. They wanted civilian involvement in all significant aspects of the program to be directed by leaders who were either elected by beat residents or somehow emerged from locally prominent organizations. They saw resident involvement in the city's community policing program as one vehicle for building the autonomous capacity of residents to help themselves and lobby effectively in the corridors of power for the outside resources they needed to address their most pressing problems. Because all of this would take time and energy, they also wanted grants and contracts to support the professional organizers it would take to carry off this vision of resident involvement. The police and city leaders would have none of this, and because it was a one-sided struggle, Chicago proceeded with a "depoliticized" version of representational involvement.

But that raises the hard questions. Unlike formally constituted bodies— made up, for example, of heads of a list of formal organizations, official nominees of the mayor, or elected representatives—beat meetings are composed of those who happen to hear about them and choose to attend. Attendance at beat meetings has remained remarkably stable. Between their inception in 1995 and the end of 1999, Chicagoans attended beat meetings on about 325,000 occasions. But inevitably, only a small percentage of beat residents will attend the meeting. Although in 1998 the average beat was home to about 7,000 adults, a good meeting by Chicago standards draws about 30 residents. This is only about 0.4 percent of the adult population. (By contrast, in the average beat about 28 percent of age-eligible residents turned out for the 1995 general mayoral election.) So, although sheer numbers are important, it is also important that beat meetings represent the interests of residents. Even a small meeting can do this effectively, if those who attend adequately articulate the concerns of the general public. This chapter addresses three representational questions about beat meetings: Do they reflect the composition of the beat?

Do they represent the problems facing the beat and residents' views of the quality of police service? Can involvement in beat meetings have any impact on neighborhood conditions that residents care about, by affecting the priorities of service providers?

A variety of data is used to address these questions. The results of surveys represent the views of neighborhood residents, and the findings of questionnaires distributed at beat meetings describe who attended and what their concerns were. The Appendix describes all of the surveys and the wording of questions addressing neighborhood problems and perceptions of police. Observers attended a large sample of beat meetings, and what they recorded is examined, as well. City agencies contributed data on their cleanup efforts. Finally, demographic information from the 1990 Census, updated where possible, portrays the race and class composition of the beats. All of the data are centered around 1998, the year beat meetings participants were surveyed.

REPRESENTATION OF RESIDENTS

The first question is: to what extent do those who attended beat meetings resemble community residents? The answer involved comparisons such as those made in Figures 3.1 and 3.2. They describe the relation between the demographic composition of the beats and the characteristics of those who attended meetings there. Information about beat residents is based on U.S. Census data for 2000. The contrasting data on beat meeting participants is drawn from questionnaires completed by 4,673 residents who attended meetings in 195 beats for which complete data are available for this study. The questionnaires were distributed by observers who attended beat meetings during 1998.

Figure 3.1 examines the match between the percentage of beat residents and meeting participants who owned their home, an important feature of any neighborhood. As it indicates, home owners were significantly overrepresented at the beat meetings we observed. At the average meeting, 75 percent of the participants were home owners, compared with a beat average of 40 percent. More than 90 percent of the meetings had a greater percentage of home owners present than lived in the beat, and home owners were the majority group at 87 percent of the meetings. The overrepresentation of home owners is especially apparent at low levels of beat home ownership; this is signaled by the decelerating regression line that is the best statistical description of the relation between the two measures. As the arrows in Figure 3.1 illustrate, beats that averaged about 30 percent home owners were represented by meetings where about 70 percent of the participants were home owners.

Figure 3.2 presents similar data charting the representation of the city's Latinos. Latino is the locally preferred term in Chicago for reference to historically Spanish-speaking peoples whose origins lie largely in Mexico, with smaller groups representing Puerto Rico, Central and South America, and the Caribbean. At the end of the 1990s, the city's Latinos totaled about 730,000—

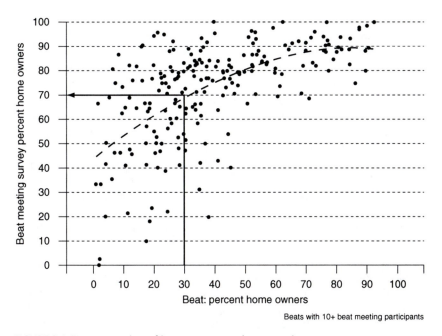

FIGURE 3.1 Representation of home owners at beat meetings.

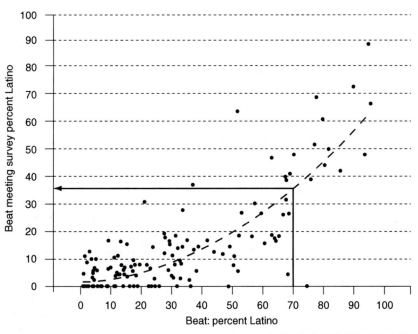

FIGURE 3.2 Representation of Latinos at beat meetings.

a group larger than the total population of all but thirteen American cities. They are also the only large racial or ethnic group that is growing in numbers, and it is anticipated that before 2010 they will constitute the second largest racial or ethnic group in Chicago. However, Figure 3.2 indicates that Latino participation in beat meetings tends to be low except in beats where a "critical mass" of Latinos live. There it skyrockets, as illustrated by the rapidly accelerating regression line in Figure 3.2. But there are relatively few concentrated Latino beats in the city above the take-off point (35 beats in the city were more than 60 percent Latino by 2000), so gross underrepresentation of Latinos is the norm. As Figure 3.2 illustrates, even at 70 percent Latino, the proportion of Latinos at beat meetings is generally about half their fraction in the population.

Beat meetings overrepresent other groups as well. The biggest gap is education, because residents with more education turn out heavily. For example, in beats where about 30 percent of residents have a college education, almost 75 percent of beat meeting participants reported having a college degree, and college graduates made up a majority at 70 percent of the meetings. Older neighborhood residents were also overrepresented. The areas examined here averaged about 12 percent over age sixty-five, but the beat meetings averaged 25 percent, double the population figure. Like home ownership, the link between the beat and meeting age leveled off at higher figures; for example, in beats where residents over sixty-five make up about 20 percent of the population (a high number), about 35 percent of meeting participants reported being in that age range. On average, meeting participants had lived in their neighborhood nine years longer than the average area resident. Women were the biggest group at about 75 percent of the meetings. The meetings attended by observers ranged from 25 percent to almost 90 percent women, and averaged 60 percent women. Women were more overrepresented in African-American areas, in poor beats, and in public housing areas.

In short, on many dimensions, involvement in Chicago's beat meetings demonstrates a strong middle-class bias. In many social programs that rely on volunteers, better off and more established members of the community are the quickest to get involved and take advantage of the effort. Research on involvement in neighborhood anticrime organizations find that higher income, more educated, home-owning, and long-term area residents more frequently know of opportunities to participate and are more likely to get involved when they have the opportunity (cf. Skogan, 1989). In the case of beat meetings, the largest discrepancies in involvement favored college graduates, home owners, and older, long-term residents. Latinos were the most underrepresented racial or ethnic group. Chicago has certainly made efforts to involve Latinos more deeply in its community policing effort. The publicity campaign supporting the program features a component aimed at Spanish-speaking residents. It includes paid promotional announcements and a police-staffed talk show on Spanish-language radio; booths at festivals held in Latino neighborhoods; and wide distribution of posters, flyers, and newsletters in Spanish. Spanish-speaking community organizers work for the city to generate involvement in beat meetings and problem solving. The city's emergency communication system is staffed to handle foreign-language calls, and the police department itself has about 800 Spanish-speaking officers. Beat meetings held in predominately Latino areas routinely are conducted in both languages, although the translators are almost always police or resident amateurs, and the meetings run at a slow pace. The department's cadet diversity training includes some role playing exercises revolving around linguistic issues. Despite these efforts, the integration of the city's Latino residents into CAPS has proven difficult.

REPRESENTATION OF CONCERN
ABOUT NEIGHBORHOOD CONDITIONS

The second question is: to what extent did those who attended beat meetings represent the views of residents concerning the problems they faced? We have seen that the meetings overrepresent more established members of the community, based on a comparison of beat populations with profiles of meeting participants. The same kinds of comparisons can be made between reports of neighborhood problems gathered in surveys of beat residents and meeting participants. The data indicate that meeting participants were more concerned about problems than were the residents of their beat: those who attended gave higher ratings than did their neighbors to a broad range of problems. Second, the data indicate that those who come to the meetings broadly represent the views of beat residents, but more accurately for some issues than for others.

To make these comparisons, the results of citywide surveys conducted during 1997, 1998, and 1999 were aggregated to the beats in which the respondents lived. The yearly surveys were large, averaging about 3,100 completed interviews, but because the respondents were scattered throughout Chicago, many beats were still sparsely represented. Not all beats had a full set of participant data, either, because the observers could not attend and successfully survey all of them and because some meetings were only sparsely attended. This chapter requires ten survey respondents as the minimum number for characterizing a beat. As a result, it examines 195 beats (70 percent of the city's 270 residential beats) where at least ten meeting participants completed questionnaires and ten residents were interviewed in the city surveys. As a group, these beats were better off with lower crime than the 75 beats that were excluded, but the biggest difference between the two groups is population size. The beats represented in the study are about one-third larger than those that are not, because residents there were more likely to be sampled in the citywide surveys.

Comparisons between residents and beat meeting participants could be made for assessments of the magnitude of seven neighborhood problems that were included in both surveys. Both groups were asked to rate whether each was a "big problem," "some problem," or "no problem" in their neighborhood. The largest gap between meeting participants and residents concerned street drug sales. Almost half of those who attended beat meetings reported that street

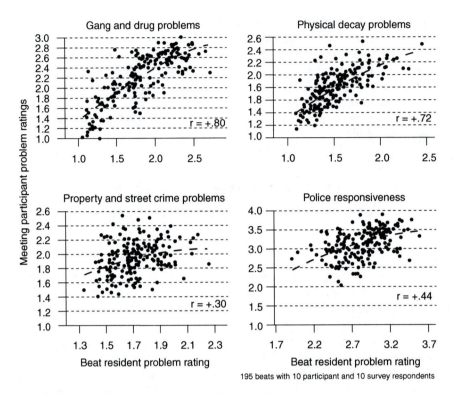

195 beats with 10 participant and 10 survey respondents

FIGURE 3.3 Representation of interests at beat meetings.

drug sales were a big problem in their neighborhood, compared with 32 percent of residents. Gang violence and graffiti came next; the gap between residents and participants was about 12 percentage points for both problems. Other gaps were smaller, but those who came to meetings were more concerned than were run-of-the-mill residents about all seven problems.

Three panels in Figure 3.3 address the extent to which residents' perceptions of beat problems were reflected in the level of concern that participants brought to beat meetings. Beat by beat, they compare ratings of problems gathered in the city surveys with ratings of the same problems supplied by meeting participants. Responses to questions about three forms of physical decay—abandoned cars, abandoned buildings, and graffiti—were combined to form a neighborhood physical decay index. Questions about the extent of problems with burglary and street crime formed a personal and property crime index, and questions about gangs and drugs constituted a measure of their own. Figure 3.3 presents average resident and beat meeting participant scores on these measures for each beat.

The strong relation between resident and participant ratings of gang and drug problems is apparent in Figure 3.3. The correlation between the two measures was +.75. Likewise, there was a strong link between beat and participant assessments of the extent of physical decay in their area; that correlation was +.72. In these domains, where residents are concerned, so are those who show up at meetings; where they are not, many participants share that view, as well. Chicagoans can feel fairly confident that those who attend meetings in their beat reflect their views about the seriousness of gang, drug, and neighborhood physical decay problems.

The link was weaker between beat meeting participant's views of crime problems and what the general public thought about burglary and street crime. As Figure 3.3 indicates, the two were correlated only +.30. Public concern about street crime translated to the meetings a bit more directly (the correlation between the two measures was +.48 for street crime and +.22 for burglary), but neither linkage was particularly strong. Careful inspection of Figure 3.3 also reveals that there was less variation across beats in the views of both groups when it came to crime. The high-to-low range for each group was smaller, and more beats were clustered near the city average.

There are at least two plausible explanations for the limited correspondence between resident and activist concern about crime. One is visibility. Most of the remaining problems probed by the surveys have visual manifestations. Graffiti, abandoned cars and buildings, street drug sales, and even some aspects of neighborhood gang activity can be clearly visible neighborhood issues. Seeing them provides evidence of their magnitude that can be shared by broad segments of the community. Graffiti has as its "victim" everyone who views and is offended by it, and unless it is cleaned up they will see it over and over again. By contrast, burglary and street crime victimize individuals and households, and they are crimes of stealth. People may hear and gossip about victims of these offenses, but they rarely see such crimes in progress, and after the fact they leave few visible scars. They do not present the kind of shared, visible, repetitive experience that other problems in our inventory can manifest, even if they are widespread in a community.

Another possible explanation for the relatively weak link between residents' views of crime and those of beat meeting participants is representational. The issue is, to what extent do biases in the representation of groups account for any lack of correspondence between the views of the general public and those that are carried into beat meetings? The views of beat meeting participants vary, depending on who they are, so the demographic imbalance in representation we have already observed may have an impact on the correspondence between the priorities of the general public and the issues that concern just those who show up.

To examine this involves contrasting the impact of imbalances in the representation of various groups at the meetings on the fit or lack of fit between the views of meeting participants and their neighbors. The group that made the largest difference was older people. Their overrepresentation affected the views of the group, for they tended to see fewer crime problems than did their younger counterparts. Residents over age sixty-five were only half as likely as those aged eighteen to twenty-nine to report that street crime was a big problem in their neighborhood, and the gap was almost as wide for burglary. The varying mix of younger versus older participants at the meetings thus had a substantial effect on the gap between beats and meetings, the strongest effect of any demographic factor. The correlation between the average age gap between beat meeting participants and residents and the underrepresentation of crime problems at the meetings was .21. In contrast, there were only small differences between older and younger people when they were asked about neighborhood physical decay or drug and gang problems; therefore, age misrepresentation had a much smaller effect on the match between the views of residents and beat meeting participants.

REPRESENTATION OF CONCERN
ABOUT POLICE

Beat meetings do not simply serve as a forum for identifying and prioritizing neighborhood problems. They also play a role in monitoring police activities in the area. An official agenda item for each meeting is a report by police about what they have been doing in response to problems identified at previous meetings. Our observers watched for them, and found that feedback reports were actually made at 61 percent of the beats they attended. The police also suggested solutions to the problems discussed at the meeting 58 percent of the time.

Although not on the agenda, complaints about police also came up frequently; the observers noted that they were discussed at meetings in 47 percent of the beats. There was also specific praise for police at a third of the meetings. The most commonly cited concern was response to 911 calls, and in particular the speed with which police arrive at the scene. There was some dissatisfaction voiced about how well police treated people who had called, and with how carefully police followed department policies designed to protect the anonymity of callers who provided them with information. The perception that there are not enough police on patrol was voiced at about one in five beats, and dissatisfaction with the implementation of various aspects of CAPS came up in 12 percent of the beats. At about a third of the meetings there was discussion of problems with the extent of citizen involvement in CAPS. Beat meeting turnout, a lack of police-citizen cooperation, and the need for more follow-up on problems that were discussed headed that list, and there was frequent discussion of the issue of retaliation against residents who become visibly associated with the police.

Beat meetings, thus, can actually provide a forum for residents to voice their concerns and try to hold police accountable for working on them, both separately and in partnership. Representing the satisfaction or dissatisfaction of residents with policing in their area should be one of their most important functions. In practice, however, this form of interest representation does not appear to be a very direct one.

The lower right-hand panel in Figure 3.3 illustrates the relation between resident views of the quality of police service in their neighborhood and the views carried into beat meetings by those who attended. The index of opin-ion about police presented in Figure 3.3 is based on responses to questions about how well police dealt with problems of concern to residents, worked with residents to solve local problems, and responded to community concerns. Figure 3.3 indicates that beat meetings provided this link in the most general sense. The correlation between beat and participant attitudes was +.44, provid-ing a direct but not particularly strong link between the two. The correlations between the individual components of the index were all in about the same range, between +.36 and +.43.

There are at least two reasons for this tenuous linkage. First, meeting par-ticipants were more optimistic than their neighbors about the quality of police service in their neighborhood. For example, about 70 percent of those attend-ing meetings in these beats thought police were doing a good or very good job at dealing with problems that concerned beat residents, but the comparable fig-ure for residents was 60 percent. The divide was greater—about 15 percentage points—in the proportion who thought police were doing a good job work-ing with residents to solve problems. Although we have seen that those who attend the meetings were more concerned than were their neighbors about a broad range of local problems, they were less concerned about the police.

This optimism probably has several sources. Those who choose to attend beat meetings in the first place may be more optimistic about police, whereas those who are not favorably inclined toward the police stay away. The gap may grow because those who attend and have a bad experience do not come back, and critics who speak up may feel unwelcome to return. Their voices are less likely to be heard. Alternately, those who attend may come to know and appre-ciate the concern shown by the police who are there. They would also see any positive accomplishments that stem from the meetings. These explanations are consistent with the finding that people who attend beat meetings frequently are more positive about the police than are those who attend only once or twice, and infrequent participants are in turn more optimistic than those who do not come at all. The gap in optimism about police that emerges between participants and the general public is also consistent with the extremely high levels of satisfaction that participants report with what takes place at the meet-ings. In citywide surveys, 85 percent or more routinely report that they learn something at the meetings, that action has taken place in their neighborhood as a result of the meetings, that they are useful for finding solutions to prob-lems, and that they improve the community's relationship with the police.

A second source for this optimism gap is that there were strong racial dif-ferences in views of the police, and racial differences in the size of the gap between residents and activists from their own community. The first—sheer racial differences in views of the police—are large, and meetings that overrep-resented White Chicagoans were more optimistic as a result. For example, in 1998 almost 70 percent of White residents thought police were doing a good job "working together with residents . . . to solve local problems." The com-parable figure for African-Americans was 41 percent, and for Latinos, 48 per-cent. However, neighborhood racial segregation is so extreme in Chicago that

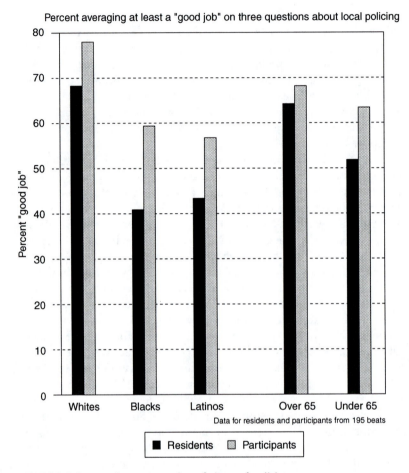

Percent averaging at least a "good job" on three questions about local policing

Data for residents and participants from 195 beats

■ Residents　　▨ Participants

FIGURE 3.4 Race and representation of views of policing.

the overrepresentation of Whites in predominately African-American beats was not a factor in very many places. More important is that the distance between African-Americans who showed up at beat meetings and their African-American neighbors who did not attend was particularly noticeable when it came to views of the police. The gulf between residents and participants was almost as great for Latinos. The differential gap between beat residents and CAPS participants, depending on their race, further attenuated the link between beat meeting participants and their neighbors.

The magnitude of the gap can be seen on the left-hand side of Figure 3.4. It presents the percentage of respondents who on average rated the police as doing at least a good job on the three measures of perceptions of the quality of police service. The difference between each pair of bars represents the gap between neighborhood residents and beat meeting participants of the same race in the 195 beats where both were well represented in the data. The gulf between the two groups was greatest—17 percentage points—among African-Americans. It was smallest—9 percentage points—among Whites. The gap between residents and CAPS participants was 14 percentage points for Latinos, close to the divide for African-Americans. Because large numbers of less satisfied segments of the public stay away, the representation of residents' views of police service is less effective in African-American and Latino communities, where the climate of opinion at beat meetings may make police-community relations appear to be rosier than they really are.

As Figure 3.4 indicates, the overrepresentation of older residents also attenuated the link between resident and beat meeting opinion. Attitude surveys usually find steep age gradients in views of policing, both among the general public and those who are stopped by police, and Chicago is no exception. In 1998, 74 percent of residents over sixty-five reported that, on average, police were doing a good job on the three aspects of police work summarized in Figure 3.4. The comparable figure for those under age thirty was 45 percent, and for thirty- to fifty-year-olds it was 53 percent. The correlation between the average age gap between beat participants and residents and the understatement of concern about policing was .29. As in the case of problem priorities, the link between age and attitudes toward police means that beat meetings provide a more favorable venue for police than they would if adults of all ages were more fully represented.

IMPACT ON NEIGHBORHOODS

The last issue addressed by this chapter is whether any of this makes a difference for the city's neighborhoods. This is a difficult question to address, for the character of neighborhoods in a large city like Chicago is influenced by a broad range of macro- as well as micro-level forces. In contrast to factors like large-scale immigration, a shift from manufacturing to services as the economic engine of the city, and the exodus of the child-rearing middle-class to the suburbs, the representativeness of beat meetings probably is not very consequential. At the local level, beat meetings compete with a long list of policies and practices for affecting the course of neighborhood development, and probably they do not account for as much as many other factors. The proper place to look for the effect of beat meetings is closer to home, in their impact on how the community policing program that embraces them is conducted. Does the program respond effectively to the concerns of residents, as they are articulated through beat meetings and other venues? Do "the goods get delivered" in response to citizen priorities? Even then, there inevitably will be other forces at work affecting how the program operates and who enjoys its benefits, so the question becomes: what is the role of beat meetings as compared with other factors determining who gets what from the program?

One important place to look for the effect of these forces is in the delivery of city services. Although both police and residents are concerned about crime, an important feature of Chicago's program is that the problems it addresses do not have to be serious criminal matters. Community policing inevitably involves an expansion of the police mandate to include a broad range of concerns that previously lay outside their competence. By the time CAPS began, everyone locally believed that crime is rooted in a range of neighborhood conditions and events, and that it is necessary to address both criminal and criminogenic problems in practical fashion if the city is to take its mission of preventing crime seriously. A department publication noted,

> CAPS recognizes that graffiti, abandoned vehicles and buildings, malfunctioning street lights and other signs of neighborhood disorder do have an adverse effect on both crime and the public's fear of crime. By addressing these relatively minor problems early on, police and other government agencies can prevent them from becoming more serious and widespread crime problems. (Chicago Police Department, 1996:2)

An expansion of the police mandate is also required by the department's commitment to open itself to public input and scrutiny. If officers responded to community concerns with remarks such as, "Well, that's not a police matter," no one would show up for another meeting. Therefore, police in Chicago find themselves involved in orchestrating neighborhood weekend cleanups and graffiti paint-outs. The districts have problem-buildings officers who inventory dilapidated and abandoned structures and track down the owners of the property. Police stand with residents at prayer vigils and guard barbeque "smoke-outs" on drug-selling corners. They distribute bracelets that would identify senior citizens if they fall unconscious and take note of street lights that are out and trees that need trimming. They are steered by residents toward problems such as the sale of loose cigarettes and individual cans of beer, as well as toward the open-air drug markets that plague too many neighborhoods.

But to make this work, community policing could not be just the police department's program; it had to have the assistance of other city agencies. So, from the beginning, Chicago envisioned that the delivery of city services would be an integral part of community policing. The mechanism is a quick and easy service request procedure involving only one sheet of paper. Officers' service requests trigger a prioritizing and case-tracking process that increases the responsiveness of other city agencies. Making this function smoothly was difficult at first. An interagency task force worked on the logistics of coordinating agency efforts against problems while programmers developed a software system that logged in, tracked, and recorded the final disposition of police service requests and generated user-friendly reports that could be double-checked in the field. District commanders and agency troubleshooters met weekly to iron out interagency communication problems. Changes were made in city ordinances to facilitate expedited building demolitions and car tows. During the program-development period the service-delivery component was one of the most successful elements of CAPS. The evaluation found that, in contrast to matched comparison areas, physical decay went down in the worst off prototype areas, and several districts made effective use of the process to target specific problems, including abandoned buildings, trash, and graffiti (see Skogan and Hartnett, 1997). More recently, the city's civilian CAPS Implementation Office stations service coordinators across the city to see to it that problem-solving projects have the support that they require. Beginning in early 2000, service requests were entered directly into the city's service-tracking system using computers located in police district stations. The system allows station personnel to check the status of individual requests and print out reports on service requests for distribution at beat meetings.

Data from the city's information system can be used to monitor two high-volume services that address problems of concern to the public and are widely discussed at beat meetings: graffiti and abandoned cars. The 1998 citywide survey found that half of Chicagoans thought graffiti was either some problem or a big problem in their neighborhood, and 32 percent expressed similar concern about abandoned cars. Residents who turned out for beat meetings were more emphatic; in the same year, 76 percent of residents who attended beat meetings thought graffiti was a problem in their neighborhood, and 59 percent were concerned about abandoned cars. The question is: how closely does the delivery of services track the priority that residents of various beats give to these two problems?

To examine this, city data banks contributed indicators of the distribution of the relevant service responses for 1997 and 1998. In those two years there were almost 180,000 graffiti site cleanups and 83,000 car-tow requests, and the data indicate that over the period the average beat was cleaned 646 times and car-tow requests were filed 225 times. Because beats vary greatly in size (they were drawn to equalize police workloads rather than population), rates of service per 1,000 residents were calculated using updated estimates of the population for each beat. These rates can be contrasted with the measures of concern about graffiti and abandoned car problems gathered in surveys of beat residents and beat meeting participants.

Figure 3.5 describes the general relation between some of the factors that may influence the distribution of city services. Behind the two "need" measures—the concern expressed by beat residents and those who attended beat meetings in the surveys—lies something that we cannot observe directly: the actual extent of the problems that bother them. This presumably drives public concern, as expressed through beat meetings but also through complaints to politicians or calls to city hotlines. The extent of the problem also affects officers' observations and priorities set for city agencies, and have influence through other channels that steer services in response to local priorities. Another factor that may affect who gets what from community policing is beat activism—the extent to which residents turn out and get involved in beat affairs. This is represented by the 1998 beat meeting turnout rate (the number of participants per 1,000 adults). In Chicago, politics provides another priority-setting process that channels benefits to this neighborhood or that, and it needs to be taken into account in any portrait of the distribution of city services. In this case it is represented by the percentage of each beat's vote that went to the incumbent (and ultimately successful) mayoral candidate in the 1995 general election.

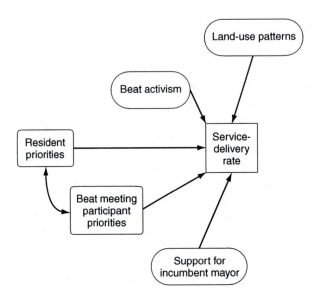

FIGURE 3.5 Beat factors and service-delivery patterns.

Finally, Figure 3.5 anticipates that land-use patterns will also affect the extent of service delivery. Many beats in Chicago contain a mix of residential and nonresidential buildings, so it is important to control for this factor before examining the effect of people-based factors such as beat meeting attendance and resident priorities. Graffiti and cleanups are both affected by the density of buildings in a beat, and small businesses provide a common target. The statistical analysis also controls for land uses (such as parking lots, automobile repair facilities, and others) that concentrate cars in a beat. The impact of those control factors is presented at the bottom of Table 3.1.

The statistical relation between these factors is described in Table 3.1. It indicates the strength of the correlations between service delivery and the factors sketched in Figure 3.5, and their relative impact when taken together in multiple regression. It documents that the link between service-delivery rates and the two ancillary components of the model summarized in Figure 3.5, politics and beat activism, varied from service to service. Being part of the mayor's electoral coalition was linked to graffiti cleanups independent of residents' priorities and the priorities of beat meeting activists. On the other hand, beat meeting attendance rates were strongly linked to action against abandoned cars, but the political complexion of the beat was not. However, in both cases there were substantial direct links between beat residents' priorities and who got what from the city. It was the strongest factor affecting car tows and followed politics for graffiti-related services. In addition, where beat meeting participants were especially concerned compared with their neighbors, service-delivery rates were higher still. The impact of both beat meeting attendance rates and the priorities of meeting participants suggests that the squeaky wheel is indeed being greased by Chicago's community policing program.

Table 3.1 Correlates of Beat Service Delivery Rates

VARIABLE	(LOG) GRAFFITI CLEANUP RATE		(LOG) CAR-TOW RATE	
	STANDARDIZED REGRESSION COEFFICIENT	BIVARIATE CORRELATION	STANDARDIZED REGRESSION COEFFICIENT	BIVARIATE CORRELATION
Resident Priorities	.30	.58	.29	.48
Meeting Attendee Priorities	.18	.57	.29	.52
Meeting Attendance Rate	.21	(–.06)	.20	.42
Vote Share for the Incumbent Mayor	.36	.63	–.22	–.34
Nonresidential Land Use	.18	.46	–.18	–.13
Percent of Parcels Small Businesses	.18	.32	—	—
Building Density	.13	.20	—	—
Percent of Parcels Automobile Uses	—	—	.34	.22
R^2 (adj.)	.65		.54	

Note: Table reports standardized regression coefficients. All coefficients and correlations are significant $p < 0.05$ unless indicated by parentheses; $N = 195$.

Of course, other factors were correlated with service-delivery rates, as well. There was a strong association between the size of the Latino population and both resident and meeting participant's ratings of graffiti problems, and Latinos voted heavily in favor of the incumbent mayor. Only in the multivariate analysis was beat activism, which is relatively low in many Latino communities, also significantly related to the delivery of graffiti services. On the car-tow side, relatively few complaints were lodged in the city's better off White neighborhoods; they were moderately concentrated in Latino and African-American areas, and voters in the latter were particularly indisposed to vote for the incumbent in 1995.

SUMMARY

This chapter finds that the representational structure created by Chicago's beat meetings to a significant extent translates residents' priorities into the program in action. There is a strong middle-class bias in participation in the meetings. Beat meetings do a better job at representing already established stakeholders in the community than they do at integrating marginalized groups with fewer mechanisms for voicing their concerns. The priorities that participants bring to the meetings sometimes reflect those of their neighbors, but it is ironic that neither concern about crime nor dissatisfaction with the quality of police service is particularly well represented in this community policing program. This being said, there were strong correlations (.48 to .58) between residents' priorities and the delivery of city services that speak to two widely discussed neighborhood problems: graffiti and abandoned cars. Neighborhoods plagued by these problems received more help.

CITATIONS

Chicago Police Department. 1996. *The Role of City Services in the CAPS Problem-Solving Model.* Chicago: Chicago Police Department.

Skogan, Wesley G. 1989. "Community Organizations and Crime." In Michael Tonry and Norval Morris (Eds.),

Crime and Justice: An Annual Review. Chicago: University of Chicago Press, 39–78.

Skogan, Wesley G. and Susan M. Hartnett. 1997. *Community Policing, Chicago Style.* New York and London: Oxford University Press.

APPENDIX ON DATA SOURCES

OBSERVATIONS AND PARTICIPANT SURVEY

During 1998, trained observers attended 459 beat meetings in 253 beats. Some beats that were involved in a parallel study were observed more than once. The data for beats with multiple observations were weighted so that all areas are represented equally, and the unit of analysis here is the police beat. At the meetings the observers completed an observation form that systematically recorded important aspects of what took place at the meeting. They also counted the number, race, and gender of residents and police who were there, and took note of city service representatives, local politicians, and other nonresidents who attended.

The observers also distributed questionnaires to the residents and police officers who were present. They contacted district neighborhood relations offices and civilian beat meeting facilitators before each meeting to ensure that they would be on the agenda. A primary goal was to not interfere with the flow of meetings, so observers were flexible in the administration of the survey. At the appointed time they arose to explain who they were and briefly described the purposes and goals of the evaluation. The questionnaires were necessarily short, so they would not take up much time, and they were designed and worded to be as accessible as possible to a wide audience. Questionnaires were available in both English and Spanish. Observers were instructed to assist any respondent who could not read the form, apart from the rest of the meeting's participants to avoid a breach of confidentiality. Police officers who were present filled out longer questionnaires while residents completed theirs.

The observers kept no formal records of refusals, noncompletions, or survey-completion rates beyond informal reports made to the project manager. Beat meetings have a fluid character. Residents and police officers come late and leave early, and they often stand and stretch or mill around in the back and conduct personal business out of the room. As a result, the simple question of how many are in attendance is a problematic one. Observers would generally recount meeting participants when they could to gauge survey response, but they were very busy during this period. Because the questionnaires were anonymous, it was not possible to determine who did not complete one or supplied only partial information. Also, although observers handled inquiries from officers or residents on any number of issues regarding the questionnaire, in no case were potential respondents pressured into completing a questionnaire if they did not desire to do so. In a few instances the observers reattended meetings in beats where the ratio of participants to completed interviews appeared to be low, and they offered surveys to those who had not completed one previously.

RESIDENT SURVEYS

The city surveys were conducted by telephone using random-digit-dialing procedures that ensured that unlisted households would be included in the sample. In 1998 and 1999 the random component of the sample was augmented by approximately 250 telephone numbers that were selected at random from published lists of numbers to increase the number of completed interviews in a few low-population police districts. They are excluded from citywide analyses but were included in the aggregated beat data examined here. The most conservative survey completion rates ranged from 40 percent to 60 percent, declining over time. The 1997 survey included 3,066 respondents, in 1998 it included 3,071 respondents, and in 1999 it included 3,101 respondents. Of this group, about 6,800 residents lived in the 195 beats for which there was complete information for this study. The questions were administered in both English and Spanish. The surveys were conducted by the Survey Research Laboratory of the University of Illinois.

The resident and beat meeting participant surveys shared three questions about the quality of police service:

How responsive are the police in your neighborhood to community concerns? Do you think they are [very responsive to very unresponsive]?

How good a job are the police doing in dealing with the problems that really concern people in your neighborhood? Would you say they are doing a [very good job to poor job]?

How good a job are the police doing in working together with residents in your neighborhood to solve local problems? Would you say they are doing a [very good job to poor job]?

Responses to these questions went together consistently. In the 1998 resident survey they were correlated an average of +.65, and at the individual level the combined index had a reliability of .85.

The resident and beat meeting participant surveys shared seven questions about neighborhood problems. Respondents were requested to rate a list of things "that you may think are problems in your neighborhood." They were asked to indicate whether "you think it is a big problem, some problem, or no problem in your neighborhood." Responses to three of these questions were used to assess the extent of neighborhood physical decay.

Abandoned cars in the streets and alleys.

Abandoned houses or other empty buildings in your area.

Graffiti, that is, writing or painting on walls or buildings.

Responses to these questions went together consistently. In the resident survey they were correlated an average of +.45, and at the individual level the combined index had a reliability of .76.

Two questions about neighborhood crime drew strongly consistent responses, and they were more closely linked to each other than to any of the remaining questions. At the individual level, responses to these questions were correlated +.71 in the resident survey. Combined, they formed an index of neighborhood gang and drug problems.

Shootings and violence by gangs.

Drug dealing on the streets.

The resident and beat meeting participant surveys shared two questions about property and street crime. At the individual level, responses to these questions in the resident survey were correlated an average of +.56.

People breaking in or sneaking into homes to steal things.

People being attacked or robbed.

PART III

Will Police Officers
Buy In?

4

Can Police Adapt? Tracking the Effects of Organizational Reform over Six Years[1]

DENNIS P. ROSENBAUM AND
DEANNA L. WILKINSON

INTRODUCTION

The rhetoric of community policing was transformed into concrete action when Congress passed the Crime Control and Law Enforcement Act of 1994 and proceeded to spend roughly $9 billion dollars over the next six years to support local law enforcement agencies in pursuit of this agenda. The four main community policing goals of the newly created federal COPS Office were to help police organizations build "police-community partnerships, problem-solving, crime prevention, and organizational support for these programmatical objectives" (Roth and Ryan, 2000). These are sensible goals, but for more than two decades academics and police experts had cautioned that new programs and practices would be short-lived without the appropriate organizational and administrative changes to support a new style of policing (Greene, 2000; Goldstein, 1979; Geller, 1985; Kelling and Moore, 1988; Moore and Stephens, 1991). Recommendations include the introduction of new organizational values, management styles, operational strategies, performance-assessment systems, and technologies that encourage police officers to build partnerships with the community and other agencies, and to engage in data-driven problem solving and crime prevention at the neighborhood level. As Mastrofski (1998) notes, community policing models often call for deformalizing, decentralizing, delayering, and despecializing the organization.

Whether this reform movement has been successful at changing police organizations or their employees is an empirical question. Too often cosmetic changes are introduced as part of an impression-management scheme that will draw favorable public reactions (cf. Manning, 1997). Hard evaluations of impact are also lacking. The literature is full of excellent theoretical discussions about desired processes and outcomes (e.g., Greene, 2000; Goldstein, 1990;

[1]This research was supported by grants from the National Institute of Justice and the Illinois Criminal Justice Information Authority. Points of view expressed are those of the authors and do not necessarily reflect the views of the funding agencies.

Mastrofski and Ritti, 2000; Moore, 1992), yet there remains a paucity of solid empirical work (see Rosenbaum, 1994; Alpert & Piquero, 2000). Finally, the "black box" approach to evaluation often looks at the effects of community policing initiatives on police or neighborhood residents without measuring the presumed mechanisms involved.

It is surprising that some important questions remain unanswered: Can progressive police administrators, committed to reform, achieve the desired "buy in" from line officers and their supervisors? Can police officers be "retooled" to think and act in a manner more consistent with the basic tenants of community policing? In this chapter we report the findings of a six-year longitudinal study of community policing reform efforts in two Midwestern police departments—findings that focus on the psychological and behavioral responses of police officers. Our fieldwork documented a wide array of organizational changes that were, in fact, introduced during the study period (see Rosenbaum et al., 1999; Rosenbaum et al., 1999). The question asked in this chapter is whether these changes had any noteworthy and sustained impact on police officers' attitudes and behaviors as would be predicted from organizational or action theory.

The theories of change that go with in community policing models assume that engineered changes in police attitudes, perceptions, and behaviors are important mechanisms through which police organizations will be able to operate more effectively, efficiently, and equitably. Hence, we must examine whether new initiatives for training, socializing, rewarding, and deploying officers can make sizable and sustained differences in officers' attitudes and behaviors with respect to community policing? In essence, can these reforms really change the "occupational subculture" of policing (cf. Skolnick, 1966), or do they simply add to the list of ineffective changes that litter the history of police "reforms"?

Engineering Change

Job Enrichment Theory The general theory of change being tested here is grounded in a long line of research on job satisfaction, as well as popular notions in the private sector about how to achieve organizational excellence (e.g., Peters and Waterman, 1982). Beginning in the late 1920s, management experts began to reject the mechanistic view espoused by Fredrick Taylor, noting that organizational success depends on motivated employees whose individual needs have been satisfied on the job. The new "human relations school" emphasized that employees will be unhappy and unmotivated unless the organization allows for good supervision, cohesive work groups, and positive employee-management relations. The subsequent "growth school" brought attention to the work itself and the importance of employees having the opportunity to get involved in challenging tasks that will engender growth in skill, efficacy, and responsibility. Psychologists such as Chris Argyris, Frederick Herzberg, and Douglas McGregor argue that good pay and job security are not enough—an organization must create "enriched" jobs that satisfy the psychological and social needs of its employees (Morgan, 1997).

Applying this job enrichment model to policing, Rosenbaum, Yeh, and Wilkinson (1994: 333) postulate that police officers are more satisfied and motivated to perform "when their individual needs are met by the organization—needs such as independence, recognition, responsibility, challenge, accomplishment, participation, compensation, and others." Additionally, the job enrichment model suggests that individual needs are more likely to be met when the police organization gives its officers the freedom to think creatively, without fear of punishment, and provides them with the necessary supports and opportunities for professional growth.

Local Theory of Change Although the job enrichment model provides a general framework for understanding and measuring program effects, the local police departments in this study shared what could be called a local theory of change at the ground level. This local theory of action specified the causal mechanisms by which job enrichment and enlargement could be achieved. In the two agencies we examined, organizational support was translated as opportunities for participatory management, supervisory feedback and encouragement, improved communication between units, training programs that focus on new knowledge and skills, geo-based deployment, and (in some cases) freedom from handling calls for service. Hence, the assumption is that lasting changes in officers' attitudes and behaviors are more likely in organizational environments that encourage and support such changes. We were fortunate to study the impact on police personnel in two settings where serious efforts were made to reform the organizations in a direction consistent with community policing models (see Wilkinson and Rosenbaum, 1994).

The most visible and primary component of the local theory of change is the introduction of special community policing units. Although cognizant of the difficulties associated with special units in police organizations, both agencies created such units at the outset as vehicles of change under the assumption that departmentwide reform would be too drastic and would backfire. The special units were envisioned as a central mechanism for reform during the first phase of implementation. The expectation was that such thinking and action would be contagious and, with the right incentives, would eventually spread departmentwide during the second phase of implementation. These units were designed to serve a number of purposes: (1) providing an incubation chamber to protect new ideas and innovative practices from the adverse effects of a potentially hostile police culture; (2) offering organizational supports in terms of extra training, nontraditional supervision, and freedom from traditional roles; (3) using officers as role models to exhibit the style of policing that is now expected; and (4) providing a mechanism for training and socializing (or resocializing) officers into the emerging community policing culture. Thus, on the basis of this special unit model, we predicted that beneficial effects would accumulate over time as more officers were exposed to the special unit. We also hypothesized that officers who participate in special units would show larger gains than officers without this experience.

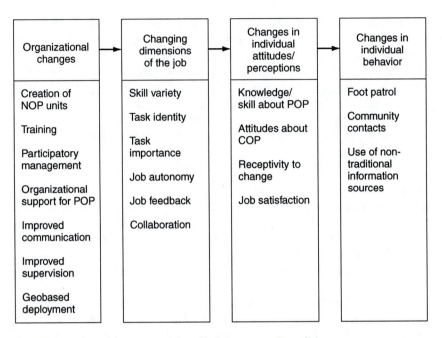

Organizational changes	Changing dimensions of the job	Changes in individual attitudes/ perceptions	Changes in individual behavior
Creation of NOP units	Skill variety	Knowledge/ skill about POP	Foot patrol
Training	Task identity	Attitudes about COP	Community contacts
Participatory management	Task importance	Receptivity to change	Use of non-traditional information sources
Organizational support for POP	Job autonomy	Job satisfaction	
Improved communication	Job feedback		
Improved supervision	Collaboration		
Geobased deployment			

FIGURE 4.1 Job enrichment model applied to community policing.

The theory of change operative in Aurora and Joliet, Illinois, included the notion that there would be a learning curve associated with community policing and problem-solving approaches, and that new attitudes and behaviors must be nurtured organizationally if long-term effects are to be expected. At the outset, the general climate within the departments was skeptical or resistant to community policing reform, although there were pockets of interest and curiosity among the rank and file. Hence, consistent and firm leadership was considered critical to the success of these initiatives. The departments' top administrators believed that the community policing and problem-solving philosophy offered a viable model for reform, although the intensity of this commitment was stronger in Joliet than in Aurora during the start-up period.

In sum, the general hypothesis being tested here is that changes in organizational structure (e.g., creation of special units), management style, and training programs, beyond other factors, will enlarge and enrich the line officers' job, as well as create a supportive work environment. This new environment will, in turn, yield positive changes in officers' attitudes, perceptions, and behaviors with respect to community policing and problem solving. This model of organizational change is summarized in Figure 4.1.

This model was first tested in one of the two cities (Joliet) approximately two years after the start of the reform program. Using a "nonequivalent pre-test/post-test control group design with repeated measurement" (which is explained later), we detected a few positive changes among officers assigned to the special Neighborhood-Oriented Policing (NOP) unit (e.g., more favorable attitudes about community policing), and some change within the non-NOP officers, especially in terms of perceived job enlargement (Rosenbaum, Yeh, and Wilkinson, 1994). But the main story was the failure to detect program effects. As we noted, after two years, "The gains associated with community policing, however, should not be overplayed. The fact remains that the absence of change was the norm rather than the exception" (p. 349).

Although these null results could be due to various design problems (e.g., measurement error or failure to measure the right outcomes), a comprehensive measurement plan and a controlled research design weaken the credibility of these explanations. More likely, either the community policing theory of change articulated here is defective in some way or the implementation of reform was insufficient after two years. The authors argued, on the basis of considerable fieldwork, that implementation was far from complete and that the "dosage level" needed to register more impressive departmentwide effects is likely to be achieved several years down the road. Hence, the long-term follow-up study reported here provides an important test of this widely held notion that community policing is difficult to implement and that researchers must be patient to observe noteworthy effects. The current research investigates the impact of police reform on police officers after six years of sustained implementation.

Organizational Setting and Reforms

The cities of Aurora (pop. 143,000) and Joliet (pop. 106,000) are located approximately forty miles west and southwest of Chicago, respectively. Both communities have substantial urban crime problems, including gang violence, drug markets, and disorder. In 1990 the two police chiefs joined forces and obtained a four-year grant from the Illinois Criminal Justice Information Authority to develop a model "Neighborhood-Oriented Policing and Problem-solving Demonstration Project." At the same time, the research team at the University of Illinois at Chicago was funded to conduct a thorough process and impact assessment of these reform efforts. Data collection continued for six years, from 1991 to 1997.

Extensive field observations by members of the research staff provided careful documentation of the planning and implementation activity at both sites. The research team documented how key process components relevant to community policing reform changed over time, including: organizational structure, organizational fit of community policing, organizational readiness for reform, training and technical support, officer selection criterion, articulation of policies and values, dynamics of new specialized units as vehicles of change, and geographic-based resource allocation.

Both departments began to implement a four-year plan in 1991, which was conceptualized a two-phase implementation process. A focal point for Phase I was the creation of a specialized NOP unit in each department, with officers assigned to small, high-crime areas, whereas Phase II would see the expansion of community policing and problem-solving departmentwide. Although much of the early attention would be on the NOP units, the initial proposal also called for agencywide training in community policing and problem solving, cultural diversity, and advanced crime prevention techniques within the first year. To further minimize the gap between special units and patrol and to encourage some sharing of ideas, the special units were located, organizationally, within the Patrol Division.

A description of the specialized unit in Joliet is provided to illustrate the program in action. In 1992, the Joliet NOP unit initially consisted of sixteen officers (all hand-picked volunteers) and three supervisors serving nine target areas. By 1996, this unit grew to twenty-four officers (selected via interview process) serving fourteen target neighborhoods. The NOP unit, although technically part of the Patrol Division, was specialized and separate from this group. In general, most NOP officers were young, had two to ten years of experience, and considered this unit to be an important career move. NOP officers were allowed to have flexible schedules to become more familiar with residents' concerns and problems at different times of the day. During much of the first year, this unit of full-time problem solvers was freed from the responsibility of answering calls for service, enabling them to devote their attention to local crime and drug problems. Over time, however, NOP officers became the primary call responders in their areas and even began to assist with calls in surrounding zones as a means of encouraging better relations with patrol officers. NOP officers were expected to have a general familiarity with area residents, know about problems in their areas, know about scheduled community meetings, and be familiar with resources that could be used for problem solving. They were also expected to know the status of their own problem-oriented policing projects. NOP officers used a variety of tools, including foot and bicycle patrols, to make officers more accessible and approachable to citizens. NOP officers had greater access to a variety of training and career development opportunities to equip them for their role as community policing officers. Finally, the NOP approach was expanded into a program called "Schools Are for Education" (SAFE) operating with ten officers assigned to ten school-neighborhood zones. The story is more complex in Aurora because special units were created, disbanded, and then created again.

Serious efforts were made to overcome the internal resistance to special units. Although most community policing activities were initiated by the NOP units as self-contained activities, our field observations found evidence of both cooperation and collaboration between NOP officers and other segments of the police department. Officers from both departments reported being deeply immersed in problem solving in the classroom and on the street. A range of problem-oriented policing strategies were pursued, but the primary approaches were: (1) order maintenance (e.g., towing abandoned vehicles, graffiti removal, enforcement of loitering, traffic and liquor laws), (2) CPTED (e.g., blocking streets and entrances to parking lots, removal of shrubs, installation of security devices), (3) code enforcement and nuisance abatement (e.g., creating police-local government building inspection teams, tenant-landlord training), (4) partnership activity (e.g., working with city agencies and community groups), and (5) basic problem-solving approaches within the patrol function.

Each department sought to build an infrastructure that would sustain its reform efforts. Over the first few years both departments struggled to develop effective differential response policies, computer upgrades, office space acquisition and renovation, community organizing and outreach, community training, and leadership development. At the outset, the Police Executive Research Forum (or PERF, a well-known Washington, D.C., consulting group) provided on-site technical assistance in assessing the needs of the organizations and facilitating program implementation. A PERF consultant initially worked half-time in each department and then worked exclusively with Joliet after the second year. Technical assistance with planning and research played a vital role in Joliet and was further enhanced by the addition of a second technical advisor in the fourth year.

Each site struggled to develop its own operational definition of community policing and problem solving through trial and error and by cross-fertilization of implementation expertise around the region and nation. Both sites sent officers to other cities and played host to visiting police officers. Community-oriented styles were also reinforced through training in cultural diversity (both sites) and community organizing (one site). Departmentwide training was held in both sites during the first year of the project. Follow-up or refresher training was typically available to officers and supervisors assigned to the NOP units, and additional recruit training was needed, especially in light of the large number of new officers who had joined the departments by the mid-1990s.

The planning process was fairly similar in these two cities. Both departments created at least two types of committees—one representing a cross-section of the organization to receive input and feedback, and one management-level committee for strategic planning. Both departments committed to experimenting with participatory styles of management by shifting traditional roles down the organizational hierarchy. Our fieldwork documented drastic differences between NOP units and patrol in the supervisory style exhibited. NOP unit supervisors were described as coaches or team leaders rather than disciplinarians or task masters.

In 1995, both departments decided to implement community policing citywide by reorganizing the patrol division from primarily shift-based to geographically based service, thus increasing the level of geographic accountability expected of patrol officers and supervisors. (Geographic management accountability has since become a popular trend in policing.) This move did not occur without problems, including competition for scarce resources among units/areas, beat integrity violations, inadequate coordination among supervisors, and conflict over the division of labor between patrol and NOP officers. Although many expected this change to be followed by the dismantling of the special NOP units, the units remained intact. The next several years were characterized by either a heightened tension between NOP and patrol units regarding who was responsible for a particular geographic zone or the development of complementary working relationships. Administrative officials in both cities considered the transition to geographic deployment successful despite the complaints at the street level.

Overall, we observed strong support from upper management for community policing during this transition period. The field research documented a renewed enthusiasm among upper level managers who, as a result of the reorganization, experienced a perceived increase in responsibility, autonomy, and empowerment. The decentralization, giving supervisors and commanders full responsibility for geographic areas, seemed to reinvigorate this group. Management used promotions and job assignments to demonstrate its strong commitment to problem solving and community policing as a new way of doing business. Some patrol supervisors began to take notice of problem-solving activities that certain officers were engaged in and encouraged those efforts, so long as officers attended to their other patrol duties.

Although the departments' plans were well conceived and informed by the literature on best practices, their first year of implementation illustrated the classic gap between theory and practice (see Wilkinson and Rosenbaum, 1994, for details). For example, a lack of organizational readiness and internal conflicts seriously delayed the implementation processes in Aurora. Moreover, NOP officers in both departments, who were perceived to be the recipients of special opportunities and privileges, were resented by many of their colleagues. The departments struggled to overcome many of these issues and were adversely affected by a number of factors, including changes in leadership, steady growth in and turnover of personnel, multiple demands on resources, and political issues. Furthermore, efforts to establish more participatory management mechanisms often fell flat during the first year when too few personnel were either knowledgeable enough or comfortable enough with community policing to participate fully. Nevertheless, the planning process at both sites included a serious effort to obtain input and "buy in" from rank and file officers (initially in Joliet and then in Aurora during the second year). These efforts expanded and shifted over the next four years, reflecting different organizational strengths and philosophies.

In sum, our process evaluation illustrates clearly that attempting major organizational reforms is not a straightforward, logical process, but rather a complex, sometimes erratic, nonlinear set of activities and events. Given this reality, the relative success with implementation can be attributed to careful planning, strong leadership, good coordination, and unwavering persistence. In retrospect, these were learning organizations—learning to be aware of their strengths and weaknesses, learning to redirect resources to meet emergent needs, and learning to build a viable structure to support community policing strategies. These demonstration projects also underscore the reality that change is a slow and (hopefully) continuous process, requiring a multiyear, if not multidecade, time frame.

Aurora and Joliet were among the first cities to attempt community policing reform on a large-scale and intensive basis. In the early 1990s there existed little organized, practical knowledge to guide police departments through the reform process. Each department tackled what it felt were the more important issues and started down what it thought would be "the path of least resistance," namely, specialized unit. These organizations attempted to build an infrastructure to sustain community policing and, at the same time, get their employees actively engaged in problem-solving and community-focused work. In the process they found an operational definition of community policing that worked for their organizations.

Although extensive reform efforts were under way, predicting the effects on employees was difficult. Some departmentwide effects were hypothesized because all employees were exposed to community policing training programs, but larger effects were expected for persons assigned to NOP units and for managers most deeply involved in the planning process. For those on the fringe, not involved at all, or hostile to reform, predicting negative effects would not be unreasonable. We relied on the job enrichment model and the local theory of change to guide our hypotheses, as articulated earlier.

Organizational differences were also expected. Because of divergent styles and timing of implementation, we hypothesized more positive changes in Joliet than in Aurora (see Wilkinson and Rosenbaum, 1994, for more details). The factors that facilitated stronger implementation in Joliet included: consistently supportive leadership, a flatter hierarchy, less rigidity and formality in communication, and the exploitation of the NOP unit as the primary vehicle for reform.

METHODS

To measure the nature and extent of program implementation, several methodologies were employed in the field, including in-person interviews with key participants, focus group interviews, observations, monthly monitoring, and a comprehensive review of documents. Local newspapers and existing police department and program records were also examined. Each process methodology served a purpose in the overall research design. This qualitative work provided critical data on context and process that would facilitate the interpretation of the impact findings reported here.

Evaluation Design

Five waves of survey data were collected to estimate the effects of the interventions on police personnel. Initially, program effects were estimated using a nonequivalent pre-test/post-test control group design (Shadish, Cook, and Campbell, 2000). The first set of results (Rosenbaum, Yeh, and Wilkinson, 1994) examined changes between the pre-test (Wave 1, 1991) and the second post-test (Wave 3, 1993) using a panel design and comparison groups inside and outside the department. However, the threats to validity became excessive when the external comparison city introduced new community policing programs and a new community-oriented police chief. Thus, Aurora and Joliet each served as its own comparison group in subsequent analyses. Also, because of the growing time lag and associated sample attrition, the Wave 4 and Wave 5 panels were supplemented by independent samples of officers in each department to achieve a total sample of approximately 100 to 120 officers.

A comprehensive questionnaire was administered to police personnel in 1991, 1992, 1993, 1995, and 1997 in Aurora and Joliet. The police survey samples were collected to represent a broad cross-section of police personnel, including both rank-and-file officers and management. The evaluation staff attended daily roll call for each shift over several consecutive days in an attempt to get full representation of the entire police department. At Wave 1, approximately 63 percent of all sworn personnel were interviewed ($N = 115$ in Aurora and $N = 118$ in Joliet). Attrition at Wave 2 and Wave 3 averaged 13 percent and 22 percent, respectively. Because of the time lag and further attrition problems, new independent samples were drawn at Wave 4 and Wave 5 to maintain a total sample size similar to Wave 1. Again, the sample sizes represented more than 60 percent of the departments' total sworn personnel. The Wave 4 sample included approximately 64 percent of officers surveyed at Wave 1, whereas the Wave 5 sample had a 41 percent overlap with the original sample. The data presented in Table 4.1 illustrate the stability of the samples across the five waves of data collection.

Police Survey Measures

Measures used in the police survey instrument reflected the influence of extensive research in organizational behavior and, more recently, research in community policing. For the organizational and job satisfaction measures, we relied heavily on the work of Dunham and colleagues (Dunham et al., 1989; Dunham and Herman, 1975; Dunham, Smith, and Blackburn, 1977), as well as Hackman and colleagues (Hackman and Oldham, 1975, 1976). For attitudes about community policing, we drew on the work of Wycoff and Skogan (1993) and tailored it to local circumstances.

Our measures were designed to capture the following constructs: (1) *dimensions of the job* (i.e., skill variety, task identity, task significance, autonomy, working with others, and job feedback), (2) *implementation of management policies* (i.e., participatory management, supervisory and peer feedback, satisfaction with supervisor, organizational support, communication with detectives, and satisfaction with organizational practices), (3) *job satisfaction* (i.e., job involvement, amount of work, compensation and benefits, relationship with peers, promotion opportunities, organizational commitment, extraorganizational immobility, work motivation, individual growth needs), (4) *attitudes toward community policing* (i.e., general attitudes, priority assigned to community policing activities, support for traditional policing, and receptivity to change), and (5) *problem-solving knowledge and behaviors* (i.e., knowledge of problem-oriented policing, problem-oriented policing capabilities, problem-oriented policing activities, use of diverse sources of information, number of police-citizen contacts, hours spent on foot patrol, hours spent on patrol, meetings with community, meetings within the organization). A description of these measures can be found in the Appendix to this chapter.

Table 4.1 Sample Demographics: Changes from 1991 to 1997

	AURORA POLICE DEPARTMENT					JOLIET POLICE DEPARTMENT				
	1991	**1992**	**1993**	**1995**	**1997**	**1991**	**1992**	**1993**	**1995**	**1997**
Sample Size (independent)	115			135	115	118			123	119
Sample Size (panel) (and % of original)	115	102 88.7	89 77.4	78 67.8	41 35.6	118	101 85.6	93 78.8	71 60.2	55 46.6
% Already in NOP	2.6	8.9	5.7	16.4	12.2	7.0	12.2	11.3	39.1	30.4
% White	89.5	88.2	93.3	80.3	84.7	82.2	83.0	88.2	81.7	78.8
% African-American	3.5	2.9	1.1	3.0	5.4	11.9	9.0	8.6	9.2	11.9
% Hispanic	6.1	5.9	5.6	12.1	4.5	4.2	5.0	2.2	1.7	5.1
% Female	5.2	4.9	5.6	7.5	12.3	6.8	5.9	4.3	4.1	4.2
% Age 29 or Less	14.8	12.7	12.4	21.8	23.7	22.9	18.0	17.2	19.0	18.5
% 5 Years or Less in Assignment	48.7	56.9	52.8	71.1	71.8	65.3	67.0	64.4	75.0	66.1
% Rank = Officer	68.7	61.4	59.6	63.4	71.8	59.5	56.3	52.2	49.6	61.5
% College Grad. or Above	30.9	33.7	39.3	36.7	37.8	38.1	45.5	47.1	38.7	37.8
% Seniority 15 Years +	48.7	49.0	48.3	42.9	39.3	44.9	50.0	54.9	52.1	49.6

Data Analysis Strategy

In the beginning, we had the luxury of testing program effects several ways, depending on how exposure to the program was defined (see Rosenbaum, Yeh, and Wilkinson, 1994), but the passage of time eliminated some options. The reform efforts started in special units, which provided a comparison group of officers not assigned to these units. But departmentwide implementation was soon pursued, first through training programs and later through geo-based deployment of personnel. Thus, as both internal and external comparison groups were eliminated over time, our analysis plans were restricted to an assessment of within-group changes from 1991 to 1997. Hence, the primary sets of analyses examine departmentwide effects over time, using officers as their own controls. Scores on each of the four post-tests (1992, 1993, 1995, 1997) were compared with the group's Wave 1 baseline scores (1991) in a multiple regression framework. Covariance analyses were used to estimate the effects of the reform initiatives among subgroups within the department. These analyses include important comparisons between NOP officers (i.e., those who reported being involved in an NOP unit at any of the five waves of the data collection) and non-NOP officers.

The changing nature of the sample drove our choice of analytic techniques. Because panel data were supplemented with independent (replacement) samples, sophisticated analytic procedures were needed. A multilevel random-effects analysis was performed to account for the clustering of data, because of repeated measurement on some subjects (see Hedeker and Gibbons, 1994). Typically, researchers assess change by making comparisons among independent samples of different respondents or by testing for change within correlated samples using only the same respondents at different in times. The present study used both types of samples and therefore we could not easily analyze the data with conventional statistical techniques. Treating the five waves of survey data as independent, when this is only partially true, would result in an underestimation of standard errors. This bias would increase the probability of committing a Type 1 error, falsely concluding that statistically significant effects exist. Alternatively, if only the panel (repeat) sample were used to conduct a repeated-measures analysis, considerable statistical power would be lost, as the sample sizes would decline considerably.

The optimal solution to this problem was to use a multilevel, random-effects regression analysis strategy, which takes into account the nonindependence of data for some respondents while retaining the statistical power associated with the full sample. In addition to controlling for fixed covariates, this type of model is able to estimate and control for differences in variance at the individual level (see Hedeker, Gibbons, and Davis, 1991; Hedeker and Gibbons, 1994). For this purpose, we used Hedeker's MIXREG program, which uses a maximum marginal likelihood solution and produces substantially more precise estimates than conventional hierarchical linear models. The random effect and residual variance estimates were significant for all tests, confirming the need for multilevel analysis.

Binary variables representing each of the last four waves were created so that the model would control for change at each of these points, relative to the initial wave. Change hypotheses were tested by comparing means at each wave against the Wave 1 baseline. (Deviations from Wave 1 are measured as unstandardized regression coefficients). The model also controlled for, and estimated the effects of, officers' rank, seniority (more than fifteen years on the force), education (college graduate or above), and demographics (African-American, Hispanic, and female). The NOP variable was measured by assigning a 1 when the respondent indicated he or she is working (or has worked) in the NOP unit, and 0 otherwise.

RESULTS

Management and Supervisory Changes

The first set of hypotheses addressed the question of whether organizational changes were noticed and appreciated by police personnel. A variety of measures were used to assess whether the organization has been responsive to the needs of officers and has provided the type of support considered necessary for problem-solving and community policing activities. The surveys measured the extent to which officers saw management as supportive, offering good supervision with regular feedback on job performance, and providing opportunities to participate in management decisions. Over time, with cumulative increases in the dosage of the intervention, officers were expected to report: a more significant role in management decision making, greater satisfaction with feedback from supervisors and peers, greater satisfaction with their supervisors, greater management support for their problem-solving activities, more opportunities to exchange information with detectives, and a more favorable overall assessment of management's policies and practices regarding employees.

Overall, the results were mixed. In Aurora, there were virtually no changes over time on these dimensions (4 percent of the comparisons were statistically significant, and 5 percent would be expected by chance). In fact, there was some evidence of decline in levels of organizational support and supervisor and peer feedback. In Joliet, indicators of management changes over time exhibited significant change on three of five dimensions in the expected direction. Specifically, gains in employees' perceived organizational support for problem solving, increased supervisor and peer feedback, and increased satisfaction with supervisors occurred at Wave 4 (relative to Wave 1). Increases in supervisor and peer feedback and satisfaction with supervisors were sustained at Wave 5, but the increased sense of organizational support was lost. No changes, however, were observed for employee satisfaction with the organizational policies and practices or for perceived participation in management. In Joliet, 21 percent of the statistical comparisons were statistically significant.

Strong predicted differences were apparent between NOP and non-NOP officers in both departments. On virtually all dimensions, officers assigned to the special units reported greater satisfaction with management policies and practices than did non–NOP officers. Similarly, rank was positively associated with beliefs about current organizational support, but only in Aurora. There were few significant differences that could be attributed to seniority, education, gender, or race.

Receptivity to Change

One of the major barriers to organizational reform is employee resistance to change and to community policing strategies in particular. Receptivity to change was at its highest level before the introduction of reforms (Wave 1). Significant declines in openness to change were registered at Wave 5 in both departments. Members of the NOP units and persons of higher rank reported significantly greater receptivity to change than did their counterparts.

Changing the Dimensions of the Job

Seven indexes were used to assess whether officers perceived changes in the dimensions of their work—changes that might provide the basis for enhancing job satisfaction and performance. These measures provided an important test of the job enrichment/job enlargement model. If the police role is enlarged to better fit the demands of community policing and the psychological needs of individual officers, one would predict that officers will be more likely to report that: their job involves a variety of tasks and skills, their work leads to a complete product rather than serves as a small part of a larger product, their job is important and has a significant impact on other people, they have more autonomy and discretion in their daily work, they have more opportunities to work together with other employees, and they are more frequently involved in tasks that provide intrinsic feedback.

The findings provide no real support for these hypotheses. No changes were observed in Aurora, and only four changes (of twenty-eight) were observed in Joliet. At Waves 3 and 4, Joliet officers reported significantly more task identity and job autonomy over time, but these effects dissipated by Wave 5. This is illustrated in Figure 4.2, which charts task identity scores over time in the two cities, and in Figure 4.3, which looks at trends in job autonomy.

Again, a look at the covariates indicates that NOP officers are distinct from other officers. NOP officers expressed greater skill variety, task identity, a stronger belief that their work affects others, greater job autonomy, a stronger sense of working closely with peers, and job feedback. Thus, participation in a special NOP unit is strongly associated with many of the desired organizational perceptions and behaviors. Similarly, these same positive feelings about the dimensions of work were uniformly more common among ranking officers than among nonranking officers. Few, if any, differences in perceived job dimensions were associated with officers' seniority, education, gender, or race.

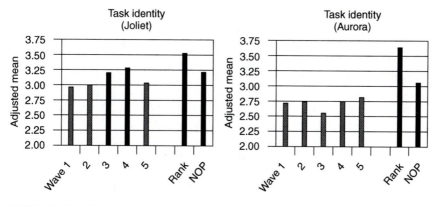

FIGURE 4.2 Task identity.

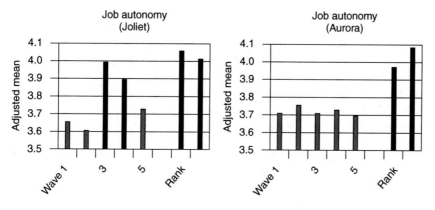

FIGURE 4.3 Job autonomy.

Job Satisfaction

Diverse job satisfaction scales and items were used to assess the extent to which employees: are involved in and enjoy their work, feel satisfied with the quantity of work expected of them, are motivated by the satisfaction derived from doing their jobs well, feel committed or attached to the organization, and believe that the job provides opportunities for individual growth and promotion. According to the job enrichment model, when positions are redesigned to provide more opportunities for individual growth and intrinsic motivation (as implied by new community policing roles), employees should report higher levels of job satisfaction. In addition, we hypothesized that officers would perceive improvements in peer relations over time (e.g., more positive regard for, and less friction among, coworkers).

The results fail to support the general hypothesis that job satisfaction will improve over time. Changes in job satisfaction over the six-year period were rare and likely due to chance. If anything, there was some evidence of declines in work motivation and fondness for coworkers.

The findings also provide little evidence that participation in the NOP unit is associated with greater job satisfaction, with the exception of two measures in Aurora (motivation and individual growth). Officers' rank, however, is linked to several job satisfaction measures in both departments. Ranking officers reported greater job involvement, increased individual growth needs, and greater promotional opportunities than did nonranking officers. Conversely, they also expressed less satisfaction with the amount of work required by their jobs and less commitment to the organization.

Individual Attitudes, Skills, and Knowledge

The initial community policing reforms in Aurora and Joliet were directed at changes within the police organizations. The next major step was to turn attention outward to the community and begin the process of community engagement and empowerment, partnership building, and problem solving. Organizational reform, if successful, should eventually produce changes in officers' perceptions of their relationship with the community, their definition of police and community roles, and their attitudes about community policing.

Views of Community and Police Roles Whether police officers hold stereotypical images of the roles of citizens and police in crime control is important for estimating the degree of success that can be expected in changing the organizational climate and style of policing, and in creating strong working partnerships with the community. Some key assumptions in the community policing model are that citizens must be recognized by the police as knowledgeable and valuable partners in the fight against crime and drugs; disorder, fear, and other noncrime issues should be given higher priority on the police agenda because of their importance to the community; and police need to establish truly collaborative relationships with other agencies and organizations to improve their effectiveness in fighting crime and disorder. Through a series of "agree-disagree" statements, we were able to gauge officers' attitudes on these subjects and capture their overall view of the community and their relationship with it. Four measures of officers' perceptions of their role and responsibilities were examined, including officers' opinions about engaging in problem-solving and community policing strategies, officers' opinions about foot patrol in policing, officers' views on the quality of their relationships with citizens, and officers' views on traditional policing strategies.

The results provide little support for the hypothesis that officers will, over time, exhibit stronger community-oriented attitudes toward the roles of police and citizens. In fact, as shown in Figure 4.4, attitudes toward community policing activities showed a significant negative trend in both cities, with significant change beginning at Wave 4 and continuing through Wave 5. Attitudes about foot patrol were more positive at Waves 2 and 3, but these effects dissipated as well. Beginning in Wave 3, attitudes became more negative about aggressive

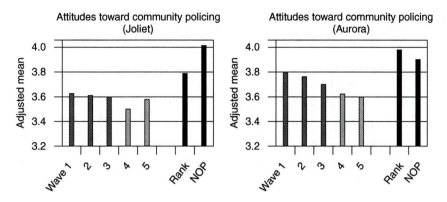

FIGURE 4.4 Attitudes toward community policing.

enforcement (Aurora) and drug enforcement (Joliet), and these effects were sustained through Wave 5.

NOP officers reported significantly more favorable attitudes toward problem-solving and community policing functions than did their non-NOP counterparts, including more positive views about foot patrol. They also held unique attitudes about citizens, at least in Joliet: NOP officers expressed a greater appreciation for informal contacts with citizens, were less reliant on citizens to ask for police services, and attached greater importance to assisting citizens. Demographic subgroup differences were inconsistent across the two sites.

Priority Assigned to Community-Oriented Activities

If community policing philosophies and training information begin to shape the attitudes and beliefs of the police force, one might expect these changes to translate into opinions about the relative importance of specific types of police activities. One would hypothesize that community-oriented activities, such as getting to know juveniles, explaining crime prevention to the public, and coordinating with other agencies, would become more valued over time, and that officers would be more inclined to support the expenditure of funds for such activities. Through a series of questions, police officers were asked to indicate how much of the department's resources should be devoted to specific activities. The four-point scales ranged from "none" to "a large amount." Eight items associated with problem-solving and community policing activities, such as foot patrol, understanding minority groups, and working with other groups to resolve problems, were combined in a single NOP activity scale, with higher scores indicating a higher funding priority given to community-oriented and problem-oriented policing activities. Responses to five items related to traditional policing were analyzed separately.

The data provide no support for the hypothesis that officers will, over time, assign an increased funding priority to community-oriented policing activities.

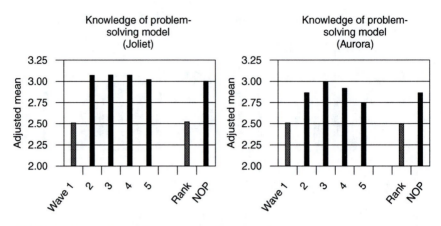

FIGURE 4.5 Knowledge of the problem-solving model.

Across all waves, police personnel in both departments consistently placed higher priority on handling calls for service, providing emergency assistance, and conducting criminal investigations.

In both departments, NOP officers were more likely than non–NOP officers to feel their department should allocate more resources to problem-solving and community policing activities, and in Joliet these officers also wanted fewer resources assigned to handling calls for service and random patrolling in squad cars. Similar to NOP officers, Hispanic and African-American officers expressed a preference for devoting more resources to community and NOP activities.

Problem-Solving Knowledge and Skill

Changes in policies, training, and field experiences were hypothesized to increase officers' knowledge and skills in problem solving. Results in Figure 4.5 show that, in both departments, officers' knowledge of problem-oriented policing was significantly higher, relative to Wave 1, at all four post-test waves, although it reached a peak and leveled off. The composite scale measuring officers' problem-solving capabilities was also significantly higher at Wave 2, but Waves 3, 4, and 5 did not differ from Wave 1. This finding suggests that departmentwide training during the first year significantly increased officers' perceived problem-solving competency, but that the effect was only temporary and began to slide back to baseline levels.

NOP officers reported significantly greater familiarity with problem-oriented policing than did non–NOP officers, and they rated themselves as more qualified on the problem-solving efficacy scale. There were no significant effects that could be attributed to rank, seniority, education, gender, or race.

Street-Level Community Policing Behavior

The translation of community policing from theory to practice should involve activities that reduce the physical and psychological distance between the beat officer and community residents. Foot patrol and participation in community

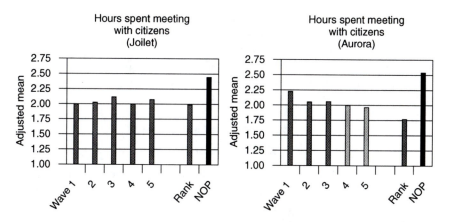

FIGURE 4.6 Hours spent meeting with citizens.

meetings are two examples of police behaviors that help achieve this objective. Community policing at the street level should mean an increase in the number of hours spent on foot patrol, a decrease in hours spent in the office or the car, and an increase in the number of contacts with various groups and agencies within the community. Some of the behavioral changes we examined include how officers engage in problem solving (e.g., what types of data sources they use), their level of contact with citizens on patrol, and their use of other agencies and organizations to help solve neighborhood problems.

In both sites, some positive behavioral changes were registered (29 percent and 21 percent of the comparisons in Aurora and Joliet, respectively). Changes in foot patrol activity were inconsistent. Both departments showed a significant increase in foot patrol hours at Wave 3 but lost ground at Wave 4 (Aurora regained this higher level at Wave 5). There was no significant change over the six-year period in the amount of time officers spent in squad cars, but Aurora officers reported a decline in the number of office hours beginning at Wave 4.

The frequency of meetings with citizens was erratic. Figure 4.6 charts trends in the average number of hours officers spend in meetings with citizens, an important component of the community policing program in both cities. Joliet increased at Wave 3 but then dropped back to baseline levels, whereas Aurora showed declines beginning at Wave 4. With a general training emphasis on police-driven problem-oriented policing projects, the lack of change in community contacts is not surprising. Both departments showed fairly consistent patterns in other contacts: committee meetings remained stable (although dipping at Wave 5 in Aurora), whereas the frequency of meetings with supervisors declined. A sizable jump in the number of meetings with other police officials started at Wave 2 and was sustained at Waves 3 through 5.

NOP differences were apparent. NOP officers spent significantly more time on foot patrol and (in Joliet) less time in squad cars than did non-NOP officers. As expected, NOP officers reported a greater frequency of meeting with citizens and are more active in attending departmental committee or task force meetings. The frequency of meeting with other police officials and with supervisors was not related to NOP status.

As expected, ranking personnel spent less time on foot patrol and in squad cars. They also spent more time in the office, in committee meetings, and in meetings with supervisors. African-American officers spent significantly more time on foot patrol in both cities.

Approaches to Problem Solving:
Use of Information Sources

Most officers have been trained in the SARA model of problem solving in classrooms, but historically little attention has been given to expanding the conventional data sources used to identify and define neighborhood problems in practice. Ideally, community-oriented officers will give increasing attention to community input, as well as to data from other agencies, as part of the problem-definition stage.

Officers were asked to indicate how often they used different types of information to identify problems in their beat. The information sources included those as diverse as community meetings, internal supervisors, and other city agencies. The four-point response scale for these items ranged from "never" to "almost always."

The results provide little support for the hypotheses. Use of most types of information sources in problem solving remained stable over the six years. The exceptions would be an apparent reduction in use of department data (especially in Aurora) and a decline in the use of citizen complaints as a source of information.

In contrast to these trends, the use of diverse data sources for problem identification was common among officers in NOP units. In both departments, these officers were significantly more likely to use information derived from community meetings, surveys, and departmental data to guide the problem-oriented policing process. In Joliet, NOP officers also distinguished themselves from the rest of the department by relying more on data from personal observation and information from other agencies.

Few consistent patterns emerged in the subgroup analyses. Hispanic and African-American officers expressed some preference for using community meetings and surveys as information sources.

DISCUSSION

This paper provides a longitudinal look, both quantitative and qualitative, at the impact of community police initiatives on police personnel in two medium-sized departments. We examined a broad range of attitudinal and behavioral indicators to test the proposition that organizational changes and training programs can enrich and enlarge the officers' job, improve job satisfaction, strengthen problem-solving skills, and instill a variety of positive attitudes and behaviors relevant to establishing a closer working relationship with the community. The results are summarized in Tables 4.2a and 4.2b.

Table 4.2a Summary of Results: Aurora (Number of Statistically Significant Findings)

Table	WAVE				INDEPENDENT VARIABLES							
	2	3	4	5	Educ	Rank	Sen	COP	Female	AA	Hisp.	Pct. Support
Mgt. Changes (6 models)	0	1	1	2	1	6	1	5	1	0	0	4%
Job Dimensions (7 models)	0	0	0	0	0	6	0	6	0	0	1	0%
Job Satisfaction (9 models)	0	0	1	1	0	6	0	2	0	2	0	3%
Role Attitudes (9 models)	0	2	2	1	3	5	3	2	1	2	0	8%
Resources (6 models)	1	1	0	2	1	1	1	1	2	0	1	8%
Knowledge (2 models)	2	1	1	1	0	0	1	2	0	0	0	62%
Behavior (7 models)	2	3	3	6	0	5	2	3	0	1	0	36%
Info Sources (7 models)	1	1	0	3	1	5	3	3	3	3	2	18%
TOTALS (54 models)	6	9	8	16	6	26	11	24	7	8	4	12%

Note: Pct. Support is the percent of all comparisons supporting the change hypothesis.

Departmentwide Effects

A few noteworthy and stable changes were observed among rank-and-file officers as a whole, controlling for membership in community policing units. Although the number of significant changes on key outcome measures is only slightly above what we would expect by chance, it does appear to grow over time, up to a point. Combining the findings from Tables 4.2a and 4.2b, the number of statistically significant hypothesized changes grew from eleven at Wave 2 to nineteen at Wave 4, and then leveled out at sixteen for Wave 5. Little improvement is noted after Wave 4 in either department, and in fact, some of the important changes were lost with the subsequent passage of time (e.g., improved attitudes toward community policing and increased knowledge and perceived competency in problem solving). Possible reasons for this leveling off or decline on several key outcome measures include:

1. A tendency to fall back into old ruts and forget recent learning. Previously, we have documented this effect after successful police training programs in Detroit (Lurigio and Rosenbaum, 1992; Rosenbaum,1987).

2. A desire to remain at a new plateau and resist reform overload. Clearly, many patrol officers experienced stress as a result of the switch to geo-based deployment, which occurred near Wave 4 when the plateau emerged. Reform may be tolerated when it involves other people, but

Table 4.2b Summary of Results: Joliet (Number of Statistically Significant Findings)

Table	WAVE				Educ	Rank	Sen	NOPT	Female	AA	Hisp.	Pct. Support
	2	3	4	5								
Mgt. Changes (5 models)	0	0	4	5	0	3	1	4	0	0	0	30%
Job Dimensions (7 models)	0	2	2	0	0	6	0	6	0	1	0	14%
Job Satisfaction (9 models)	0	0	1	3	0	5	2	0	0	2	2	5%
Role Attitudes (11 models)	2	5	5	4	2	5	4	8	1	4	3	23%
Resources (6 models)	0	1	1	1	1	0	0	3	3	1	1	4%
Knowledge (2 models)	2	1	1	1	0	0	0	2	0	0	0	62%
Behavior (7 models)	2	3	2	1	1	5	1	4	0	1	0	25%
Info Sources (8 models)	0	3	1	2	0	2	3	5	1	0	2	9%
TOTALS (55 models)	6	15	16	17	4	26	11	32	5	9	8	17%

Note: Pct. Support is the percent of all comparisons supporting the change hypothesis.

when it affects you personally (as this reform eventually did), a higher level of resistance may be activated.

3. Some resentment of the special units may have produced a boomerang effect on attitudes. We could speculate that all of the change and creativity occurring around (but not including) patrol officers may have caused them to feel less secure in their jobs and less satisfied with the policing tasks they were left to fulfill. Our fieldwork documented the classic frustration among non-NOP officers with regard to resources drains and perceived resource inequities.

Implementation Issues

With respect to testing our theoretical models, implementation integrity issues become paramount. One might conclude that the types of interventions employed in these experimental sites did not activate (or set in motion) the hypothesized mediating processes (especially for officers who did not participate in a NOP unit), and therefore, a reasonable test of the theory was not possible. There was little evidence in Aurora, for example, that management changes were noticed by the officers and, correspondingly, that the nature of their jobs has been altered in any measurable way. In Joliet, management changes were more noticeable, and more positive effects were found, yet the bigger picture is still one of limited effects on personnel attitudes and behavior.

The typical response to null results in community policing, and one that we resorted to at earlier stages of this research (Rosenbaum, Yeh, and Wilkinson, 1994) is, "Give them more time—it takes a long time to reform a police organization." Although no one here is challenging the assertion that police reform is difficult, our fieldwork tells us that significant changes were made in these two organizations during six years of intensive reform, and yet only limited effects were observed on police officers. The case histories of these two departments, developed through extensive fieldwork, point to a substantial amount of planning, training, leadership, coordination, and commitment on the part of the change agents. Each managed to overcome major obstacles to bring about real reforms. Although much work remained to be done at the conclusion of the study, a lot had been accomplished. Despite these efforts over six years, the impact of these changes on police personnel remains limited and, in fact, may have reached a peak in the middle of the project.

These findings raise several questions. First, what is a reasonable theory of implementation? What constitutes "implementation success," and when should we expect to see changes due to these interventions? Practitioners are tired of being beaten up by evaluators who claim the reformers have failed at implementation, yet rarely does anyone provide guidelines or criteria for success. We, too, are guilty of this omission. We hope researchers can build a body of reliable findings that will help to predict when, and if, a certain frequency, dosage, and duration of treatment will achieve maximum impact, and when, and if, this arrangement will lose its effectiveness. Second, we are lead to ask, what types of effects can we reasonably expect from these police reform initiatives? Stated differently, what effects might we miss by relying exclusively on the types of quantitative outcome measures reported here? In part, we are able to answer this question because of our extensive, qualitative fieldwork. Certainly, we have narratives from individual officers who report near-religious experiences after becoming absorbed in this new style of policing. Perhaps different survey measures would have captured this phenomenon better. Also, we know that community policing officers successfully executed numerous problem-oriented policing projects and built new and lasting relationships with other city agencies (e.g., landlord associations, city inspectors, and others). Although these activities may not have changed officers' feelings and attitudes about their work, they are potentially beneficial to the community.

Theoretical Implications

Another possible explanation for the limited officer effects we observed, beyond implementation integrity, is the potential inadequacy of our theoretical models. First, perhaps our assumptions about mediating processes, as delineated in the job enrichment model, are incorrect. For example, one might argue that job enlargement and job satisfaction are not key variables in the process. To change street-level behavior, perhaps organizational reforms (e.g., training, new work units) do not have to change specific work-related attitudes and perceptions, but rather should have a direct effect on certain community-oriented behaviors. This study is inconclusive on this issue. Organizational changes were successfully introduced and some dimensions of the job were significantly improved (especially in the department with the strongest implementation), but these job changes had little effect on attitudes and perceptions about work or on street-level behaviors.

The second theoretical test focused on the special unit (local) theory of change. The special unit model of reform starts with a small core of competent individuals who, with management support, are expected to demonstrate the value of this new policing style to the rest of the department. By placing a high value on this type of policing, administrators intended that these concepts and practices would spread to the entire police force. The results provide limited evidence of departmentwide improvements in community-oriented attitudes and behaviors. From the subgroup analyses reported here, one might be tempted to conclude that officers who benefited the most from community policing reforms were those who joined special NOP units. NOP officers scored significantly (and dramatically) higher than non-NOP officers on more than thirty scales in the direction expected by community policing theory. The critical question is whether these differences are due to self- (or departmental) selection, post-selection treatment, or some combination (after all, the initial NOP team members were volunteers). To provide a partial test of this question, we conducted a series of trend analyses on the officers in these special units on variables for which they differed significantly from their counterparts. The results provide no compelling evidence that NOP officers are improving over time. In Aurora, virtually no changes occurred, and in Joliet five hypothesized increases were counterbalanced by seven unexpected declines. The simple fact is that NOP officers registered substantially higher scores than non-NOP officers at the baseline, that is, before program implementation.

Research and Policy Implications

The research and policy implications of this work have been scattered throughout this chapter, so we limit our comments here. First, we do not see these departments as failures because they were unable to make lasting changes in the attitudes of their employees. They mounted impressive interventions and, arguably, were successful on outcomes that had little connection to the thoughts and behaviors of their officers. Second, this work has caused us to think about whether research and intervention strategies are justified in focusing on departmentwide personnel effects. Perhaps police reformers should, instead, turn their attention to the selection, training, and supervision of a new core of individuals who will eventually become a "critical mass." The implication of this replacement model of change (vs. individual within-person change model) is that substantive changes on key outcome measures may require ten to twenty years. Intervention effects will likely be conditioned by rates of hiring and retirement, which alter the dominant norms of police culture. In

Chapter 6 of this book, Richard Wood and his colleagues discuss the fragmentation of traditional police culture and emerging battle for hegemony among subgroups, and it is clear that researchers also need to track the views and activities of different subcultures (e.g., paramilitary vs. community policing) through both field observation and surveys to determine whether they are receptive to, or actively seek to undermine, particular interventions.

One thing is clear from the findings of the present study. We can identify a large group of officers for whom community policing, creative problem solving, and data-driven planning are appealing and easily adopted. These individuals have distinguished themselves repeatedly on a number of survey dimensions. Arguably, they are the new "super cops" of the community policing era—that is, they exhibit many of the idealized attitudes and behaviors advocated by community policing advocates. What we don't know is whether these characteristics can be created and shaped or can only be discovered and supported. This study clearly identifies them attitudinally and our fieldwork documented the distinctive behavioral repertoire among several model officers; however, a closer look is needed, via ethnographic and other methods, to define their distinctive behavioral repertoire.

These findings, along with the nature of the organizational interventions being investigated, reopen Pandora's Box on the question of special units as a vehicle for police reform. Although special units have been universally condemned as a mistaken strategy for reform, our fieldwork and survey data do not necessarily support this conclusion. This subject is too big for this limited space, but we conclude here with a few comments. First, in one of these case studies, the NOP unit provided an incubator for ideas that otherwise would have been crushed by the mainstream police culture. Second, administrators were able to create a work environment throughout the department in which participation in this type of unit was viewed as desirable and rewarding. Yes, special units have developed an ugly reputation in the history of police organizations, often viewed as elitist, isolationist, and the beneficiaries of special treatment, but all such units are not inherently evil. Granted, the isolation of specialized community policing units seems to be an important management issue that needs to be confronted with rigor. Community policing units of the type used in Aurora and Joliet generally operate in the city's highest crime areas and thus require more police resources than other geographic areas. Given limited resources, coordinated and collaborative efforts are necessary for efficient policing. Without a doubt, special units as a vehicle for community policing reform are not for every department. We learned from Aurora and Joliet that special units may serve a desirable function as change agents and role models, as well as vehicles to deliver new services to the community.

Even when reforms have achieved their goal of departmentwide implementation, a split force may be necessary to allow the types of long-term planning, complex problem-solving, and multiagency partnership-building activities that are simply not possible for the majority of urban patrol officers who are "prisoners of 9-1-1." Within this framework, the goal is to find those individuals who are skilled at performing community-oriented roles and recognize that other officers may be better qualified and happier in more traditional domains. Through the iterative process of self-selection, department selection, transfers, attrition, and promotions, departments should be able to identify and support the "right people" for the "right jobs." In addition, efforts need to be made to ensure that all police officers who work for an organization that has special NOP-type units are educated as to the goals and methods of officers engaged in proactive problem solving and community policing. This knowledge is important because specialized units are reliant on patrol officers for information, support, and follow-up. The exemplary problem-solving cases documented as part of this study were generally those in which community policing officers worked closely with patrol officers, supervisors, other city agencies, and the local community to tackle a complex neighborhood problem.

CITATIONS

Alpert, Geoffrey P. and Alex R. Piquero (Eds.). 2000. *Community Policing: Contemporary Readings,* 2nd edition. Prospect Heights, IL: Waveland Press.

Dunham, Randall B. and Jeanne B. Herman. 1975. "Development of a Female Faces Scale for Measuring Job Satisfaction." *Journal of Applied Psychology,* 60: 629–631.

Dunham, Randall B., Frank J. Smith, and Richard S. 1977. "Validation of the Index of Organizational Reactions with the JDI, the MSQ and the Faces Scales." *Academy of Management Journal,* 20: 420–432.

Dunham, Randall B., J. Grube, D. G. Gardner, and J. L. Pierce. 1989. "The Development of an Attitude Toward Change Instrument." Paper presented to the 49th Annual Meeting of the Academy of Management, Washington, DC.

Geller, William A. (Ed.). 1985. *Police Leadership in America: Crisis and Opportunity.* New York: Praeger.

Goldstein, Herman. 1979. "Improving Policing: A Problem-Oriented Approach." *Crime and Delinquency,* 25: 236–258.

Goldstein, Herman. 1990. *Problem-Oriented Policing.* New York: McGraw-Hill.

Greene, Jack R. 2000. "Community Policing in America: Changing the Nature, Structure and Function of

the Police." In Julie Horney, John Martin, Doris L. MacKenzie, Ruth Peterson, and Dennis P. Rosenbaum (Eds.), *Criminal Justice 2000, Volume 3.* Washington, DC: U.S. Department of Justice, Office of Justice Programs, National Institute of Justice, 299–370.

Hackman, J. Richard and Greg R. Oldham. 1975. "Development of the Job Diagnostic Survey." *Journal of Applied Psychology,* 60: 159–170.

Hackman, J. Richard and Greg R. Oldham. 1976. "Motivation Through the Design of Work: Test of a Theory." *Organizational Behavior and Human Decision Processes,* 16: 250–279.

Hedeker, D. and R. D. Gibbons. 1994. "A Random-effects Original Regression Model for Multilevel Analysis." *Biometrics,* 50: 933–944.

Hedeker, Donald, R. D. Gibbons, and J. M. Davis. 1991. "Random Regression Models for Multicenter Clinical Trials Data." *Psychopharmacology Bulletin,* 27: 73–77.

Kelling, George L. and Mark H. Moore. 1988. *The Evolving Strategy of Policing.* (Perspectives on Policing, No. 4). Washington, DC: National Institute of Justice and Harvard University.

Lurigio, Arthur J. and Dennis P. Rosenbaum. 1992. "The Travails of the Detroit Police-Victims Experiment:

Assumptions and Important Lessons." *American Journal of Police,* 11: 1–34.

Lurigio, Arthur. J. and Dennis P. Rosenbaum. 1994. "The Impact of Community Policing on Police Personnel: A Review of the Literature." In Dennis P. Rosenbaum (Ed.), *The Challenge of Community Policing: Testing the Promises.* Thousand Oaks, CA: Sage, 147–166.

Manning, Peter K. 1997. *Police Work: The Social Organization of Policing,* 2nd edition. Prospect Heights, IL: Waveland Press.

Mastrofski, Stephen D. and Richard Ritti. 2000. "Making Sense of Community Policing: A Theory-based Analysis." *Police Practice,* 1: 183–210.

Mastrofski, Stephen D. 1998. Community Policing and Police Organization Structure. Chapter in J. Brodeur, ed., *Community Policing and the Evaluation of Police Service Delivery,* pp. 161–189. Thousand Oaks, CA: Sage.

Moore, Mark H. 1992. "Problem-Solving and Community Policing." In Michael. Tonry and Norval Morris (Eds.), *Crime and Justice: A Review of Research* Chicago: University of Chicago Press, 99–158.

Moore, Mark H. and Darrel Stephens. 1991. *Police Organization and Management: Towards a New Managerial Orthodoxy.* Washington, DC: Police Executive Research Forum.

Morgan, Gareth 1997. *Images of Organizations,* 2nd edition. Thousand Oaks, CA: Sage.

Peters, Thomas J. and Robert H. Waterman, Jr. 1982. *In Search of Excellence: Lessons from America's Best-Run Companies.* New York: Warner.

Rosenbaum, Dennis P. 1987. "Coping with Victimization: The Effects of Police Intervention on Victims' Psychological Readjustment." *Crime and Delinquency,* 33: 502–519.

Rosenbaum, Dennis P., Deanna L. Wilkinson, Sandra K. Costello, Gordon S. Hanson, Donald D. Stemen, Katie Roussos, and Maureen E. Allen. 1999. *Community Policing in Aurora: Results of a Longitudinal Evaluation.*

Chicago, IL: Center for Research in Law and Justice, University of Illinois at Chicago. Final report to the National Institute of Justice.

Rosenbaum, Dennis P., Deanna L. Wilkinson, Sandra K. Costello, Gordon S. Hanson, Donald D. Stemen, Maureen E. Allen, and Kathleen K. O'Connell. 1999. *Community Policing in Joliet: Results of a Longitudinal Evaluation.* Chicago, IL: Center for Research in Law and Justice, University of Illinois at Chicago. Final report to the National Institute of Justice.

Rosenbaum, Dennis P., Sandra Yeh, and Deanna L. Wilkinson. 1994. "Estimating the Effects of Community Policing Reform on Police Officers." *Crime and Delinquency,* 40: 331–353.

Rosenbaum, Dennis P. (Ed.). 1994. *The Challenge of Community Policing: Testing the Promises.* Newbury Park, CA: Sage.

Roth, Jeffrey A. and Joseph Ryan. 2000. "The COPS Program After 4 Years— National Evaluation." *Research in Brief,* Washington DC: U.S. Department of Justice, Office of Justice Programs, National Institute of Justice.

Shadish, Willam R., Cook, Thomas D., & Campbell, Donald T. (2002). *Experimental and Quasi-Experimental Designs for Generalized Causal Inference.* Boston: Houghton-Mifflin.

Skolnick, Jerome 1966. *Justice Without Trial.* New York: Wiley.

Skolnick, Jerome and David Bayley. 1988. *Community Policing: Issues and Practices around the World.* National Institute of Justices, Issues and Practices. Washington, DC: U.S. Department of Justice.

Wilkinson, Deanna L. and Dennis P. Rosenbaum. 1994. "The Effect of Organizational Structure and Climate on Police Reform: A Comparison of Two Cities." In Dennis P. Rosenbaum (Ed.), *The Challenge of Community Policing: Testing the Promises.* Newbury Park, CA: Sage, 110–126.

Wycoff, Mary Ann and Wesley G. Skogan. 1993. *Community Policing in Madison: Quality from the Inside Out.* Washington, DC: National Institute of Justice.

APPENDIX

This Appendix presents a number of technical details supporting the conclusions in the main body of the chapter. Many readers may wish to skip over these materials.

THE OFFICER SURVEY MEASURES

Numerous composite indexes were constructed to measure changes in officers' attitudes, perceptions, beliefs, and behaviors. The response formats for most individual items used a five-point ordinal scale ranging from "strongly disagree" to "strongly agree." Principal components factor analysis and reliability analysis were conducted to establish the unidimensionality and internal consistency of the scales (see Rosenbaum, Yeh, and Wilkinson, 1994, for scale properties).

Dimensions of the Job A variety of measures were used to determine whether officers perceived changes in the dimensions of their work that might increase the meaningfulness of their jobs, their responsibility for work outcomes, and their knowledge of how well they are performing. If such changes in job dimensions occur, prior research on organizations suggests that employee motivation and performance would improve by enhancing job satisfaction. Using Hackman and Oldham's (1976) job-characteristics model, questions focused on the five core dimensions of the job. The following scales are shortened versions of those developed by Hackman and Oldham (1975):

> *Skill Variety:* the extent to which officers' jobs require a variety of different activities and skills (three items)
>
> *Task Identity:* the extent to which employees feel their work involves completing an entire task from start to finish (three items)
>
> *Task Significance:* the extent to which employees feel their work has a significant impact on the lives or work of other people either inside or outside of the organization (two items)
>
> *Autonomy:* the extents to which employees feel their jobs provide independence and discretion in scheduling work and approaches to work (three items)
>
> *Working with Others:* how closely the officers work with their peers (two items)
>
> *Job Feedback:* the extent to which officers see their jobs as providing feedback about work performance independent of supervisory or peer feedback (three items)

Implementation of Management Policies A variety of measures were used to assess whether the police organization and management team were responsive to officers' needs and provided the type of communication opportunities and support considered necessary for problem-solving and community policing activities (Dunham, Smith, and Blackburn, 1977; Hackman and Oldham, 1975).

> *Participatory Management:* the extent to which employees feel able to participate in the organization's decision-making processes (three items)
>
> *Supervisory and Peer Feedback:* the extent to which employees believe their supervisor and peers give feedback regarding job performance (three items)
>
> *Satisfaction with Supervisor:* the degree to which employees feel satisfied with their supervisor (nine items)
>
> *Organizational Support:* the extent of organizational support officers receive for their problem-solving efforts (i.e., scheduling flexibility, supervisor approval, recognition, needed resources or personnel, etc.) (single item)

Communication with Detectives: the frequency of organizational opportunities for officers and detectives to share information (single item)

Satisfaction with Organizational Practices: officers' level of satisfaction with the organization, especially with how it treats employees (five items)

Job Satisfaction The survey contained a wide range of job satisfaction scales (Dunham, Smith, and Blackburn, 1977; Wycoff and Skogan, 1993). Longer versions of these scales have been used with industry and police organizations.

Job Involvement: the extent to which employees are involved in and enjoy the type of work they do (six items)

Amount of Work: officers' satisfaction with the quantity of work expected or required for their job (three items)

Compensation and Benefits: officers' satisfaction with the level of pay and benefits received (three items)

Relationship with Peers: officer satisfaction with coworkers (three items)

Promotion Opportunities: perceptions of promotion opportunities (single item)

Organizational Commitment: level of commitment to the organization (i.e., whether employees feel a strong sense of emotional attachment or belonging to the organization (three items)

Extraorganizational Immobility: officers' perception of how difficult it would be to leave the department at this time (two items)

Work Motivation: the degrees of personal satisfaction officers receive from doing their job well (single item)

Individual Growth Need: the extent to which employees need a job that provides opportunities for personal growth (e.g., a job that is challenging, requires creativity, provides opportunities to learn, etc.) (six items)

Attitudes Regarding Community Policing Several scales were used to measure officers' attitudes about new forms of policing and openness to change (Wycoff and Skogan, 1993).

Attitudes Toward Community Policing: the extent to which officers express attitudes supportive of community policing and problem-solving activities (10 items)

Priority Assigned to Community Policing Activities: the extent to which officers believe department resources should be spent on a variety of policing activities that community oriented (eight items)

Support for Traditional Policing: the extent to which officers believe department resources should be spent on traditional, incident-driven policing (four items)

Receptivity to Change: officers' receptivity or, conversely, resistance to change (nine items)

Problem-Solving Knowledge and Behaviors Several scales were used to measure officers' knowledge of, and involvement in, problem-solving activities (Wycoff and Skogan, 1993).

Knowledge of Problem-Oriented Policing: the extent to which officers are familiar with the concept of problem-oriented policing (single item)

Problem-Solving Capabilities: the extent to which officers feel qualified to engage in various problem-solving activities ranging from problem identification to solution evaluation (four items)

Problem-Solving Activities: the quantity of problem-solving activity for individual officers (thirteen items, with scale range of 0 to 13 problems)

Use of Diverse Sources of Information: the extent to which officers rely on a wide variety of information sources, such as community meetings, to identify and define community problems (eight items)

Number of Police-Citizen Interactions: number of informal police-citizen contacts, other than calls for service, per eight-hour day (single item)

Hours Spent on Foot Patrol: estimate of how many hours officers spend in an average week on foot patrol (single item)

Hours Spent on Patrol: estimate of how many hours officers spend in an average week in marked or unmarked squad cars (single item)

Meetings with Community: the extent of community engagement as defined by the number of meetings held with various community groups, service agencies, business groups, and individual citizens (eight items, with scale range of 0 to 8)

Meetings with Internal Groups and Individuals: number of meetings held with department committees, other officers and detectives, and supervisors (three items, with scale range of 0 to 3)

5

Working the Street: Does Community Policing Matter?[1]

WILLIAM TERRILL AND
STEPHEN D. MASTROFSKI

Community policing curbs police brutality.

(TROJANOWICZ, 1991: 1)

No more nightstick justice in Motown.

(SKOLNICK AND BAYLEY, 1986: 50)

The Commission heard from several experts in police administration who urged adoption of the community policing model as a means of combating excessive use of force and improving relations between the LAPD and the people it serves (Independent Commission, 1991: 100). . . .Community based policing's emphasis on patrol officers interacting positively with the public should have the effect of "humanizing" officers' perceptions of those whom they police. As suggested by many of the clergy who spoke to the Commission, community based policing would both increase the effectiveness of the police and diminish the tension between the public and the LAPD by eliminating the view of the "community as enemy."

(INDEPENDENT COMMISSION, 1991: 105)

For many people, thanks in part to how it has been presented by many police leaders, community policing is viewed as "soft" policing comparable to community relations or, worse yet, social work. . . .This failure to understand the inherent assertiveness of community or problem oriented policing, and equating it with soft policing, has greater consequences than just alienating line police officers. The equation of "community" and "soft" leads to public confusion when tough police action is required to deal with severe crime or disorder problems.

(KELLING, 1999: 10)

[1]Data for this chapter come from the Project on Policing Neighborhoods, supported by Grant No. 95-IJ-CX-0071 by the National Institute of Justice, Office of Justice Programs, U.S. Department of Justice. Points of view in this document are those of the authors and do not necessarily represent the official position or policies of the U.S. Department of Justice.

*Reduce disorder and you WILL reduce crime. The strategy is
sending a strong message to those who commit minor crimes that they
will be held responsible for their acts. The message goes like this:
behave in public spaces, or the police will take action.*

(BRATTON, 1996)

Three decades ago Egon Bittner (1970: 46) asserted that what distinguishes police from other occupations is their capacity to distribute "non-negotiably coercive force employed in accord with an intuitive grasp of situational exigencies." If that is so, one might ask whether and how the overwhelmingly popular movement toward community policing is influencing the application of this most fundamental police capacity. This chapter presents an empirical assessment of the consequences of community policing for the practice of coercion. We wish to learn the impact of involvement in community policing on the day-to-day exercise of coercion by patrol officers. Does the department leadership's community policing philosophy influence the use of coercion by the rank and file? Are officers assigned specific community policing responsibilities more, or less, likely to coerce suspects they encounter? Are those trained in community policing more, or less, likely to engage in coercion? Do those officers who embrace community policing's values exercise coercion differently from those who do not?

Answering these questions will help us understand the challenges of bringing officers' coercive practices into conformance with the expectations set forth by community policing advocates. What makes this an interesting task is that—as one can tell from this chapter's introductory quotations—the nature of those expectations depends on how top police leadership defines community policing. We identify two approaches to community policing, one that expects to reduce the frequency and intensity of coercion, and another that encourages coercion at a lower intensity. We analyze police coercion in two departments, one that embraces each approach. This comparison enables us to determine whether the two community policing philosophies really produce differences in the way officers behave with the public. More specifically, we attempt to determine whether differences in the use of coercion at the street level can be attributed to certain management choices, such as the creation of community policing specialist assignments or the amount of community policing training given to officers. In addition, we examine whether officers who embrace community policing values exercise coercion differently from those who do not.

We begin by considering in principle the implications of community policing for coercion by police. We then review what empirical research is available to reflect on this. Finally, we present an analysis of systematic field observation of patrol officers in face-to-face interactions with suspects during their routine work shifts in two cities, each of which employs a different philosophical approach to community policing.

THE RELATIONSHIP OF COMMUNITY
POLICING TO COERCION

By coercion, we mean the use or threat of force (Muir, 1977). In his seminal essay, Bittner (1970) notes that contemporary Western culture finds coercion offensive, preferring to achieve peace by peaceful means, but that state-sponsored violence is nonetheless sometimes necessary to accomplish peace, justice, and other worthwhile objectives. Investing the police with broad coercive authority when society finds coercion offensive makes police work ironic (Klockars, 1988: 240). Contemporary Western society expects police to be economical in the distribution of coercion, applying only that amount required to achieve peace and justice, a fine calibration that is difficult given the high uncertainty about the particular circumstances, the relatively crude tools available to officers, and the need to act "now!" Even if society recognizes the need for police to use coercion under some conditions, its actual practice is so repugnant that both society and the police find the need to legitimate police actions in ways that obscure their true nature.

If we adopt Bittner's (1970) perspective, we should not be surprised that different views have emerged about what community policing's relationship to coercion should be. Some define it in such a way that coercion becomes a less prominent aspect of what police do, or that police should apply it in more subtle ways, drawing more heavily on "peaceful," scientific, and preventive methods (Klockars, 1988). Others, however, embrace a model that gives coercion a more explicit, indeed, central role in the construction of what community policing is about—as an essential means of protecting the community and fulfilling its will (Crank, 1994). Both schools of thought draw on currently popular yearnings for community, social cohesion, and order (Manning, 1984), but they are nonetheless competing to wear the mantle of community policing. There are significant stakes in terms of which model becomes ascendant or, alternatively, whether the reform continues to be defined in terms that allow leaders so divergent as Presidents Reagan and Clinton to subscribe to it, each using it to further different agendas. Our purpose here is not to enter into this debate, but merely to use it as a starting point for learning what happens to police coercion under community policing.

Because the meaning of community policing can vary, its relationship to coercion is complex. One perspective focuses on the need to partner with the community (Skolnick and Bayley, 1986: 212) or to solve long-term community problems (Goldstein, 1990) by working on the underlying causes of those problems using situational crime prevention (Clarke, 1993) and other methods that focus attention on activities far removed from the actual application of force—working with neighborhood groups, studying crime statistics and analyzing problems, and relying more heavily on other service organizations to participate in preventive interventions. Other community policing advocates argue that this reform is precisely what is needed to infuse police with the will, skill, and community support to make force unnecessary in many situations where it otherwise might have been used. Responding to the Rodney King incident, Robert Trojanowicz (1991: 1) asserts:

> Most of the discussion about solutions [to police brutality] so far has focused on training and minority recruiting and on the need for police chiefs to send an unambiguous message that abuse and harassment will not be tolerated—that "police brutality begins where resistance ends." All are essential pieces of the puzzle, yet equally if not more important is the need for fundamental reform in the relationship between people and the police—a shift from confrontation to cooperation that only Community Policing can provide.

Developing stronger community partnerships was the centerpiece of reforms recommended by the Los Angeles blue ribbon commission to eliminate brutality and racism in that city's force (Independent Commission, 1991). It has since been characterized by some of its critics as the "officer friendly" approach to community policing, one that "would respectfully resume contact with the community, courteously listen to people's problems, and immediately find appropriate solutions" (Bratton, 1996: 198).

Jack Greene (2000: 320) notes that although some departments have followed the sort of community partnership and problem-solving model described earlier, others have pursued a different approach, one that gives coercion center stage. Aggressive order-maintenance practices have been popularized among the police under the rubric of "broken windows" policing, a term introduced by James Q. Wilson and George Kelling (1982). Their essay advocates forceful police intervention to stop minor public disorders, hypothesized as the root cause of the social and economic decline of urban neighborhoods. Police are encouraged to target public drunks, panhandlers, rowdy juveniles, prostitutes, and other street people. They recommend a wide range of interventions: making arrests, issuing citations, conducting stops, interrogating, warning, rousting individuals, and taking whatever force is legally justifiable to control those whose behavior disrupts orderly neighborhood life. It is a style that presumably satisfies a community's "taste for order," one that answers "No!" to the rhetorical question, "Do we want police officers to develop a 'What the hell' attitude toward disorderly or dangerous behavior, even if it is not technically illegal?" (Kelling, 1987: 91). Advocating higher levels of police intervention to prevent disorders, even more than to repair them, Kelling later asserts that the broken windows argument has been misconstrued by some as "combative or militarized policing," when it is really "preventive interventionist" or "assertive" policing that calls for "careful and judicious use of law enforcement" (1999: 11). In their broken windows model, Kelling and Coles (1996:23) argue,

> Neighborhood rules were to be enforced for the most part through non arrest approaches—education, persuasion, counseling, and ordering—so that arrest would only be resorted to when other approaches failed.

Still, the greater risk of misrepresentation of community policing from Kelling's perspective is to interpret it as soft policing, for that ignores the fundamental coercive function of police and leaves the reform's flank vulnerable to those who prefer policing that is largely unfettered by legal constraints, returning instead to tough, militaristic policing where police authority is unchecked (Kelling, 1999: 11).

The broken windows model was highly publicized when New York City adopted it, and the city's leaders credited it with substantial declines in crime and even the city's economic revitalization (Bratton, 1998; Kelling and Coles, 1996; Kelling and Sousa, 2001). Touted by some as a zero-tolerance approach to minor public disorders (Greene, 1999), many other police departments around the nation have since adopted programs based on the broken windows assumptions. The broken windows model has recently come under attack in New York City precisely because some believe it promotes a culture too permissive of police coercion (Reibstein, 1997). In the wake of the Louima and Diallo incidents, New York City police were accused of brutalizing an in-custody suspect in the first case and the wrongful and excessive use of lethal force in the second. In addition, the department has been criticized by various community groups, the state attorney general, and the U.S. Civil Rights Commission for racial bias against minority citizens in the application of aggressive order-maintenance tactics. Critics claim that the department has been infused with a culture that promotes coercive and intrusive tactics that go too far, especially when dealing with minority citizens (Spitzer, 1999). Advocates of aggressive order maintenance, including prominent former mayor Giuliani of New York City, have denied that this approach has fostered police brutality (Lyons, 1999: 3).

Our review of the partnership and problem-oriented models and broken windows models indicates that the direction of community policing's impact depends on the model a department or an officer chooses to follow. Where community partnership and problem-solving approaches are embraced (hereafter referred to as the partnership model), coercion should be less likely. Where the broken windows approach is supported, coercion should be more likely, especially in its lower, less intrusive verbal forms that involve no physical contact or restraint.

PAST RESEARCH ON COERCION
AND COMMUNITY POLICING

Most research assessing the effects of community policing examines its impact on crime, fear of crime, the public's view of the police, and the degree of connectedness and cooperation among citizens and private and public organizations (Greene, 2000). There is little research that assesses the direct consequences of this reform for coercion by police officers. Nonetheless, a handful of recent inquiries sheds some light on the relationship. A 1999 study conducted by the New York Attorney General's office examined New York City Police stop-and-frisk records to determine the relationship between aggressive police tactics under the broken windows, zero-tolerance approach and race (Spitzer, 1999). In total, 175,000 stop-and-frisk reports, covering January 1998

through May 1999, were examined. The report concludes that officers dispro-
portionately stop and frisk minority citizens, often with little or no legal justification. Whites, who constitute 43 percent of the city's population accounted
for only 13 percent of all stop and frisks. Furthermore, a more detailed analysis of 10,000 stop and frisks in eight precincts uncovered that nearly 40 percent of all stops failed to meet the legal standard of reasonable suspicion. Testi-
mony by a number of minority residents, some of whom had been stopped by
police, suggested to the study's authors that the minority community tended
to view the department's practices as unnecessary and unwarranted intrusions.

A few past inquiries explore officer attitudes that reflect on coercion and
community policing. The Police Foundation conducted a national survey of
more than 900 police officers in the mid-1990s involving various attitudes
toward the use of police authority (Weisburd et al., 1998). Patrol officers were
asked whether community policing increases, decreases, or has no impact on
excessive force incidents. Only 2 percent of the responding officers stated they
believed community policing increases the likelihood of excessive force,
whereas 51 percent believed community policing decreases the likelihood, and
47 percent felt it had no impact. More interesting was that Black officers compared with White officers were more inclined to believe community policing
would decrease excessive force, whereas White officers were more likely to
believe it would have no impact.

A study of the effect of community policing on the use of arrest was done
in Richmond, Virginia, during the early 1990s (Mastrofski, Worden, and Snipes,
1995). The authors examine the effect of officers' attitude toward community
policing on their decision to make an arrest with nontraffic suspects. The
Richmond department was pursuing a community partnership approach. Officers positively oriented to community policing values were less likely to make
an arrest compared with those who were not positive about community policing, other things being equal. The behavior of procommunity policing officers
was less influenced by legal considerations, such as the strength of the evidence,
but extralegal influences (such as the suspect's race) were no more influential
than for officers who were less positive about community policing.

Finally, Robert Worden (1995) looks at a host of potential influences on
police force, analyzing Police Services Data from the 1970s. One such attitude
was officer perception of the police role. Worden posits that officers with a narrow police role orientation (e.g., limited to crime fighting and law enforcement) are more likely to engage in coercive behavior compared with those
who had a wider view (e.g., expanded to include the handling of a wide array
of service activities). Although a bit of a stretch, one might associate a narrow
view of the police role as falling into line with an aggressive policing style,
whereas those on the opposite end would lean more heavily toward community partnership. Worden finds no effect for aggressive policing style.

Most prior research on police coercion focuses on the effects of situational influences and officer characteristics. Among the most frequently
measured situational cues are: citizen race, gender, class, age, demeanor, sobri-
ety, mental state, and emotional state; number of officers present; number of

citizens present; location of encounter; and type and seriousness of offense (Chevigny, 1969; Friedrich, 1977; Reiss 1968; Terrill and Mastrofski, 2002; Toch, 1969; Westley, 1953; Worden, 1995). The factors most consistently predicting police coercion include citizens who are male, display a disrespectful demeanor toward the police, are antagonistic or aggressive, and show signs of intoxication.

Another line of research explores the possibility that officers with certain traits and background characteristics (e.g., officer race, gender, education, training, age, length of service, patrol assignment) respond differently in similar situations (Cascio, 1977; Cohen and Chaiken, 1972; Croft, 1985; Friedrich, 1977; Garner et al., 1995; Terrill and Mastrofski, 2002; Worden, 1989, 1995). Research in this area provides mixed results. For instance, Worden's (1995) analysis shows that officers with a four-year degree were significantly more likely to use physical force classified as "reasonable," whereas Terrill and Mastrofski (2002) find that encounters involving officers with higher levels of education were significantly less likely to resort to force (physical and verbal).

THIS STUDY

Taking the past literature on police coercion into account, this study considers what community policing adds to our ability to predict officers' use of coercion, both verbal (commands and threats) and physical (where police apply force or restraint or are intrusive using physical contact). We assume it makes sense to order forms of police behavior according to the degree of coercion applied: coercion applied physically is more coercive than coercion applied verbally, which in turn is more coercive than occasions when police display neither.

Data available to us allow a test of the impact of community policing on an encounter-by-encounter basis, as officers engage citizens suspected of wrongdoing face to face. We are able to consider several ways community policing might manifest an influence over officers' behavior with suspects. Community policing can abide in many places and in many ways in an organization. At the most general level, we consider a department's approach to community policing as evidenced by top management's policies and exhortations. We have data available from two departments, one in which the leadership pursued a broken windows orientation and another in which the leadership pursued a community partnership approach. If the police leadership's approach to community policing is more than mere public relations, officers in the broken windows department should, other things being equal, be more inclined to resort to force whereas officers in the community partnership department should be less likely to use force. The stronger the effects of department policy, the greater credence the data lend to the argument that top leadership influences the routine decisions made about coercion on a case-by-case basis at the street level, an argument set forth by Wilson in his classic 1968 study.

How do management priorities play out at the street level? At the officer level we consider several ways community policing may affect the use of coercion. First is a combination of opportunity and job responsibility (DeJong, Mastrofski, and Parks, 2001; Mastrofski, Ritti, and Snipes, 1994). Some officers are given specialist assignments that free them from the routine responsibilities of answering calls for service so that they can engage in community policing. Because their job tasks are defined in terms of community policing, they should be more motivated to perform the model of community policing advocated by the department. In the department where management advocated a broken windows approach, specialists should be more inclined to use coercion; in the department where management advocated community partnership, specialists should be less likely to use coercion.

Regardless of their job assignment, officers may vary in the degree to which they are skilled at community policing. Research on drunk driving arrests suggests that officers with greater skill levels (measured by training in handling drunk driving incidents) tend to make more arrests (Mastrofski, Ritti, and Snipes 1994). Similarly, officers with greater skill in community policing should demonstrate more of the type of behavior supported by the department's model of community policing, although a recent test of this effect on the amount of time officers spent on problem solving failed to show significant effects (DeJong, Mastrofski, and Parks, 2001). Here we hypothesize that highly trained officers in the broken windows department should be more inclined to use coercion, whereas highly trained officers in the community partnership department should be less inclined to use coercion.

A third way to assess community policing's impact is to determine the extent to which officers themselves embrace the philosophy of each model. Although police departments tend to project themselves in the image of a single model, an individual officer may in fact accept or reject both. In general, the stronger the officer's personal commitment to the broken windows model, the more coercion the officer is likely to use; the stronger the officer's commitment to the partnership model, the less coercion the officer is likely to use.

We might well expect that the effects will be more complex than the simple relationships posited. Community policing's influence may differ across the full range of coercion possibilities. It is conceivable that both the broken windows and community partnership models have an impact, albeit each at a different level of coercion. If, as Kelling (1996) suggests, broken windows strategies promote greater "preventive intervention," we would expect it to produce higher rates of low-level—that is, verbal—coercion without escalating to physical force. If, as proponents of the community partnership model argue, community policing "curbs brutality," we would expect it to suppress the more extreme levels of coercion: physical force. If, as some skeptical officers argue, the partnership model produces "grin and wave" policing that avoids coercion generally (a concern also voiced by Kelling), we would expect that model to produce less coercive interventions of all sorts.

Finally, there is the null hypothesis indicating that community policing is irrelevant to the practice of coercion at the street level. To the extent that this is so, measures of community policing should have no bearing on officers' practice of coercion, other things being equal.

RESEARCH SITES

Indianapolis, Indiana, and St. Petersburg, Florida, were the research sites for the Project on Policing Neighborhoods (POPN), the study from which our data are drawn, and from which Chapter 9 in this volume also draws. Field research was conducted in 1996 in Indianapolis and in 1997 in St. Petersburg. These sites were selected because both had committed to implementing community policing, both had diverse populations in terms of race and wealth, and both were receptive to hosting a large research project. Indianapolis had 1,013 officers, about twice the level of St. Petersburg. Details on department and community characteristics are provided by Mastrofski and colleagues (2000: 318).

The departments' chiefs were similar in some respects. Both had been appointed on their reputations for promoting community policing, and both considered improving community relations their top priority. Both stressed the need to decentralize service delivery, and both had attempted to achieve long-term stability in officers' beat assignments to facilitate closer police community working relations. Finally, both had declared that all patrol officers would engage in community policing but had also created specialist units given full-time responsibility to do it.

The departments also showed important differences in their approaches to community policing. The Indianapolis department had taken several steps consistent with the broken windows model. The department's top leadership encouraged the suppression of public disorders, drug crime, gang activity, and illegal weapons by intrusive law enforcement methods. District commanders were given considerable latitude in how they pursued these objectives. Although all officers were expected to do community policing, each district also deployed community policing specialist teams. One district emphasized bike patrol as a way to catch offenders more effectively and to establish better rapport with the public. Another focused on drug dealing, illegal firearms, and quality-of-life offenses, relying heavily on aggressive traffic enforcement and order maintenance (much of which was performed by a specially designated squad). Another district also used aggressive order maintenance, using crime and calls for service data to target hot spots and track the progress of interventions. These were supplemented with an array of community outreach endeavors (foot patrol, crime watch, prayer vigils, school programs, and a citizen advisory task force). Finally, one district concentrated on drug problems by using code enforcement to condemn properties used for illicit dealing. A civilian employee worked closely with sworn officers to identify such properties and mobilize the city's code enforcement.

St. Petersburg's top leadership emphasized a community partnership approach to community policing. Officers were assigned to beats with considerably smaller residential populations than in Indianapolis. It appointed a community policing officer specialist for each beat. Each community policing officer was expected to coordinate the community policing efforts of all officers assigned to that beat across all work shifts. Unlike Indianapolis, where district commanders played a central role in shaping the selection of field tactics, district commanders and lower level supervisors played only a small, supporting role in overseeing the problem-solving process. Community policing officers were to identify problems using crime and calls for service data and by working closely with community groups. Surveys of projects reported by officers indicate that illicit drugs were the most frequently targeted problem, but these accounted for less than half of the projects initiated. Disputes and disorders, theft, burglary, robbery, traffic, and a host of miscellaneous problems accounted for the majority of projects reported. Whereas Indianapolis relied more heavily on civilian employees for working with neighborhood groups, St. Petersburg expected its community policing officers to fulfill this responsibility. They participated in a variety of partnership and community-building activities, such as neighborhood watch groups, antidrug marches, and neighborhood group meetings.

It is important to note that the two departments were not exclusively attached to separate models of community policing. It is likely that in a given department these two approaches could compete, as in Lyons's (1999) description of Seattle. However, management at both sites had clearly emphasized one model over the other, and they had structured community policing in ways that differentially facilitated the two models. By assigning community policing officers to a few homogeneous specialist teams with their own supervisors, Indianapolis made it easier to coordinate aggressive order maintenance on a larger and more visible scale. By assigning each community policing officer to a beat-focused team, including all the generalist patrol officers assigned to that beat, and by requiring that they maintain ongoing contact with neighborhood organizations to develop individualized responses to those problems, St. Petersburg facilitated a partnership approach. With this in mind, we characterize Indianapolis's approach as broken windows and St. Petersburg as partnership.

COLLECTING THE DATA

This study uses two data sets from the POPN: systematic observation of patrol officers and in-person interviews of those officers. Patrol observation was conducted in twelve beats in each city. The sample of beats was matched as closely as possible across the two sites according to the degree of socioeconomic distress (measured as the sum of the percentages of families with children headed by a single female, the adult population that is unemployed, and the population below 50 percent of the poverty level)—an index similar to one used by Sampson, Raudenbush, and Earls, (1997). The sample excluded beats with the lowest socioeconomic distress; observations concentrate in areas where police citizen interactions are most frequent. Field observers were graduate students and honors undergraduates with a semester's training in systematic observation of the police plus on-site orientation rides.

Observation was conducted in summer months according to procedures described elsewhere (Mastrofski et al., 1998). Researchers accompanied officers throughout a matched sample of work shifts in each of the selected beats (approximately 240 hours per beat). Busier times of the day and week were over sampled. General patrol officers and community policing officers were observed in rough proportion to their representation in the allocation of officers to the study beats. Observers took brief field notes and spent the next day transcribing them into detailed accounts and coding them according to a protocol. Observers' detailed narrative accounts were used to capture the sequencing of events within a police citizen encounter.

Observers noted officers' encounters with the public. An encounter was a face-to-face communication between officers and citizens that was more than a passing greeting. Observers recorded contact with approximately 6,500 citizens in Indianapolis and 5,500 citizens in St. Petersburg, those events ranging from less than a minute to several hours. We focus on those interactions with people whom police or other citizens present placed in the role of suspect (wrongdoers, peace disturbers, or persons for whom complaints were received). Field observers recorded 3,255 encounters between suspects and 276 police officers. The officers involved in the study received our assurance of confidentiality. In only .5 percent of the encounters did observers detect evidence suggesting that officers had changed their behavior because of the researcher's presence. Far more common were instances where the observed police behavior could have been cause for disciplinary action, also noted in previous field studies of patrol officers (Reiss, 1968). Typically observers reported cordial relations with police during ride-alongs. Only 12 percent of their observation sessions began with a negative officer attitude about the observer's presence, dropping to 2 percent by the end of the session.

Finally, data on officer characteristics and attitudes are taken from in-person interviews conducted in private by researchers who did not conduct field observations. Interview data were merged with observation data in this analysis, causing only a few cases to be lost because officers refused to be interviewed or were otherwise unavailable.

MEASURING POLICE COERCION

This section describes how we measured police coercion, and the following section describes how we measured the various factors we hypothesize will influence the amount of coercion police use in their encounters with suspects. Table 5.1 provides an overview of how these variables were defined, and Table 5.2 provides descriptive statistics broken down by site.

Table 5.1 Description of the Explanatory Variables

Variable	Hypothesized Effect	Definition
Community Policing		
Broken windows department	+	1 = Indianapolis, 0 = St. Petersburg
CPO assignment	+/–	1 = CPO assignment, 0 = general patrol
CP training	+/–	Amount of community policing training: 1 = none, 2 = < 1 day, 3 = 1–2 days, 4 = 3–5 days, 5 = > 5 days
Aggressive patrol values	+	"A good patrol officer is one who patrols aggressively by stopping cars, checking out people, running license checks, and so forth": 1 = disagree strongly, 2 = disagree somewhat, 3 = agree somewhat, 4 = agree strongly
Community partnership values	–	"A good patrol officer will try to find out what residents think the neighborhood problems are": 1 = disagree strongly, 2 = disagree somewhat, 3 = agree somewhat, 4 = agree strongly
Control Variables		
Officer Characteristics		
Male	+	1 = male, 0 = female
Non-White	+/–	1 = non-White, 0 = White
Experience	–	Years of experience in department;
Education	–	1 = less than high school, 2 = high school graduate/GED, 3 = some college/no degree, 4 = associate degree, 5 = > 2 years college no B.S., 6 = bachelors degree, 7 = some graduate work, 8 = graduate degree
Legal restraints	+	"In order to do their jobs, patrol officers must sometimes overlook search and seizure laws and other legal guidelines": 1 = disagree strongly, 2 = disagree somewhat, 3 = agree somewhat, 4 = agree strongly
Suspect Characteristics		
Male	+	1 = male, 0-female
Non-White	+	1 = non-White, 0 = White
Age	–	1 = 0–5 years, 2 = 6–12 years, 3 = 13–17 years, 4 = 18–20 years, 5 = 21–29 years, 6 = 30–44 years, 7 = 45–59 years, 8 = 60+ years
Wealth	–	Observed level of wealth: 1 = chronic poverty, 2 = low, 3 = middle, 4 = above middle

(continued)

Table 5.1 Description of the Explanatory Variables *(continued)*

Variable	Hypothesized Effect	Definition
Community Policing		
Drug/alcohol	+	1 = Suspect shows behavioral effects of drug/alcohol, 0 = all other
Mentally impaired	+	1 = Suspect shows behavioral effects of mental impairment, 0 = all other
Fear/anger	+	1 = Suspect displays a heightened state of emotion—fear or anger, 0 = all other
Conflict	+	1 = Suspect in conflict with another citizen on scene; 1 = none, 2 = calm verbal, 3 = agitated verbal, 4 = threatened assault, 5 = assault
Disrespect	+	1 = Suspect disrespectful to police in language or gesture, 0 = all other
Resistance	+	Level of suspect resistance: 1 = none, 2 = passive, 3 = verbal, 4 = defensive, 5 = active
Weapon	+	1 = Suspect has weapon, 0 = all other
Evidence	+	Summative index (0–7) of the evidence of the target's or requester's violation of the law. Points assigned for each factor present and summed: officer observed citizen perform an illegal act (3), citizen gave officer a full confession (2), citizen gave officer a partial confession (1), officer observed physical evidence implicating citizen (1), officer heard testimony from other citizens implicating the citizen (1).
Arrest	+	1 = Suspect is arrested, 0 = not arrested
Encounter Characteristics		
No. of officers	+/−	Number of officers on scene
No. of bystanders	+/−	Number of citizen bystanders on scene
Violence anticipated	+	1 = Indication of violence from dispatcher, other officers, or observed officers' own knowledge (revealed by comments); 0 = all other
Proactive encounter	+	1 = Officer initiates encounter, 0 = all other
Potentially violent situation	+	1 = Problem involves a dispute, traffic incident, or suspicious person, 0 = all other

Table 5.2 Descriptive Statistics

Variable	Range	Indianapolis Mean (S.D.)	St. Petersburg Mean (S.D.)
Dependent Variables			
Highest level of force	0–3	.874 (.815)	.713 (.793)
None, verbal, physical force	0–2	.849 (.761)	.697 (.758)
Community Policing			
CPO assignment	0–1	.048 (.214)	.239 (.426)
CP training	1–5	3.34 (.990)	2.69 (1.30)
Aggresive patrol values	1–4	2.98 (.860)	2.95 (.874)
Community partnership values	1–4	3.68 (.562)	3.48 (.654)
Control Variables			
Officer Characteristics			
Male	0–1	.843 (.363)	.852 (.355)
Non-White	0–1	.243 (.429)	.145 (.352)
Experience	1–32	7.58 (6.14)	7.66 (5.78)
Education	1–8	4.62 (1.71)	4.34 (1.55)
Legal restraints	1–4	1.77 (.928)	1.36 (.732)
Suspect Characteristics			
Male	0–1	.743 (.437)	.687 (.463)
Non-White	0–1	.689 (.462)	.555 (.497)
Age	1–8	5.12 (1.31)	5.38 (1.38)
Wealth	1–4	2.37 (.546)	2.34 (.584)
Drug/alcohol	0–1	.201 (.400)	.221 (.415)
Mentally impaired	0–1	.018 (.135)	.004 (.214)
Fear/anger	0–1	.242 (.428)	.424 (.494)
Conflict	1–5	1.14 (.596)	1.12 (.545)
Disrespect	0–1	.007 (.271)	.119 (.325)
Resistance	1–5	1.23 (.705)	1.17 (.595)
Weapon	0–1	.001 (.122)	.001 (.120)
Evidence	0–7	1.19 (1.60)	1.49 (1.80)
Arrest	0–1	.115 (.320)	.105 (.306)
Encounter Characteristics			
No. of officers	1–26	2.30 (1.76)	2.10 (1.38)
No. of bystanders	1–100	4.53 (5.89)	3.82 (5.38)
Violence anticipated	0–1	.007 (.270)	.107 (.309)
Proactive encounter	0–1	.471 (.499)	.404 (.491)
Potentially violent situation	0–1	.516 (.499)	.420 (.493)

We define coercion as acts that threaten or inflict physical harm on citizens, similar to the National Academy of Science definition of violence generally (Garner et al., 1995: 152). We order different police acts according to the amount of coercion exerted: none, verbal (commands and threats), physical restraint or search (handcuffing, firm grip, pat downs and searches), and impact (pain compliance techniques, takedown maneuvers, strikes to the body with or without a weapon). From least to most coercive, these levels reflect the amount of harm imposed on the suspect. Observers recorded no instances of firearm discharges at suspects. Police attempts to question, advise, persuade, or suggest did not qualify as coercion unless they included an explicit command or threat. We consider only the coercion used by the officer selected for observation.

Police often used more than one level of coercion with a given suspect (see Terrill, 2003). For this analysis, we are interested in the highest level used. Our dependent measure does not reflect attempts by officers to use lower levels, either before or after the highest level was applied. Thus, this analysis does not distinguish officers who began with low levels of coercion, such as commands or threats, escalating only to higher levels of physical force when lower levels failed to achieve their objectives. Although the dynamics of coercion within an encounter are worthy of inquiry (see Terrill, 2001), we are interested only in how much coercion was ultimately applied so that we may judge the impact of community policing on coercion generally.

INFLUENCES ON POLICE COERCION

Community Policing Factors

We measure community policing in five ways. First, we distinguish officers according to the department leadership's dominant model: broken windows for Indianapolis and community partnership for St. Petersburg. For the remaining four measures, we have available several items that reflect ways that police organizations try to implement community policing by affecting officers' work responsibilities, skills, and values. Hence, our second measure distinguishes between two categories of patrol officer job responsibility: community policing specialists (whose sole responsibility is community policing work) and general patrol officers (who are expected to engage in community policing among many other responsibilities, including answering calls for service). The third measure is the amount of training in community policing principles officers received. Although this is not a direct measure of officers' skills in community policing, it indicates officers' formal preparation and serves as a proxy. As with the job assignment, the direction of the effect of the training variable is expected to be suffused with the department leadership's dominant philosophy—more coercion in a broken windows department and less in a community partnership department. Finally, we have two survey items that indicate the officer's personal attachment to each of the two models of community policing. One item asks officers to state the degree of their concurrence with a statement that places high value on aggressive patrol. Another item asks officers to indicate their level of agreement that officers should "try to find out what residents think the neighborhood problems are." Officers agreeing with the former (aggressive patrol) should be more inclined to use coercion, whereas those agreeing with the latter (resident perceptions) should be less likely to rely on coercion.

Officer Characteristics

Aside from our measures of community policing, there are a number of other officer characteristics that have been thought to influence the use of force. We use officer gender, race, years of experience, highest level of education, and the officer's attitude about ignoring legal restraints to control for several presumed officer predispositions to use force. With the exception of the legal restraint measure, each is linked to police coerciveness in prior inquiries. The legal restraint measure allows us to control for officers' willingness to overlook legal guidelines in the course of their duties. This item offers some indication of the officer's proclivity to let the ends justify violating rules about the means. Those agreeing with this statement should be more inclined to resort to coercion with greater frequency.

Suspect Characteristics

Researchers expend considerable effort to assess the impact of a citizen's social status on his or her prospects for being punished by police. Donald Black (1976) posits that the application of punishment by legal agents can be explained by various types of social characteristics of the subjects of control. Black's theory predicts that the police will be more punitive, hence coercive, toward those with lower economic or marginal cultural status, such as the poor, minorities, and the young. Those who appear to be guilty of wrongdoing (the degree of culpability reflected in the strength of the evidence), intoxicated, mentally deranged, disrespectful, resistant, or filled with anger or fear are viewed negatively by police (as well as society generally). This means that they offend standards about proper behavior or they appear to lack the requisite self-control and in either case are more deserving of police-applied control and punishment. Observers made judgments about the presence or absence of these factors from the evidence presented at the scene to them and the officers they were observing.

Those who possess weapons are considered dangerous and especially needful of forceful control. Those who are arrested are, of course, formally certified as criminal wrongdoers, and both departments required a degree of physical force (handcuffing) when this occurred. Although this did not always take place, the inclusion of an "arrest" variable allows us to control for that level of physical force required by department procedure to accomplish the arrest, an act that in all cases legitimates physical control.

Encounter Characteristics

Certain features of the police-citizen encounter may influence the police proclivity to use force. The number of both officers and citizen bystanders present on the scene of an encounter can influence the likelihood or level of police force, although the direction of the effect is open to interpretation. In one respect, additional officers may lead to increased force as the observed officer may be inclined to raise the level knowing he or she has sufficient backup should the suspect ultimately resist. Conversely, backup support from fellow officers may lower the level of force as the observed officer may feel less need to take control of the suspect, because others are on the scene to help should the suspect increase the level of resistance. Similar effects may take shape in terms of bystanders. As the number of citizens increase, an officer may feel the need to demonstrate being in control by applying more force. However, additional bystanders also means an increased number of potential witnesses to the force being applied.

When officers anticipate violence, they may be quicker to resort to coercion themselves (Fyfe, 1978). If the dispatcher indicated the possibility of violence, or if the officer picked up on some other cue, such as the suspect's reputation, observers coded that violence was anticipated. When the encounter is officer initiated, police legitimacy is lower than when the officer is invited (Reiss, 1971). Consequently, we anticipate that police would be quicker to assert their authority and do it more forcefully. Finally, when a suspect was in conflict, disrespectful, resistant, possessed a weapon, or arrested, we coded only those instances that occurred before the police used the highest level of coercion, to be able to make the proper inference about cause and effect.

THE EFFECTS OF COMMUNITY POLICING ON COERCION

Table 5.3 shows the distribution of police coercion in the two cities. The pattern is similar in both, but Indianapolis, the department promoting the broken windows approach, relies more heavily on coercion at all levels than does St. Petersburg, the department promoting the partnership model. Over all, the odds are 21 percent greater that a suspect would be coerced in Indianapolis (not shown in table)—19 percent greater for verbal coercion, 20 percent greater for physical restraint or control, and 73 percent greater for physical impact. The difference between the two cities is striking, although it is based on only sixty-nine cases and thus should be interpreted with caution. A multivariate ordered probit regression and multinomial logistic regression (not shown) with all predictors in the models confirm that this pattern of relationships remains statistically significant when all other factors are taken into account. Thus, at this stage of the analysis, there is no support for the notion that broken windows policing promotes more verbal coercion while reducing levels of physical coercion.

Next we wish to learn what, if anything, the four measured community policing mechanisms contributed to the patterns of coercion previously noted. Ordered probits were estimated separately for each department, including in the model the four officer-level community policing variables and all of the control variables; the results are presented in Table 5.4. Of the eight community policing coefficients estimated for the two sites, only two were statistically significant. Contrary to expectations, officers with a community policing assignment in St. Petersburg tended to use more coercion, whereas, consistent with expectations, officers with more community policing training in Indianapolis were inclined to use more coercion. However, as shown in the table's last column, neither coefficient was statistically distinguishable from its counterpart at the other site at the conventional standard of $p < 0.05$ (requiring a t value of 1.96 or higher).

It is possible that the effects of at least some community policing variables are not the same throughout the full range of the coercion scale, and this may account for the general absence of specific community policing influences in

Table 5.3 Distribution of Coercion Levels by City

	Indianapolis	St. Petersburg	Odds Ratio
No coercion	37.7%	48.4%	.78
Verbal	39.7	33.5	1.19
Physical restraint/search	20.0	16.6	1.20
Physical incapacitation	2.6	1.5	1.73
N	1,829	1,426	

Chi square = 39.27, $p < 0.001$

Table 5.4 Ordered Probit of Police Coercion: Comparison of Indianapolis and St. Petersburg

	Indianapolis		St. Petersburg		
Community Policing	b_1	SE	b_2	SE	t_{b1-b2}
CPO assignment	−.022	(.131)	.186*	(.091)	−1.30
CP training	.064*	(.029)	.019	(.030)	1.07
Aggressive patrol	−.009	(.040)	.009	(.043)	−0.30
Community partnership	.042	(.058)	−.040	(.057)	1.00
Control Variables					
Officer Characteristics					
Male	.014	(.081)	.205	(.107)	−1.42
Non-White	.032	(.074)	.018	(.100)	0.11
Experience	−.014*	(.005)	−.013	(.007)	−1.11
Education	−.064*	(.017)	−.021	(.026)	−1.38
Legal restraints	−.022	(.030)	.001	(.047)	−1.41
Suspect Characteristics					
Male	.296*	(.072)	.226*	(.074)	0.67
Non-White	.166*	(.065)	.077	(.066)	0.96
Age	−.129*	(.023)	−.058*	(.025)	−2.09
Wealth	−.117*	(.051)	−.165*	(.057)	0.62
Drug/alcohol	.307*	(.070)	.337*	(.078)	−0.28
Mentally impaired	−.140	(.232)	−.043	(.157)	−0.34
Fear/anger	−.004	(.069)	.126	(.072)	−1.30
Conflict	.065	(.053)	.189*	(.081)	−1.28
Disrespect	−.008	(.103)	−.093	(.110)	0.56
Resistance	.357*	(.042)	.374*	(.061)	−0.23
Weapon	.841*	(.239)	.343	(.264)	1.39
Evidence	.078*	(.018)	.578*	(.019)	0.80
Arrest	.996*	(.080)	1.480*	(.100)	−3.78
Encounter Characteristics					
No. of officers	.101*	(.018)	−.010	(.026)	3.51
No. of bystanders	−.004	(.005)	.003	(.007)	−0.81
Violence anticipated	.034	(.100)	.003	(.111)	0.20
Proactive encounter	.097	(.057)	.287*	(.068)	−2.14
Potentially violent problem	.077	(.056)	−.088	(.067)	1.89
Intercept	.219	(.322)	−.638	(.371)	
N	1829		1426		
Pseudo R^2	.281		.267		

Note: b represents the regression coefficient; SE represents the standard error of each coefficient; * indicates statistical significance at $p < 0.05$.

Table 5.5 Multinomial Logit of Police Coercion: Comparison of Indianapolis and St. Petersburg

| | Indianapolis | | | | St. Petersburg | | | |
| | Verbal | | Physical | | Verbal | | Physical | |
Community Policing	*b*	SE	*b*	SE	*b*	SE	*b*	SE
CPO assignment	−.040	(.278)	−.218	(.392)	.331	(.186)	.355	(.266)
CP training	.167*	(.061)	.132	(.081)	.003	(.057)	.109	(.086)
Aggressive patrol	.031	(.080)	−.105	(.109)	−.091	(.084)	.184	(.129)
Community partnership	.103	(.119)	.142	(.166)	−.012	(.114)	−.190	(.164)
Control Variables								
Officer Characteristics								
Male	.087	(.166)	−.076	(.217)	.202	(.219)	.475	(.326)
Nonwhite	.092	(.149)	.010	(.202)	.179	(.192)	.029	(.297)
Experience	−.024*	(.010)	−.043*	(.015)	−.011	(.013)	−.046*	(.022)
Education	−.171*	(.035)	−.133*	(.047)	−.061	(.053)	.001	(.077)
Legal restraints	−.027	(.064)	−.037	(.086)	−.027	(.096)	.102	(.135)
Suspect Characteristics								
Male	.134	(.127)	1.06*	(.207)	.104	(.138)	.818*	(.226)
Non-White	.169	(.128)	.505*	(.181)	.156	(.134)	.215	(.196)
Age	−.202*	(.046)	−.354*	(.060)	−.017	(.049)	−.219*	(.074)
Wealth	−.233*	(.106)	−.266	(.143)	−.213	(.114)	−.516*	(.168)
Drug/alcohol	.496*	(.163)	.834*	(.198)	.325	(.173)	1.050*	(.222)
Mentally impaired	−.441	(.466)	−.171	(.590)	.033	(.307)	−.333	(.481)
Fear/anger	−.032	(.155)	−.008	(.197)	.331*	(.143)	−.008	(.205)
Conflict	.377*	(.122)	.172	(.160)	.677*	(.152)	.438*	(.219)
Disrespect	−.028	(.264)	−.184	(.322)	.034	(.224)	−.166	(.334)
Resistance	.765*	(.151)	.802*	(.162)	.794*	(.173)	.823*	(.210)
Weapon	1.620*	(.805)	2.870*	(.810)	.263	(.645)	1.720*	(.670)
Evidence	.182*	(.038)	.202*	(.048)	.200*	(.037)	.050	(.054)
Arrest	−1.410*	(.353)	1.960*	(.232)	−3.100*	(1.03)	3.090*	(.277)
Encounter Characteristics								
No. of officers	−.087	(.052)	.271*	(.053)	−.242*	(.063)	.080	(.069)
No. of bystanders	−.017	(.013)	−.013	(.014)	.013	(.015)	−.009	(.018)
Violence anticipated	.369	(.235)	.092	(.297)	−.514	(.267)	.392	(.309)
Proactive encounter	.199	(.127)	.216	(.162)	.377*	(.141)	.684*	(.201)
Potentially violent problem	.393*	(.116)	.059	(.152)	−.143	(.139)	−.158	(.202)
Intercept	.293	(.665)	−.824	(.887)	−1.29	(.736)	−3.57	(1.11)
N	1829				1426			
Pseudo R^2	.336				.361			

Note: *b* represents the regression coefficient; SE represents the standard error of each coefficient; * indicates statistical significance at $p < .05$.

the ordered probit. Perhaps, as earlier hypothesized, community policing increases the likelihood of lower, verbal levels of coercion but has no effect or actually reduces higher, physical levels of coercion, and this could vary by the model of community policing embraced by the department. Table 5.5 presents the results of a multinomial logistic regression that explores this possibility. For ease of interpretation, the two physical coercion levels (restraint/search and impact) are combined. "No coercion" serves as the reference category for the coefficients reported.

With one exception the results in Table 5.5 do not alter the pattern shown in Table 5.4. With the exception of the training variable, community policing effects do not produce statistically distinguishable differences in levels of coercion when the likelihood of verbal and physical coercion are compared with no coercion. In Indianapolis, community policing training significantly increases the likelihood of verbal coercion, and this is statistically distinguishable from the absence of such an effect in St. Petersburg ($p < 0.05$, comparison not shown in table). Training also increases the likelihood of physical coercion, but that coefficient is not statistically distinguishable from the no-coercion reference category in either city. We must therefore be cautious not to make too much of the difference between cities. Overall, these mechanisms for promoting community policing—job assignment, training, and officer beliefs—do not appear to increase verbal coercion while reducing physical coercion.

We have not dwelled on the effects of the control variables because our primary interest is in the contribution of community policing variables. However, there are some patterns worth noting. From the ordered probit results in Table 5.4, the direction of effects is consistent at the two sites for most of the control variables, suggesting a high degree of cross-site stability in the nature of influence exerted by these situational characteristics. That is, for the most part, there is no indication that the two models of community policing interact with the control variables in ways that suggest markedly different decision making in the exercise of coercive discretion. For example, we see that non-White suspects are significantly more likely to be coerced in Indianapolis and not St. Petersburg, but the difference between the effects of the two sites is not significant.

In contrast, four of control variables (age, arrest, number of officers, and proactive encounters) did produce differences between cities. Both Indianapolis and St. Petersburg officers were significantly more inclined to coerce younger suspects, but the effect was much stronger in Indianapolis, and significantly so. Arrests were more likely to produce coercion (of a physical sort, as is clear from Table 5.5) in St. Petersburg than in Indianapolis, the vast majority of these being the use of handcuffs or other restraint. As the number of other officers at the scene increased, Table 5.4 shows that this significantly increased the likelihood of coercion in Indianapolis, while having no effect in St. Petersburg. However, Table 5.5 shows that more officers present in Indianapolis stimulated more physical coercion, whereas in St. Petersburg more officers had no effect on physical coercion and suppressed verbal coercion. The reverse was true of proactive encounters; they substantially increased the likelihood of coercion in St. Petersburg but were inconsequential in Indianapolis, primarily due to differences in effects on physical coercion.

In addition, potentially violent problems showed differential effects across sites that approached significance in the probit model ($p < 0.06$) and that achieved significance when verbal and physical coercion were distinguished in the multinomial logistic regression. Indianapolis officers were significantly more inclined than St. Petersburg officers to coerce suspects verbally when an indicator of potential violence was present. This more assertive stance is consistent with the notion of assertive interventions under the broken windows model.

Otherwise, community-policing-based explanations for the few significant interaction effects between city and control variables are not obvious. One might argue that there is some evidence to support Klockars's (1988) concern that the broken windows model is more vulnerable to discrimination against socially marginal groups (1985: 319)—in this case, racial minorities—but the difference with St. Petersburg is not sufficient to achieve statistical significance. However, the pattern of greater coercion toward juveniles predicted by Klockars under a broken windows approach is found, even though officers in both cities were significantly inclined to use more coercion with younger suspects. Whether the size of the difference is sufficient to cause great concern is debatable. For example, in Indianapolis, the odds of police physically coercing a teenage suspect (13 to 17 years old) was 5.7 times that of coercing a middle-age person (45 to 59 years old); in St. Petersburg the same comparison produces an odds differential in the same direction of 5.0. The relationship of the number of officers on scene in Indianapolis to coercion could conceivably have a direct linkage to that city's approach to community policing. Table 5.5 shows that the strength of this difference is found in the application of physical force. Indianapolis's leaders actively promoted proactive interventions to seize contraband and reduce the risk of public disorder, and these kinds of activities were often undertaken in teams. The logic of this reasoning is not supported by the evidence, however, because it is in St. Petersburg, not Indianapolis, where proactive interventions increased the level of coercion, mostly of the physical sort.

The effects of officer-level community policing variables are weak in comparison with several situational factors. For example, consider the effects of training in Indianapolis—the only statistically significant community policing variable in Table 5.5. An Indianapolis officer with more than five days of training had .7 greater odds of using verbal coercion than one who had no training (odds ratios not shown in table). However, an actively resistant suspect in Indianapolis had odds of verbal coercion more than 8 times that of a citizen who showed no resistance. A suspect with the highest evidence score had 7.2 times the odds of verbal coercion as one who had the lowest score. The dominance of situational influences in models such as ours has long been commonplace in research findings (Riksheim and Chermak, 1993; Terrill and Mastrofski, 2002; Worden, 1989) and should surprise no one. Most of the variation in what a physician does with a patient can undoubtedly be accounted for by situational characteristics (e.g., the patient's symptoms and complaints). However, most patients still care about the smaller differences that training and motivation make on the doctor's performance. Similarly, small differences attributable to the officer's skill and motivation probably matter to the citizens who are treated as suspects by police.

Finally, we note that some officer characteristics, albeit not those directly related to community policing, show effects of an impressive magnitude when compared with situational predictors. For example, the Indianapolis officer without a high school education had about 8 times the odds of coercing the citizen (both verbally and physically) as the one who had a graduate degree. Comparing the far more common educational levels of high school degree versus four-year college degree produces an odds differential of 3.6. (The same pattern held in St. Petersburg, but it was not statistically significant.) Similarly, an Indianapolis rookie with one year on the force had about 3.6 times the odds of using verbal force and 2.7 times the odds of using physical force as the twenty-year veteran. This stands in sharp contrast to the more modest effects of community policing training mentioned earlier.

CONCLUSION

The model of community policing that top management promotes does seem to matter. Officers at the broken windows site (Indianapolis) showed a striking proclivity for greater coercion than did those at St. Petersburg. However, we find little support for officer-level influences and no support for the notion that either model increased verbal coercion while decreasing physical coercion—a proposition offered by some advocates who see modest increases in coercion as the ounce of prevention that obviates the need for the pound of cure.

One might question whether the difference in coercion levels between the two departments was really due to the model of community policing employed. Perhaps it was due in whole or part to some other unmeasured features of the departments and their communities. There is no way to rule out conclusively other possibilities, but we note that the two most obvious seem unlikely. One might expect more police violence where there is more crime and violence in the community (Fyfe, 1978). But Indianapolis and St. Petersburg are evenly matched for all officially recorded crimes per thousand residents (100 and 99, respectively) and for the subset of violent crimes per thousand residents (19.6 and 19.7, respectively).

Another possibility is that the cultures of the two departments regarding coercion have long been different and that the leadership of each selected the model that best suited the traditional orientation of the officers. If this were so, we should have observed in Indianapolis substantially more favorable views of aggressive patrolling and less favorable views of community partnership as compared with St. Petersburg. The reverse is in fact the case. Table 5.6 compares the two departments based on a sample of nearly all patrol officers in both departments.

Indianapolis officers were less positively disposed to aggressive patrol than St. Petersburg officers, although the difference was not statistically significant. They also averaged a substantially more positive attitude toward community partnership than did the St. Petersburg officers. Our comparison of the departments does not support the hypothesis that cultural traditions in the departments, rather than the community policing orientation of management, account for these differences. Thus, we are unable to reject the hypothesis that these department leaders' efforts to shape their officers' behavior actually had the intended effect, as Wilson (1968) posits in his classic study. What this means in practical terms is that the effects of the leader's approach to community

**Table 5.6 Officer Attitudes Toward Community Policing:
Full Sample in Both Departments**

	Indianapolis Mean Value (s.d.)	St. Petersburg Mean Value (s.d.)	p
Aggressive patrol	2.87 (.86)	2.95 (.84)	.226
Community partnership	3.69 (.52)	3.54 (.62)	.001

Note: Scale values range from 1 to 4 (higher values indicating stronger agreement) and are calculated from the full sample of respondents in each department (N = 398 for Indianapolis and N = 237 for St. Petersburg).

policing depends on the model employed. Blanket assertions that community policing will have a uniform effect on levels of coercion simply cannot be supported from this analysis. The results caution us to recognize that there are great differences among approaches that pass as community policing, and that these differences have important consequences for what happens on the street.

We hope that our exploration of the effects of officer-level characteristics might illuminate the way department-level effects were achieved. We are less successful here in identifying features of community policing attributable to individual officers that would account for different coercion levels. Officers' job assignments (community policing officer versus general patrol) seem to structure the inclination to coerce in St. Petersburg, but not Indianapolis, and the St. Petersburg effect is opposite that expected and not statistically distinguishable from the Indianapolis effect in any event. What can account for the unexpected effect that community policing officers working under St. Petersburg's partnership model actually showed higher levels of coercion? We can only note that the level of direct supervision by first-line supervisors was tighter in Indianapolis than in St. Petersburg. St. Petersburg community policing officers set their own work schedules, thus making it much harder to supervise. They were left much more to their own devices than community policing officers in Indianapolis, and hence, they may have been more inclined to engage in a work style that suited them, not top management. Also, because St. Petersburg assigned a much larger portion of its patrol force to community policing officers slots, the department could not be as selective as Indianapolis in placing officers who best fit the leadership's image of the ideal. Indeed, several middle managers indicated that it was difficult to find enough officers willing to take the job who were also sufficiently motivated and skilled to do it the way the department wanted.

The amount of community policing training had the expected effect in Indianapolis, increasing the likelihood of coercion, but no effect in St. Petersburg, and again the difference between the sites is not statistically significant. Perhaps the Indianapolis model, and hence the department's training, resonated more clearly with the predisposition and skills of officers to engage in coercive practices; perhaps the training in St. Petersburg, focusing much more on problem solving and partnership, had more resistance to overcome and therefore failed to show the expected effect there.

The officers' attitudes toward the two community policing models showed no effect at either site. The absence of attitudinal effects is not without precedence and is in fact the rule, not the exception, in prior research on police discretion (Worden, 1989, 1995). In this instance, our findings fail to support a popular argument that the accomplishment of community policing requires changing officers' values (Sparrow et al., 1990: 149) because community policing is held to be a philosophy, not a program. If this oft-heard refrain is true, the officers who were most responsive to top management's values about community policing were no more likely to share that philosophy than those who were unresponsive to their leadership. Management in these departments appears to have been unsuccessful in establishing the linkage between the hearts and minds of their officers and their practices. Put simply, as a group, officers were not inspired to act according to their own views of community policing, but they were responsive to top management's philosophy about community policing, at least as it played out in the use of coercion. As William Bratton (1998) and others suggest, it may be more important to make the organization's values and priorities clear than it is to persuade officers to adopt these philosophies. At least in Indianapolis, training may have clarified and reinforced management's views, and clarity of purpose may be enough to get the desired response. Alternatively, both of these departments may have offered incentives to perform according to management's preferences that simply were not tapped by the measures available to us.

As with any study of a small number of nonrandomly selected departments, one must not rush to conclude that what we find here represents a nationwide pattern. If resources were no object, we can imagine a study that had encounter-level observations on a much larger number of departments. This would not only increase the generalizability of the findings but would allow for a more comprehensive test of department-level effects. For example, there are undoubtedly some departments where both models prosper simultaneously and others where they are present in varying combinations of intensity. It would be interesting to examine the use of coercion in a department where officers were encouraged to pursue actively aggressive order maintenance, but working closely with the "community" to do this. If, as some suspect (Klockars, 1985; Lyons, 1999), this results in taking sides between conflicting social or economic groups, one would want to track carefully who gets coerced.

CITATIONS

Bittner, Egon. 1970. *The Functions of Police in Modern Society.* Washington, DC: National Institute of Mental Health.

Black, Donald. 1976. *The Behavior of Law.* New York: Academic Press.

Bratton, William. 1996. Quotation on the cover of George L. Kelling and Catherine M. Coles, *Fixing Broken Windows.* New York: Free Press.

Bratton, William. 1998. *Turnaround: How America's Top Cop Reversed the Crime Epidemic.* New York: Random House.

Cascio, Wayne F. 1977. "Formal Education and Police Officer Performance." *Journal of Police Science and Administration,* 5: 89–96.

Chevigny, Paul. 1969. *Police Power: Police Abuses in New York City.* New York: Pantheon.

Clarke, Ronald V. 1993. *Crime Prevention Studies,* Volume 1. Monsey, NY: Criminal Justice Press.

Cohen, Bernard and Jan M. Chaiken. 1972. *Police Background Characteristics and Performance.* New York: Rand.

Crank, John P. 1994. "Watchman and Community: Myth and Institutionalization in Policing." *Law & Society Review,* 28: 325–351.

Croft, Elizabeth Benz. 1985. *Police Use of Force: An Empirical Analysis.* Unpublished Ph.D. dissertation, University of Michigan.

DeJong, Christina, Stephen D. Mastrofski, and Roger B. Parks. 2001. "Patrol Officers and Problem Solving: An Application of Expectancy Theory." *Justice Quarterly,* 18: 31–62.

Friedrich, Robert J. 1977. *The Impact of Organizational, Individual, and Situational Factors on Police Behavior.* Unpublished Ph.D. dissertation, University of Michigan.

Fyfe, James J. 1978. *Shots Fired: A Typological Examination of New York City Police Firearms Discharges, 1971–1975.* Unpublished Ph.D. dissertation, University of Michigan.

Fyfe, James J. 1988. *The Metro Dade Police Citizen Violence Reduction Project, Final Report, Executive Summary.* Washington, DC: Police Foundation.

Garner, Joel H., Thomas Schade, John Hepburn, and John Buchanan. 1995. "Measuring the Continuum of Force Used By and Against the Police." *Criminal Justice Review,* 20: 146–168.

Goldstein, Herman. 1990. *Problem Oriented Policing.* New York: McGraw-Hill.

Greene, Jack R. 2000. "Community Policing in America: Changing the Nature, Structure, and Function of the Police." In Julie Horney (Ed.), *Policies, Processes, and Decisions of the Criminal Justice System.* Washington, DC: National Institute of Justice, 299–370.

Greene, Judith A. 1999. "Zero Tolerance: A Case Study of Police Policies and Practices in New York City." *Crime and Delinquency,* 45: 171–187.

Independent Commission on the Los Angeles Police Department. 1991. *Report of the Independent Commission on the Los Angeles Police Department,* Los Angeles.

Kelling, George L. 1987. "Acquiring a Taste for Order: The Community and Police." *Crime and Delinquency,* 33: 90–102.

Kelling, George L. 1999. *"Broken Windows" and Police Discretion.* Washington, DC: National Institute of Justice.

Kelling, George L. and Catherine M. Coles. 1996. *Fixing Broken Windows: Restoring Order and Reducing Crime in Our Communities.* New York: Simon & Schuster.

Kelling, George L. and William H. Sousa Jr. 2001. "Do Police Matter? An Analysis of the Impact of New York City's Police Reform." Civic Report, No. 22. Center for Civic Innovation at the Manhattan Institute, New York.

Klockars, Carl B. 1985. "Order Maintenance, the Quality of Urban Life, and Police: A Different Line of Argument." In William A. Geller, ed., *Police Leadership and America: Crisis and Opportunity.* New York: Praeger, pp. 309–321.

Klockars, Carl B. 1988. "The Rhetoric of Community Policing." In Jack R. Greene and Stephen D. Mastrofski (Eds.), *Community Policing: Rhetoric or Reality.* New York: Praeger, 239–258.

Lyons, William. 1999. *The Politics of Community Policing: Rearranging the Power to Punish.* Ann Arbor, MI: University of Michigan Press.

Manning, Peter K. 1984. "Community Policing." *American Journal of Police,* 3: 205–227.

Manning, Peter K. 1989. "The Occupational Culture of the Police." In Larry Hoover (Ed.), *The Encyclopedia of Police Science*. Dallas, TX: Garland Press, 349–366.

Mastrofski, Stephen D., R. Richard Ritti, and Jeffrey B. Snipes. 1994. "Expectancy Theory and Police Productivity in DUI Enforcement." *Law and Society Review*, 28: 101–136.

Mastrofski, Stephen D., Roger B. Parks, Albert J. Reiss Jr., Robert E. Worden, Christina DeJong, Jeffrey B. Snipes, and William Terrill. 1998. *Systematic Social Observation of Public Police: Applying Field Research Methods to Policy Issues*. Washington, DC: National Institute of Justice, U.S. Department of Justice.

Mastrofski, Stephen D., Robert E. Worden, and Jeffrey B. Snipes. 1995. "Law Enforcement in a Time of Community Policing." *Criminology*, 33: 539–563.

Mastrofski, Stephen D., Jeffrey B. Snipes, Roger B. Parks, and Christopher D. Maxwell. 2000. "The Helping Hand of the Law: Police Control of Citizens on Request." *Criminology*, 38: 307–342.

Mok, Magdalena and Marcellin Flynn. 1998. "Effect of Catholic School Culture on Students' Achievement in the Higher School Certificate Examination: A Multilevel Path Analysis." *Educational Psychology*, 18: 409–432.

Muir, William K., Jr. 1977. *Police: Streetcorner Politicians*. Chicago: University of Chicago Press.

Reibstein, Larry. 1997. "NYPD Black and Blue." *Newsweek*, June 2: 66–68.

Reiss, Albert J., Jr. 1968. *Police Brutality: Answers to Key Questions*. New Brunswick, NJ: Transaction.

Reiss, Albert J., Jr. 1971. *The Police and the Public*. New Haven, CT: Yale University Press.

Riksheim, Eric and Steven Chermak. 1993. "Causes of Police Behavior Revisited." *Journal of Criminal Justice*, 21: 353–382.

Roth, Jeffrey A., Joseph F. Ryan, Stephen J. Gaffigan, Christorpher S. Koper, Mark H. Moore, Janice A. Roehl, Calvin C. Johnson, Gretchen E. Moore, Ruth M.

White, Michael E. Buerger, Elizabeth A. Langston, and David Thacher. 2000. *National Evaluation of the COPS Program—Title I of the 1994 Crime Act*. Washington, DC: National Institute of Justice, U.S. Department of Justice.

Sampson, Robert J., Stephen W. Raudenbush, and Felton Earls. 1997. "Neighborhoods and Violent Crime: A Multilevel Study of Collective Efficacy." *Science*, 277: 918–924.

Skogan, Wesley G. and Susan M. Hartnett. 1997. *Community Policing, Chicago Style*. New York: Oxford University Press.

Skolnick, Jerome H. and David H. Bayley. 1986. *The New Blue Line: Police Innovation in Six American Cities*. New York: Free Press.

Sparrow, Malcolm K., Mark H. Moore, and David M. Kennedy. 1990. *Beyond 911: A New Era for Policing*. New York: Basic.

Spitzer, Eliot. 1999. *The New York City Police Department's "Stop & Frisk" Practices: A Report to the People of the State of New York from the Office of the Attorney General*. New York: New York State Attorney General

Terrill, William. 2001. *Police Coercion: Application of the Force Continuum*. New York: LFB.

Terrill, William. 2003. Police Use of Force and Suspect Resistance: The Micro Process of the Police Suspect Encounter. *Police Quarterly*, forthcoming.

Terrill, William and Stephen D. Mastrofski. 2002. "Situational and Officer Based Determinants of Police Coercion." *Justice Quarterly*, 19: 101–134.

Toch, Hans. 1969. *Violent Men: An Inquiry into the Psychology of Violence*. Chicago: Aldine.

Trojanowicz, Robert. 1991. "Community Policing Curbs Police Brutality." *Footprints*, 3: 1–3.

Weisburd, David, Rosann Greenspan, Kellie Bryant, Edwin E. Hamilton, Hubert Williams, and David Olson. 1998. *Abuse of Police Authority in the Age of Community Policing: A Preliminary Study of Issues and Attitudes*. Washington, DC: The Police Foundation.

Westley, William A. 1953. "Violence and the Police." *American Journal of Sociology,* 59: 34–41.

Wilson, James Q. 1968. *Varieties of Police Behavior: The Management of Law and Order in Eight Communities.* Cambridge, MA: Harvard University Press.

Wilson, James Q. and George L. Kelling. 1982. "The Police and Neighborhood Safety: Broken Windows." *Atlantic Monthly,* 127: 29–38.

Worden, Robert E. 1989. "Situational and Attitudinal Explanations of Police Behavior: A Theoretical Reappraisal and Empirical Assessment." *Law and Society Review,* 23: 667–711.

Worden, Robert E. 1995. "The 'Causes' of Police Brutality: Theory and Evidence on Police Use of Force." In William A. Geller and Hans Toch (Eds.), *And Justice for All: Understanding and Controlling Police Abuse of Force.* Washington, DC: Police Executive Research Forum, 31–60.

6

Diving into Quicksand: Program Implementation and Police Subcultures[1]

RICHARD L. WOOD,
MARIAH DAVIS, AND
AMELIA ROUSE

Community policing has emerged as a primary vehicle for advancing crime-fighting programs and police reform efforts during the last fifteen years. Such has been the hegemony of the concept of community policing among scholars, police leaders, and the wider public that even the hard-edged policing strategies pursued in New York and elsewhere have been justified under the community policing mantel. Though initial evaluation studies of community policing resulted in uneven reports of the model's effectiveness, more recently a well-designed study in Chicago documents that community policing can work when pursued vigorously (Skogan and Hartnett, 1997). The fundamental lesson out of these implementation studies appears to be: "It is hard to get community policing off the ground, but it can be made to work" to reduce crime, fear of crime, and police-community alienation (Skogan and Hartnett, 1997: 246).

Despite the evidence for community policing's strategic effectiveness and its widespread support among the public, within many local police departments resistance to community policing practices remains strong. Police researchers and police leaders alike have noted that police culture represents a primary obstacle to its effective implementation—even where those strategies have been relatively successful, as in Chicago (Skogan et al., 1997; Skogan et al., 1999; Chan, 1997; Wood, Davis, and Rouse, 1999). As Mark Moore argues, "Probably the biggest obstacle facing anyone who would implement a new strategy of policing is the difficulty of changing the ongoing culture of policing" (Moore, 1992; 149, see also Sparrow, Moore, and Kennedy, 1990).

[1] This research was supported by grants from the National Institute of Justice (U.S. Department of Justice #96-IJ-CX-0068 and #98-IJ-CX-0073). The authors thank research partners within the Albuquerque Police Department, particularly Roy Turpen, Karen Fischer, and sworn leaders too numerous to list, for their ongoing collaboration; the National Institute of Justice and the Department of Justice for research support; and National Institute of Justice program monitor Dr. Steven Edwards for his counsel. Jim Ron, Paul Lichterman, and Bert Useem read and offered insightful feedback on an earlier draft of this paper.

This is not to suggest that those charged with leading police departments and implementing community policing should focus exclusively on police culture. Organizational structure, job incentives, well-designed evaluation research, police training, and technology will all provide key tools for reshaping how—and how effectively—police officers do their jobs. But it is to argue for the centrality of police culture on two grounds. First, as these other tools are brought to bear, police leaders need constantly to consider how their interventions will be received by officers embedded in the police subcultures described here; failure to do so condemns leaders' intervention to irrelevance or distortion "on the ground." Second, any success had by police leaders in implementing new, more effective approaches to policing may be short lived unless they are consolidated by incorporation into a coherent police culture. That is, effective organizational change requires paying attention to the dynamics of current police culture, and consolidating that change requires the gradual construction of a coherent police culture that integrates the best of old and new.

Yet much of our understanding remains informed primarily by the ethnographic work of Jerome Skolnick (1966), James Q. Wilson (1968), John Van Maanen (1978), and Elizabeth Reuss-Ianni (1983). This literature continues to provide insight into crucial aspects of urban police culture, but it no longer illuminates the full complexity of that culture as it has evolved over the last twenty years. This chapter builds on the strengths of these accounts but seeks a more contemporary view of urban policing. We draw on a four-year ethnographic study (including 3,000 hours of police ride-alongs, participant observation in police and community meetings, and 200 interviews with police personnel) of police culture in the "Sunbelt City Police Department" (SCPD) to analyze the interaction between police culture and a long-term effort to implement community policing in an ethnically diverse metropolitan area in the Sunbelt. The chapter briefly traces the fragmentation of traditional police culture, outlines a set of subcultures of policing that today compete for hegemony, and analyzes the reception of community policing across police subcultures—that is, the way competition among these subcultures works to dissipate and undermine community policing implementation, and to capture it for the narrow interests of each subculture. We conclude by discussing plausible scenarios for the immediate future of urban policing in the United States, in light of the fact that no clear winner has emerged in the struggle for hegemony within police organizational culture.

TRADITIONAL POLICE CULTURE

The broad outlines of police culture are well analyzed. Though often termed the professional culture of policing, we use the term *traditional police culture* because today it is what older officers remember from earlier times.

Rich ethnographic work on police culture and behavior was pursued by Skolnick (1966) and Wilson (1968), both of whom have had an important influence on subsequent police scholarship. Egon Bittner (1967) shows the craft-like nature of police work and the salient place within it of keeping peace, in contrast to law enforcement. Van Maanen (1978) illuminates the experiential world of police officers and the experiences that shape their shared culture, and Reuss-Ianni (1983) analyzes the contrasting cultures of street cops and management cops. Fictional depictions (Wambaugh, 1975) and journalistic accounts (Baker, 1985; Fletcher, 1991) illuminate the social world of police officers and the behaviors that both construct and reflect that world.

Out of these and other ethnographic studies, a relatively coherent image of police culture emerges, an image that continues to inform a great deal of scholarship and teaching about the police (see, for example, the widely used articles by Kappeler, Sluder, and Alpert, 1994, and by Skolnick and Fyfe, 1994). The image that developed out of this literature was of a relatively coherent, unified culture of policing, despite Wilson's (1968) explicit emphasis on the varieties of police behavior and Reuss-Ianni's (1983) emphasis on the cop-management split. Different authors emphasize different precise details of this unified police culture, but it can be broadly characterized as combining: (1) a high—indeed, nearly insurmountable—us-them boundary between sworn officers and all others, including civilian coworkers; and (2) strongly reinforced rules governing behavior, some rooted in the official rules of standard operating procedure but the most important ones rooted in the informal norms and sanctions of peer relations with other officers. Among the latter are strong expectations of macho behavior, bravery in the face of danger, and the preservation of a code of silence in the face of accusations of police misbehavior. The overarching ethos of police culture is often depicted as an assumption that police officers represent a thin blue line protecting decent citizens in a world viewed in deeply dualistic terms as a struggle between a weak "normal" society under siege by the forces of evil and chaos. This ethos emphasizes the constant danger of police work, the thrill of hot pursuit, and police culture as preserving a kind of eternal adolescence among officers.

The data from this study cannot assess whether this depiction of a relatively unified police culture was accurate twenty years ago. Though recent critiques of the concept of organizational culture have rightly highlighted the contested, contradictory, and cleavage-ridden character of the cultures of real organizations, there does appear to have been a coherent core to the world of policing roughly corresponding to this brief sketch. However, over the last fifteen years whatever unified police culture lay at the heart of police organizational life in the past has fragmented. To analyze the basis for this fragmentation, we draw partially on Steve Herbert's (1998, 1997) ethnographic study of the Los Angeles Police Department, in which he identifies the competing and overlapping normative commitments among urban police officers.

THE FRAGMENTATION OF POLICE CULTURE:
SEVEN POLICE SUBCULTURES

Although police may have shared such a unified organizational culture in the past, in the SCPD and elsewhere, they no longer do. The traditional culture of policing has partially broken down under the influence of changing city demographics, litigation regarding minority hiring and police behavior, increasing racial and gender diversity within police ranks (Martin 1997; Reaves, 1996; Bureau of Justice Statistics, 1998), three decades of police research showing the inaccuracy of the assumptions underlying traditional police models (Trojanowicz, 1982; Kelling, 1974), reform policing models generated by police scholars (e.g., Goldstein, 1979, 1990; Fielding, 1995; Toch and Grant, 1991; Eck and Spelman 1987) and disseminated by the National Institute of Justice (1992, 1995; U.S. Department of Justice, 1994), reform-minded politicians and police managers, popular pressure from residents who are placing new demands on police agencies, and so on. But no strong organizational culture has coalesced to take the of the traditional culture of policing. Rather, SCPD organizational culture is characterized by fragmentation and competition among several subcultures.

Subcultures are nothing new in policing; what is new is that nothing like a dominant culture now integrates the SCPD subcultures together, providing overall coherence and vision to police officers. Instead, several such visions are in active competition. We draw on interview and ethnographic data to describe these subcultures of policing by summarizing how each subculture varies on five variables: sense of the police *mission* and the individual officer's role in it; the *normative commitments* that are most central to it; the *practices* of patrol and community interaction in which officers engage; the *beliefs* about policing, the community, and the department that officers hold (including who they consider legitimate actors against crime and how strongly they divide the world into us vs. them categories, itself quite variable); and the *ethos* of life as a police officer that surrounds each subculture, including its views of authority and cooperation (see Wilson, 1989, Herbert, 1999, and Geertz, 1973, on these analytic categories).

Some core orientations continue to be shared by most police officers, forming a kind of archetypal police culture, which can be thought of as the foundation of police identity that underlies the other subcultures. Thus, one officer noted in our interviews, "A cop is a cop is a cop. Some are better than others, some are worse. But we are all made out of pretty much the same stuff." This most notably includes a sense of being different from others and clearly on the side of right and a keen awareness of being at risk when in public. Though these orientations represent normative commitments to morality and safety, the particular twist given to morality and safety varies dramatically across subcultures. We discuss these subcultures in turn, noting that although some SCPD personnel operate exclusively within one subculture, others operate at the intersection of two or more.

Remnants of the Traditional Culture

I became a police officer to catch the bad guys, not to be a god-damned social worker. (Patrol officer, seven years in SCPD)

Among front-line officers, probably the most influential subculture embodies the remnants of the traditional model of policing. Its influence is rooted in the legitimacy of its long tradition and acceptance among many officers. This subculture is the one most often represented in society and media, and provides the basis for many citizens' stereotypes of police officers. Yet it no longer integrates officers into a coherent social world; rather, it is just one among competing subcultures.

Officers that subscribe to this subculture typically stated they became officers to "catch bad guys," "to protect and to serve," or simply " to fight crime." When asked how they intended to fight crime, the typical officer response was that they would catch criminals either by "doing patrol" or investigating crimes. The day-to-day practices of the traditional officer revolve around responding to calls for service, writing reports and citations, and conducting randomized patrol. Beyond these, the only strategies for action in which these officers engage on their own initiative are tactical plans—operations such as mass drug arrests, traffic enforcement, or street saturation that are executed by police in response to police-identified issues.

The belief system of traditional police culture is reflected in officers' strong identification with the brotherhood of police officers, a brotherhood from which they exclude officers that are corrupt or extremely lazy. Some traditional officers actively seek to promote that brotherhood by purposefully engaging in traditional police activities such as "choir practice," a time-honored custom of officers drinking together after work (Wambaugh, 1975). However, this subculture's status as only a remnant is reflected in how rare choir practice has become among Sunbelt City police officers: it occurs only sporadically and then as a voluntary activity, from which individual officers excuse themselves. The traditional subculture places a high value on officer autonomy, both from police administrators and from the surrounding community. Such autonomy in seen as both necessary in this line of work and as one of the key attractions of policing as a career; lack of autonomy leads to frustration. As one officer commented when his squad was instructed to meet a minimum monthly performance standard for written citations: "They give me a badge and a gun, and trust me to decide when it's appropriate to take someone's life . . . but they don't trust me enough to decide whether or not I should give someone a ticket or a warning." Likewise, the notion that officers or police departments ought to take direction from or collaborate with the communities they protect and serve is anathema in this subculture. That is, the only legitimate actors against crime are law enforcement professionals. Thus, fundamental to the traditional subculture is an us-versus-them worldview with "us" being limited to other sworn officers. As one officer noted:

I have always said that cops should get minority rights. I mean, we get treated the same as any other minority, only worse. Because we are a cop, we have to worry about scumbags shooting at us, spitting in our food.

Certain people won't hang out with us, we get treated as lepers. We always worry about our cars being scratched up, our kids being bullied . . . just because the color of our skin happens to be blue.

Thus, the ethos within the traditional subculture is one of officers who consider themselves to be professionals and who should be insulated from external demands. This ethos might be summed up as one of crime fighters operating with as much autonomy—from the community and from supervisors—as they can manage.

This subculture's dominant normative commitments are to safety, law, and morality, as seen in three facets of traditional policing. First, in this subculture, no claim is stronger than what is required to keep officers safe; thus, when changes were proposed at the SCPD academy to reflect community policing emphases, they were effectively stalled for years under the rationale that they would undermine training in officer safety. Second, the requirements of the law also strongly shape the dynamics of traditional police work—but not only in defining what is to be done. The law and standard operating procedures also provide the boundaries along which officers exercise their creativity and inventiveness—that is, violate the rules—to protect officer safety, catch bad guys, and foster officer autonomy. Third, officer's inherent goodness is rarely questioned; their honor and the honor of the department for which they work stand between social order and social chaos. However, contrary to the common stereotype, this commitment to morality can cut two ways: although it can justify turning a blind eye to officer abuse of force, in well-led departments it generates peer pressure against officers seen to be abusing force. Over the four-year term of this study, which dynamic predominated at a given time or in a given unit appeared to depend primarily on the tone set by the chief (departmentwide) and by immediate supervisors; strong leadership appeared to trigger and legitimate peer pressure against abuse.

Paramilitary Subculture

We are who the police call when they need help, the last resort when everything has gone to shit. (SCPD SWAT officer)

The paramilitary subculture is perhaps the most controversial subculture found in a police agency, the culture most revered and reviled. Indeed, some observers see this subculture as having taken over urban policing (see especially Kraska and Kappeler, 1997; also Auten, 1981; Miller, 1996; Jefferson, 1990; Chambliss, 1994). As with the traditional subculture, the ultimate mission of paramilitary officers is to fight crime. But the paramilitary style of officers adds a razor edge to their mission statement: they intend to vigorously protect society from scumbags and believe that their duty to protect and serve is a righteous war. The ethos within the paramilitary subculture can best be described as that of competitive soldiers, with officers bringing a high-energy focus and a dedication to self-betterment to that war. As one officer noted, "The way I figure it, we are the last line of defense. We try to keep the scumbags from hurting the normal, honest citizens any way we can."

In pursuing this mission, the paramilitary officer engages in a series of complex and often grueling practices. These officers are among the most physically fit on the department, spending hours each day at the gym and often taking a multitude of vitamins and supplements to increase their physical size, strength, and overall health. The high physical standards of the paramilitary officer enhance the hard-hitting work ethic of the officer, characterized by a "kick ass, take names" policing style. These officers are typically known for their on-the-job energy as well as their ability to shoot, fight, or engage in a multitude of other high-intensity police-related activities. As officers, they often have the highest arrest and self-initiated action statistics. The desire to be where the action is results in these officers working areas known for their violent crimes and "scumbag" populations. Many paramilitary style officers want to work eventually in an elite specialized unit (typically SWAT) that is composed of officers like themselves and offers recognition for their abilities and actions; others prefer to remain on patrol work, at least as long as they feel their paramilitary orientation is welcome there. The paramilitary officers already in specialized units often feel that they have finally found a home in their unit, because they are surrounded by other officers who have similar world views and work ethics. It is in their specialized units that many of the paramilitary officers begin to accept their job as a lifestyle, if not almost a calling. Thus, the feeling these officers carry of being elite is reinforced as they become more specialized in their jobs.

The practices of paramilitary policing reflect this sense of mission and these beliefs. When confronting critical incidents, officers tend to adopt relatively aggressive tactics in the belief that only such tactics are adequate to the task. During more routine activities, their practices tend toward proactive policing—initiating car stops; doing assertive foot, bicycle, or horse patrol; engaging suspected gang members—focused on establishing contact with suspicious persons. This gives these officers the opportunity to assess the person, ask for identification, check for warrants, and possibly locate weapons or drugs. Alternatively, these officers may become disaffected from routine activities and simply shun them or become openly abusive in routine interactions. The paramilitary subculture shares with the traditional subculture an us–versus–them orientation. Here, however, the "them" is more focused on those drawn together under the label "scumbag" or similar terms: criminals, those living parasitically off the wider society, and so on. Other key beliefs include a sense of paramilitary officers as a kind of fraternity within policing, dedicated to the true vision of policing, and a perception of the political system as a threat to that vision, because a suspicion that politicians do not understand the value or necessity of their working methods.

The value of teamwork represents crucial tenet of the paramilitary subculture, and the best teams work to limit overtly self-glorifying or abusive behavior. The paramilitary subculture pushes all officers to recognize that their ability to do their jobs effectively, if not their lives, depends on the officer standing next to him. This can either push officers toward the extremes of militaristic behavior or limit such behavior, if officers believe that arrogance and abuse represent a threat to fellow officers because they may provoke retaliation or alienate needed community support. In this subculture is found the greatest support for hierarchical authority. Although they hope for true leaders as their immediate supervisors, they accept that often they have to settle for a manager who has "hard stripes" and thus deserves, if not respect, at least obedience. Paramilitary style officers often hold their superiors (especially first-line sergeants) to the same high standards they hold for themselves. When these standards are not met (lack of physical ability, low shooting qualification scores, dishonesty or corruption), the officers generally do not publicly challenge their superior. Instead, they simply treat the superior as an outsider and look to the informal leaders in their squad for advice and encouragement.

The key normative commitments in this subculture include competence, adventure or machismo, and a certain kind of morality. A remarkable amount of focus and training time goes into maintaining peak competence in a variety of defensive tactics and the use of force. Likewise, the sheer physical adventure of critical incidents lie at the heart of what makes policing attractive within this subculture, and cultivating individual abilities and organizational capacities for handling such incidents are the *sine qua non* of excellent officers and leaders. Thus, body building and training in martial arts—in addition to being exercises in machismo—are valued as true policing assets. Though occasionally women are part of this subculture, it is a more one-dimensionally masculine culture than the traditional subculture, into which women have fit—not easily, certainly, but with less difficulty. Morality is seen one dimensionally: in practice, virtually nothing qualifies as abuse of force because police work represents a war against evil. The normative order of safety plays an important role in this subculture, but with a twist: officers believe their safety—especially "when everything has gone to shit"—is protected best through aggressive tactics, rather than through defensive caution.

Opportunistic Subculture

I wanted to go somewhere where I could study [for a college degree, during his patrol shift]. So, that was the carrot my supervisors held in front of me: if I would go to "Shitsville" beat and take care of problems and square that place away, then I was allowed to come up here where the call load is less. So I am hanging out up here where the only thing that is going on is rabbits fucking. (Patrol officer, eight years)

Atomization and self-interest define the opportunistic subculture: these officers focus narrowly on what the job can do for them and refuse to vest themselves in the larger interests of the organization or community. The mission statement for these officers is either self-preservation or self-promotion, taken to a degree that is far beyond that of the average officer. For these individuals, any attention to the common good of their squad, area command, department, or community is secondary to what they can do for themselves. Because these officers are usually "looking out for number one," their organizational mission depends on what they feel will increase and protect their power within the department.

These officers learn to play the system, using their supervisors to enable their actions. They also learn to play the community, knowing and using all of the perks provided to them by their position.

Opportunistic officers will often try to align themselves with other cultures to gain popularity, but they are not eagerly embraced. The actions (or lack there of) of the opportunistic officer angers some other officers, as they are forced to pick up the slack left by the opportunistic officer. These are the officers that both the traditional and paramilitary officer say give all officers a bad name. It is important to note that the opportunistic officer is not necessarily lazy. Rather, two versions of the opportunistic subculture produce two different kinds of officers. Those of the careerist variety may in fact work hard, saying or doing whatever is necessary to climb the ranks of the department, and avoid actions or situations that would hurt their chances of promotion. This happens, however, with remarkably little concern for whether their work contributes to improving the department or the community.

A more narcissistic variety of officer may be the most egregious manifestation of the opportunistic subculture, the corrupt officer. This officer feels that society owes him or her, and therefore demands the many perks that carrying a badge may offer. "I had a supervisor once who used to really lean on people. I mean, it's all right to get discounts at meals and free coffee and such, but this guy . . . he went too far. He would go into a business, any business, pick up an item and ask them how much it costs. If the price they gave him was the full price, then he would tell them that they must have misunderstood. Then he would take out his badge, and say 'No, I meant how much is this for a cop?' " Other varieties of opportunism draw on the prestige of the badge to acquire sexual favors from "badge bunnies." Without strong controls, such opportunism can degenerate into full-blown corruption, use of police authority to coerce sex, and so on.

Superficially, it may be the opportunistic officer who responds most positively to efforts at organizational change in police departments. When confronted with a change, these officers immediately ask, "How is this going to affect me?" Opportunistic officers concerned with promotion will embrace the change if someone with sufficient power to affect their careers is pushing it. But such an embrace can be so superficial as to severely limit the impact of the changes, by failing to link it to a serious focus on preventing and controlling crime. Other opportunistic officers will avoid conflict by giving lip service to any mandate while minimizing any impact the mandate would have on them, by shirking work, "milking" calls for service, and so on. Organizational leadership demands the capacity to distinguish between opportunistic and real change agents within departments.

Although officers operating within this subculture may, to advance personally, espouse commitments linked to any of the normative values of policing, fundamentally the opportunistic stance rejects them all. More accurately, opportunism subverts them all as "normative" by using them instrumentally for individual gain. Thus, it is essentially not a true subculture but rather a retreat from shared cultural commitments.

Administrative Subculture

> The guys still in the field, I know they say "He doesn't remember what it's like to be a real cop and take calls or that my common sense is fried from breathing the paint in the Main for too long." I know they say that, and it bothers me some. But I still think that the job I do is important. For them to do their job, they need people like me. I make it possible for them to do their job. (Police manager, more than fifteen years in SCPD)

Sworn and civilian members of the administrative subculture may embrace the sense of police mission of any of the other subcultures, but they emphasize doing so in a legally and fiscally efficient manner, subject to pressures from the city political system. Officers in this culture recognize that police work does not exist in a vacuum but rather in important political, legal, and economic contexts. It is within those contexts that these officers must operate, constantly balancing their socialization in the world of front-line policing, their judgment about what is best for police and community, and political pressures from above.

Those in the administrative subculture realize that it is sometimes necessary to play politics to accomplish their jobs. Sometimes, however, even these officers feel that the politics and bureaucracy work against the fundamental mission of the police department. They resent having to enforce rules and procedures that seem to be written with little thought as to their consequences. As one police manager said:

> I find my job [pause] disturbing. Before I got promoted, my job was fun. My squad was great, we worked hard but also screwed around a bunch. I was very proud of being a cop. But now, I sit up here and read some of the stuff that this department actually puts in writing, and I am trying to explain it to my people, trying to make it sound like it is not the most asinine thing I have ever read. Ever. And sometimes I just can't.

Many of those who ended up in administrative positions seemed almost surprised to have found themselves there:

> I became a police officer so I could work outdoors . . . and I like adventure and excitement. I never wanted to sit behind a desk (officer bangs hand on desk), wear a tie (officer pulls on the tie he is wearing), answer a phone (officer taps his phone) or do paperwork (officer picks up one of twenty files on his desk). But I just kept getting promoted. The day I retire (officer picks up his beeper), I am going to drive to the edge of a river, and the minute somebody beeps me, I'm going to toss this over.

Many of those in the administrative subculture said that the hardest part of their job is the separateness they feel from the rest of the sworn officers. One police manager noted, "I don't even feel like a real cop anymore. I am a secretary with a badge."

The practices of the administrative subculture are based in accountability. These officers tend to be record keepers, either by innate nature or by the necessity of their position. They gravitate toward positions with administrative responsibilities that require them to track expenditures, resources, and time. This tracking is obviously necessary and can lead to greater efficiency in an organization. It can also lead to supervisory unreasonableness, or "bean counting."

The resulting ethos takes two forms: a negative bureaucratic ethos centered on the needs and priorities of administration for its own sake, and a positive pragmatic ethos centered on making policing work within its current political, legal, and economic contexts. Of course, both are bureaucratic—the department could not function without a working bureaucracy.

The realities of organizational, political, legal, and fiscal accountability push bureaucratic control and the law front and center as the normative commitments of the administrative subculture. To the extent that bureaucratic and legal imperatives come unmoored from the other goals of policing, the administrative subculture itself loses legitimacy in the eyes of the other police subcultures. Conversely, to the extent bureaucratic and legal mechanisms are mobilized to further the other normative commitments, they attain legitimacy in the eyes of officers. During stable periods in policing, the job of police managers was relatively simple: make the bureaucracy serve the work of policing and make officers follow the law. However, during periods of transition in policing—such as the present, when old assumptions are being called into question by research, new models of policing are being elaborated, and the demographics of policing are shifting—police managers' jobs become much more complex. They must explain to their personnel the nature of the transition, help the organization sift through new initiatives and decide what works and what does not, use the norms of bureaucratic control and the law to implement valuable initiatives and fight destructive ones, and monitor the shifting internal and external political environments of their departments, all the while forging the shared normative commitments required for a new police culture.

Civilian Subculture

A lieutenant once said that, "You see these people (civilian employees)? These people are the backbone of this department, our civilian staff is the backbone. If it wasn't for our civilian staff, we would be lost. If you respect these people, there is nothing they won't do for you. You disrespect them, they will treat you like hell." And he was right, because I took two days to give an officer who was a jerk the information he needed, and I had it right there. (Police department civilian employee, thirteen years)

So far, we have focused on sworn officers, but civilians today typically constitute between one-fifth and one-third of the personnel of large police departments. Civilian employees provide the vital services that allow a department to function, whether offering legal advice, controlling the allocation of vehicles and equipment, analyzing the key evidence for criminal prosecution, prioritizing and dispatching calls for service, or coordinating the organizational planning of the entire agency. As one civilian noted:

We are the first contact that any citizen has with the department. When somebody needs help, they call 911. If they don't call us, they don't get an officer . . . and we also have the greatest impact on what happens to that person. If they had a call, the officer wrote the report, but the report doesn't get typed in, or we lose it . . . well, that is the end of their case. Whoever that officer arrested, without the report, it is thrown out of court.

In SCPD, civilians have a fairly distinct organizational subculture. Although civilians may be part of the other subcultures, the very nature of their functions in the department and their relationship to sworn officers delineates them as a separate organizational subculture.

One element was uniformly widespread in the civilian subculture: most civilians identify strongly with the department's overall mission, centered around the work of controlling crime and promoting public safety. One hears little antagonism toward—and often real respect for—the fundamental role of sworn police officers. Civilians are often proud of their own role in supporting that work and being part of that mission. As one high-level civilian manager noted, "It's rewarding for me to work on something that in an indirect way makes the city safer for some little kid riding his bike down the street, you know. We played a role in that, and that really makes me feel good. It's being able to see something that I've had a part in making the city better."

Certain beliefs unite the civilians in the police department. The most central shared belief is that the work done by civilians is crucial to the success of the department, rather than peripheral to it. But many civilians emphasized that sworn members of the department generally fail to recognize this. Civilians thus thirst for such recognition. Beyond this, civilians embrace essentially the same spectrum of organizational missions as do sworn officers, with the exception of the hardest line paramilitary stance.

The fact that civilians both embrace the police mission and feel unaccepted as equals within it produces a certain ambivalence among many civilian employees at all levels: on one hand they feel they contribute, on the other hand they must struggle to sustain their morale. This ambivalence was expressed by one supervisor when asked whether working as a civilian in SCPD was generally positive or negative: "I'd say generally positive, but with a real concern about not being peers, and not communicating the way that communication should be done in the department. That's what I see generally as the issue between sworn and civilian."

But civilian employees respond to this situation in diverse ways. Among civilian managers and supervisors, there often exists a strong sense of being excluded. This leads to conflict over how their authority, resources, or expertise should be used, and often to a sense that they are taken less seriously than sworn officers (regardless of their expertise). This exchange between civilian managers in a focus group illustrates their frustration:

Manager 1: [Officer attitudes toward civilians] relate to the brotherhood of the officers. Officers feel like, "If you haven't gone through what I've gone through, then don't tell me what to do."

Manager 2: Exactly, I think that's it. I have heard it time and time again. . . . It's exactly that: we are not of the cloth. We haven't been through the Academy, the baptism by fire. We haven't gone out and arrested people, or as [former chief] used to say, we haven't ever gone through a door with him. There's always a tacit reminder that we're just not of the cloth.

This feeling was by no means universal. Some civilian managers reported a high degree of acceptance by sworn officers. Civilian SCPD employees tend to divide starkly between those who identify strongly with the sworn-dominated culture of the department and those who are critical of it. In our focus groups, identifying strongly and uncritically with sworn officers predominated among those managers on whom sworn personnel depend directly for expertise or resources, and rank-and-file civilian employees. More alienated views predominated among managers on whom officers did not depend directly, presumably because these managers had fewer bargaining chips with which to demand respectful treatment.

The key practices of civilians vary enormously, depending upon their jobs. It is thus difficult to identify concrete practices they share. This in itself reduces the bonds of solidarity felt among civilian employees compared with sworn officers, who generally perform similar work tasks. Beyond this, however, key patterns are discernible in civilians' interactions with sworn officers. First, some civilians operate on the periphery of the sworn culture, recognizing their integral role in SCPD but accepting the centrality of the sworn culture. Second, like some sworn officers, some civilians adopt a stance of being active agents of change within SCPD, striving to move the organization forward toward better civilian-sworn relations, more effective policing, and so on. As in any organization, these reformers must find networks of support to sustain their sense of direction and effectiveness. Ideally, that network of support includes both sworn and civilian colleagues. Third, another segment of civilians become beaten down by the frustrations of their position in the agency and tire of their sense of powerlessness. Unless they can find a positive place within SCPD's organizational culture, they become alienated from their work and become resentful of the status quo. The overall ethos of the civilian subculture might be best described as being one of unequal partnership. But it plays out differently in these three groups, and thus the civilian and sworn relationships fall along three lines: those accepting of the status quo, those attempting to reform it, and those that passively resent the nature of the relationship between the civilians and the sworn.

Competence represents the core normative commitment around which the civilian subculture revolves. As a culturally subaltern group within policing, civilians gain status and legitimacy by demonstrating expert knowledge of specific tasks, particularly to the extent that their expertise is seen as directly benefiting sworn officers or aiding in catching criminals. Thus, the civilians most respected in the department include those in charge of payroll and the criminalistics laboratory. The lowest status civilian manager is the legal advisor to the department, whose job primarily involved cautioning police leaders about perpetrators' legal rights and advising them in adjudicating complaints against officers. In between, civilians gain or lose status within the hegemonic culture depending on their demonstrated competence and usefulness, as well as on whether they embrace (at least publicly) the dominant definition of morality—the assumption that officers represent the good in a struggle against evil.

Expert COP Subculture

I think our mission now is to be problem solvers and to involve the community in solving those problems. Five years ago our mission was to make arrests and get criminals off the streets. But now that simply isn't enough. So we have had to change our thinking. (Midlevel supervisor, twelve years)

In recent years, as SCPD strove to implement community policing, some officers and civilians came to embrace some of the tools of community policing so strongly that they reorganized themselves and their work around the practices and beliefs underlying it. These officers and civilians from various levels of the department have either invested considerable effort in researching and learning about community policing or its elements, or have adopted it as their primary police role after being convinced of its value through SCPD training sessions.

The people in this community-oriented policing subculture serve as local experts on community policing, both formally and informally. Some serve in formal roles on SCPD's Problem-Oriented Policing Committee or Community Policing Steering Committee (now defunct), or train other SCPD personnel in problem-solving techniques. Others serve informally as informational resources for officers trying to understand how the department wants them to incorporate community policing into their work. Their sense of the police mission often reflects official statements of community policing, whether from SCPD's mission statement, written materials from federal offices promoting community policing, or other community policing literature. Their beliefs about policing often center on the idea that by working together police and community members can lower crime rates by preventing crime. They also favor opening up police boundaries to community input and participation, and share a commitment to decentralizing the policing structure. For some, these beliefs are informed by significant reading on competing models of policing; others are more influenced by a vague sense of wanting police and community members to get along. Less common, some shed the traditionally antagonistic view toward local government and media attention common among sworn officers and view both as potential resources for generating more effective policing. They thus attempt to cultivate positive ties with those organizations.

The key practices of this subculture are the standard elements of community policing: problem solving, attending community meetings, trying to keep officers in assigned neighborhoods, and building ties to other city agencies potentially useful in crime prevention. At its best, their problem solving entails

sophisticated attention to underlying crime-generating problems and the creative development of solutions to these problems. Likewise, these officers do
not attend community meetings passively; they use their authority to draw
community members into more active collaboration in taking responsibility
for their neighborhoods, defining their problems, and devising effective solutions. At the other extreme, some officers linked nominally to the community
policing subculture engage in these practices only cursorily: they label as problem solving traditional police-centered tactics, passively attend community
meetings or use them to promote public relations without real crime prevention content, etc.

The ethos operative within this part of the community-oriented policing
subculture centers around institutional reform, that is, personal commitment to
trying to move SCPD toward more effectively reducing crime, combined with
a belief that community-oriented policing offers the best tools for doing so. At
its best, this ethos carries a spirit of collaborative empowerment as people work
together to exert constructive and effective influence in moving the department in the direction of embracing at least significant aspects of community
policing. The members of the expert community-oriented policing group are
the activists, teachers, and mentors promoting community policing within the
department.

The future of the community-oriented policing subculture, like the future
direction of policing itself, is an open question. Because the subculture of
community-oriented policing expertise is relatively new and because its adherents are widely scattered in a large department, it could still be absorbed into
the more established subcultures. Conversely, this nascent subculture may
thrive as it fights for hegemony in the organizational culture of SCPD.

A Phantom Straw Man: The Weak
Community-Oriented Policing Subculture

Finally, to understand the dynamics of policing reform in urban America today,
one must recognize a kind of phantom subculture that plays an important role
for officers and supervisors fundamentally opposed to recent reform models of
policing. These traditionalist and paramilitary opponents of community policing portray it as reducing the mission of policing to customer service alone; in
their caricature, community policing simply involves being nice to the community and the idea that police should do what the community wants. Instead
of seeing problem solving and other community policing practices as means to
more effectively fight crime, they portray community policing as asking them
to be a weak cop or Officer Friendly: glad-handing citizens, doing public relations work, being a positive presence in the community. Note that these beliefs
and practices might indeed have a role in a strong policing model; the key here
is that they are seen as all that community policing is about.

Whether a weak community-oriented policing subculture actually exists,
in the sense of officers who embrace this vision of policing, is dubious. If such
officers exist, they are a tiny minority. At least in an urban police department

with serious crime and gang problems, this subculture holds remarkably little appeal to the vast majority of officers. It certainly stands little chance of becoming the dominant model of policing in such a setting. Indeed, it carries no true ethos for urban policing; it can exist only at the margins of the department, in isolated individuals or small units carrying out specialized functions.

Yet this phantom subculture plays a vital role in the organizational culture of policing. It serves as a caricature used to undermine the notion that community policing has anything to offer contemporary urban policing. Thus, those opposed to reform seek to identify community policing with this weak community-oriented policing caricature and to emasculate community policing advocates as "empty-holster cops." If allowed to define community policing, this strategy effectively undermines any effort to implement it or even to incorporate its best insights into police practices generally.

If, on the other hand, the best aspects of community policing are to gain significant influence in police culture, community policing must escape from the clutches of the weak community-oriented policing caricature. In the grassroots police world of SCPD and many other departments, it has not fully done so.

The future organizational culture of policing will be shaped in part by the ongoing dynamics among all of the subcultures present there. By analyzing these subcultures, we may better understand the morass into which police leaders feel they are driving when striving to implement reform models of all kinds. The cross-cutting expectations, demands, assumptions, and orientations summarized here are the quicksand in which reform so often becomes mired.

Cultural Challenges to Community Policing

All those concerned with community policing implementation—police leaders, political officials, and scholars—may gain insight by paying attention to the dynamics at play between these subcultures. Such insight will not prevent departments from experiencing the quicksand of police subcultures, but it can help them navigate through it.

Perhaps most important is simply to recognize the ongoing struggle among these subcultures for hegemony in defining the organizational culture of police departments. Because they have long experience working in shifting bureaucratic and political winds, police personnel are remarkably adept at adopting the language and appearing to embrace the priorities of new models as they gain ascendancy. But officers' fundamental allegiances and assumptions change only very slowly, for they are deeply intertwined with these subcultures. As a result, a superficially smooth transition toward a new departmental strategic initiative may mask an acute struggle to capture that initiative for the interests of one subculture. Examples abound: Administrators use the rhetoric of community policing in public settings to gain legitimacy and advance their budgetary priorities while doing little to see that community policing becomes a reality on the ground. Paramilitary officers may adopt a language of community policing and form community ties to gain allies for their war on crime, then turn to those community groups for explicit political support when their budgets are threatened or they come under fire for abuse of force. Traditionalists may simply adopt problem-solving language to describe their unchanged, police-centered tactical plans, and then claim to be doing real problem solving unless they are held accountable to a more rigorous model. Even community-oriented policing experts with a tinge of opportunism may use the reform model entrepreneurially, simply as a tool to advance their own careers (or, in some cases, their interest in future political office). This research witnessed examples of these and other ways of capturing the new initiative.

Note that the practitioners of each of the capture strategies just delineated might well score highly on a quick survey of knowledge about and orientation toward community policing; they just would not be actually engaged in the concrete practices advocated under community policing. Of course, it is only those practices that have been shown to actually reduce crime, fear of crime, and police-community alienation.

To assure that these practices are implemented, police leaders must pay close attention to the real dynamics, self-interests, and meanings within each subculture. For example, officers oriented toward the paramilitary subculture carry sufficient prestige, do a large enough portion of the proactive work of policing, and are so crucial during the occasional critical incidents faced by a department that an implementation effort may be dead on arrival if it alienates them entirely. Implementation must appeal to their proactive work ethic and their commitment to reducing crime and protecting citizens, even as it also moderates or disciplines the extremists among them. Likewise, opportunists are easily led to adopt a reform stance through job incentives, but placing them in positions of authority over implementation guarantees that little will change in practice. Finally, community policing can help break down the divide between civilian and sworn employees, but if seen as essentially a civilian initiative, few sworn officers are likely to embrace it. In handling these various cultural challenges, the role of mid-level police managers will be critical (Geller and Swanger, 1995; Langworthy, 1986).

Though many police personnel implicitly identify with more than one of the subcultures depicted here, they often hold primary allegiance to one. More important, those seen as leaders—whether because of their prestige among peers or because of formal authority in the police organization—are often seen that way precisely because they champion one of these subcultures. These leaders inevitably come to be identified strongly with one subculture. Their perception of what works may then be colored by ego conflicts with other up-and-coming leaders. The organizational learning process of finding the best way forward may thus be hijacked by the personal status competition that drives the organizational politics inside of police departments. Similarly, these leaders will only embrace community policing strategies to the extent they can be convinced that those strategies either (1) advance their subculture's interests or (2) show real promise to affect crime. Of course, Option 1 is simply a version of the capture strategy. But most officers remain sufficiently committed to fighting crime that Option 2 is a viable strategy. Where hard, well-crafted social-scientific evidence documents the anticrime effectiveness of a given approach, presenting a simplified version of that evidence can gain the allegiance of leaders across subcultures.

This is not the place to rehash the findings of the vast cottage industry that has grown up around organizational change efforts in the public and private sectors. But that literature (Schein, 1992; Kanter, Stein, and Jick, 1992) and the previous discussion suggest that two kinds of leaders will play key roles in implementation efforts. First, pushing change through the quicksand of departmental politics requires change agents—zealots, true believers—who will forge ahead with new ideas and practices despite opposition and criticism. Second, doing so intelligently will require leaders who cross boundaries between subcultures, avoid being captured by any one of them, and keep a pragmatic focus on combining old and new practices while analyzing what works on the ground.

One final cultural challenge for all those responsible for generating and implementing reform models in policing lies in recognizing constantly that reform itself is a multidimensional process. It is first a *political process* requiring adept formation of coalitions among key constituencies internal to police departments (notably, the subcultures discussed here) as well as of alliances with key pressure points in city government and the wider community. It is also a *bureaucratic process*, requiring that flows of internal and external communication and the incentives of departmental life (pay, shift scheduling, status awards, assignment to prestigious units, promotions, the chief's time allocation, etc.) reflect and promote the priorities associated with the proposed reforms. Third, it is a *cultural process*. To be stable, the reform model must draw on and recombine cultural elements from all the subcultures into a set of assumptions, strategies for action, self-identities, and practices that bring meaning and motivation to the experience of departmental personnel (more on this later). Fourth, if successful implementation is to be something more than the blind imposition of a new ideology, it must be an *analytic process*. Police leaders and scholars must continuously reassess what is working, what is not, and why, as well as develop new innovations for what might work in fighting and preventing crime. Fifth, as Skogan and Hartnett (1997) point out, successful reform will necessarily be an *iterative process*, that is, based on a great deal of trial and error and diffusion of strategies successful in one setting to new locations, where they are adapted to new local realities. Finally, we must not lose site of all this as a *policing process*, that ultimately policing is simply different from most organizational settings, and reform must respond to the realities and appeal to the cultural orientations of the personnel attracted to the policing profession.

ALTERNATIVE FUTURES: FRAGMENTATION
OR CONSOLIDATION?

The interaction and competition among these contemporary subcultures of urban policing will determine a great deal about the face of policing and the outcome of police reform efforts in the years ahead. Though strong economic times and stabilizing drug markets have helped generate falling crime rates in much of American society in recent years, when the next economic downturn or round of intense competition in drug markets rolls around, we may well confront another crime explosion. As of this writing (2002), crime rates nationally have begun to rise again. Police departments have to develop the tools now to face this challenge, including strong, flexible organizational cultures that can respond adroitly. Equally important, the historic tensions between law enforcement and subaltern groups, especially poor minority and immigrant communities, show no signs of abating; the new war on terrorism may exacerbate those tensions. Empowering police departments to reduce crime while protecting civil and human rights promises to be a continuing challenge. Although political leaders, judicial oversight, and grassroots activism are important elements in drawing attention to these challenges, to confront them successfully police culture will have to coalesce around some combination of new and old practices, beliefs, and normative commitments, built on an ethos and sense of mission attuned to a multicultural, politically democratic, but economically polarized urban America.

Various models currently compete for primacy in the minds and hearts of police leaders throughout the country. The most prominent are traditional models of professional policing, community policing linked to problem solving, and quality-of-life policing linked to police-led crackdowns on disorder (Kelling and Coles, 1996). Although recent research suggests that the putative causal link between disorder and crime—the broken windows thesis (Wilson and Kelling, 1982; Skogan, 1990)—does not in fact hold up (Sampson and Raudenbush, 1999), the jury is not yet in, and in any case quality-of-life policing will continue to attract officers steeped in the paramilitary subculture or oriented toward the adventure and machismo of policing (Silverman, 1999). Therefore, the future of policing in urban America remains indeterminate; Figure 6.1 recapitulates the argument of this chapter and suggests various alternative scenarios for urban police culture:

In the immediate future, most police departments will continue to experiment with a variety of approaches. Far from a bad thing, such muddling through represents the kind of iterative approach that may lead to real success. But if done without vision and systematic analysis of what works and what does not, such experimentation may well lead to ongoing fragmentation of police organizational culture. Such a scenario may lead to undesirable outcomes for both police and community. Without strong direction, opportunism will flourish and increasing numbers of police officers may succumb to narcissistic, violent, or corrupt behavior.

Should community policing reforms consolidate only in a weak sense, unaccompanied by strong organizational direction and without generating a strong ethos and sense of mission, they too could lead to deepening corruption. Police became isolated from the communities they patrol partly because of technological changes, but also as part of the professionalization drive of the 1930s and 1940s intended to isolate them from the corrupting influence of community ties. Community ties not linked to professional ethics, personal integrity, and commitment to crime reduction—and accountable to strong

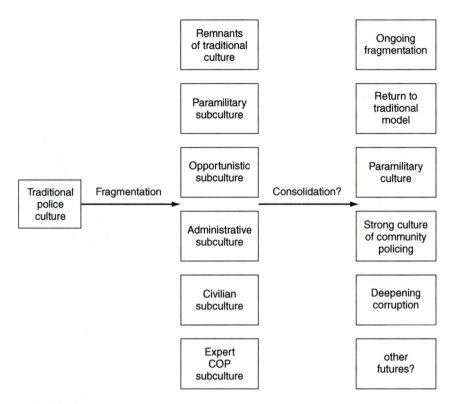

FIGURE 6.1 Development of police culture.

departmental and legal oversight—may expose officers to vast financial incentives from drug-distribution networks.

   Given the resiliency of the organizational culture of policing, another plausible future scenario is a return to something approximating traditional police culture. Many factors currently push against this outcome—the changed internal demographics of policing, legal and political pressures in favor of police reform, police leaders committed to opening their departments instead of insulating them from outside influence, and research showing that traditional police practices failed to control crime but did generate low officer morale—all make traditional retrenchment less likely. But how permanent are these factors? Nearly all depend on local or national political dynamics that could change quickly, removing any real pressure to change traditional police practices. Already, the incentive in favor of community policing provided by major federal funding tied to its priorities is a thing of the past. The new demographics of policing may be more permanent, but presumably members of non-White groups can be socialized over time into traditional police culture. The new demographics may thus have helped fragment traditional culture but may not be a particularly effective check on its return. Likewise, past research findings will not change, but future findings may, and in any case police leaders and policy makers are free to simply disregard inconvenient research findings. Thus, nothing guarantees against a return to the practices, norms, and ethos of traditional police culture. Recent developments in Chicago, where some of the best research documenting the impact of community policing has been conducted, is illuminating in this regard. Traditionalists have made inroads in stopping community policing in its tracks and rolling back some reforms (Skogan et al., 1999).

Another alternative scenario lies in the consolidation of a more strongly paramilitary culture of policing; indeed, some observers believe that precisely this is occurring under the cover of a rhetoric of community policing (Chambliss, 1994; Kraska and Kappeler, 1997). Although such a scenario is decried by most academic observers, it is pursued by some paramilitary enthusiasts in policing. The hold of the paramilitary subculture over the hearts and minds of some officers is undeniable. This has led to egregious abuses, including in the infamous Rampart division of the Los Angeles Police Department and a sequence of infamous cases in the New York Police Department. Whether such cases represent moral lapses of individual officers, as argued by the official Board of Inquiry (Los Angeles Police Department, 2000), or command-and-control failures of individual supervisors, organizational command failures, or the takeover by paramilitary culture of whole departments lies beyond this study. Although we see no good evidence that such a takeover is imminent, and significant political and legal checks are working against it, the paramilitarization of urban policing remains a constant undercurrent. If consolidated, it could become the main current of urban policing. Particularly sobering in this regard is the finding (Muir, 1979) that aggressive exertion of power on the part of police in fact attracts greater violence. Should resurgent gang violence coincide with stronger paramilitary policing and deepening alienation between police and urban communities, mutual escalation might indeed lead to such paramilitary consolidation.

Yet another plausible future scenario for urban law enforcement would involve the consolidation of a strong culture of community policing. A detailed look at what such a strong culture might entail is beyond the scope of this chapter, and in any case, it will be constructed not through academic clairvoyance but rather through the hard work of those policing, governing, and living in our cities. But the categories employed here suggest at least the following broad outlines: Such a strong culture of policing would focus its *mission* around preventing and reducing crime, while preserving a place for some measure of the adrenaline-driven crime-fighting work that officers still expect and that appears to bring in police recruits. The core *practices* of such a model of policing would include the political skills involved in informal community contact and meetings with community groups, as well as the craft-like skills of problem solving to address conditions leading to crime, disorder, and calls for service.

But some of the traditional policing skills would also remain central: defensive tactics, tactical training, handling calls for service, investigating crimes, and writing reports. Such a model would also include some of the proactive practices currently emphasized within the paramilitary subculture, disciplined by intolerance of abuse and collaborative relationships with communities being patrolled. Thus, those viewed as *legitimate actors against crime* would include police, local residents, and collaborating city agencies, and the norms for *authority and cooperation* would not only encourage police-community cooperation in reducing crime but also draw on police authority to catalyze community engagement. The *strategies for action* would include many traditional tools of policing, but these would be secondary to the collaborative, problem-focused approaches called for by recent reform models. Important, stronger analytic thinking by police leaders at all levels would inform their decisions about when to use which strategies; cultivating such analytic skills represents an important hurdle to be surmounted. The *ethos* surrounding such a police culture might be termed mutual empowerment: using police-initiated activity to blunt the worst ravages of criminal activity on neighborhoods, leveraging police legitimacy to help residents exert informal authority over their neighborhoods, but also controlling police behavior through community oversight.

The core *normative commitments* around which such a culture might revolve would no doubt include those identified by Herbert (1998), but new norms would also have to coalesce. Among them might be a commitment to empirically driven analysis of patterns of crime and disorder and police-community responses to those patterns. Such analytic policing has only begun to emerge as a significant presence in well-led police departments; systematic embrace of such an approach might go a long way toward building police departments as the learning organizations so widely promoted but so difficult to consolidate.

CONCLUSION

The current transitional period in urban policing in America has left police departments a legacy of fragmented organizational cultures, with a variety of approaches to police work pulling in contradictory directions. Police leaders charged with implementing community policing and other reform models thus risk driving into a morass of cross-cutting pressures. Given recent evidence for the effectiveness of community policing practices, widespread reports of implementation difficulties suggest that this morass may quickly become quicksand, suffocating reform efforts. This analysis of police subcultures strives to help scholars and practitioners navigate these difficulties through an ethnographic look at current cultural dynamics inside urban policing. On its face, it cannot be generalized nationally; at base, it is a one-city case study of the dynamics of organizational transition. But brief fieldwork in five other cities nationally, and conversations with police professionals, researchers, and observers of policing in Washington, D.C., suggest that these dynamics are common throughout urban police departments in America.

Despite all that police leaders and scholars already know about the subject, such an ethnographic reexamination is timely for at least three reasons: First, most of our knowledge has been built on ethnographic work now two or three decades old. Given all the changes in the ideology, demographics, and political context of policing in the interim, there is a *prima facie* case for asking whether police culture has shifted. Second, addressing the apparent resurgence of excessive police force (or at least declining tolerance for it) demands deeper understanding of the dynamics leading to officer abuse; police culture appears to be one crucial link in the causal chain leading to such abuse. Third, if our case for the fragmentation of police culture is correct, it seems likely that coming years will witness attempts to reconsolidate a more unified culture of policing, if for no other reason than overly fragmented organizational cultures find it difficult to pursue their goals effectively.

Though the primary agents for consolidating a new police culture will surely be formal and informal police leaders themselves, what culture will ultimately prevail depends significantly on conditions set by others: local political leaders who control the purse strings and leadership of local departments, the possible renewal of federal funding for reform policing models following the sunset of the 1994 Crime Bill initiatives, and the demands of diverse urban democratic constituencies. Thus, political leaders, judicial officials, and urban residents committed to protecting democratic ideals while fighting crime can probably prevent the consolidation of a one-dimensionally paramilitary model of policing. But they cannot impose a new organizational culture of policing. Only policing insiders can actually construct such a new cultural core to give direction and meaning to the work of policing. It will be the interplay between the cultural agency of police leaders and the structural conditions set by political and legal dynamics that will determine the future course of urban policing. For these reasons, understanding police culture in its contemporary complexity is an urgent democratic task.

CITATIONS

Auten, James H. 1981. "The Paramilitary Model of Police and Police Professionalism." *Police Studies*, 4: 67–78.

Baker, Mark. 1985. *Cops: Their Lives in Their Own Words*. New York: Simon & Schuster.

Bittner, Egon. 1967. "The Police on Skid Row: A Study of Peace Keeping." *American Sociological Review*, 32: 699–715.

Bittner, Egon. 1970. *The Functions of the Police in Modern Society*. Cambridge, MA: Oelgeschlager, Gunn, & Hain.

Bratton, William with Peter Knobler. 1998. *Turnaround: How America's Top Cop Reversed the Crime Epidemic*. New York: Random House.

Burawoy, Michael, A. Burton, A. Ferguson, K. Fox, J. Gamson, N. Gartrell, L. Hurst, C. Kurzman, L. Salzinger, J.

Schiffman, and S. Ui. 1991. *Ethnography Unbound: Power and Resistance in the Modern Metropolis*. Berkeley: University of California Press.

Bureau of Justice Statistics. 1998. *Local Police Departments*. Bureau of Justice Statistics, U. S. Department of Justice.

Chambliss, William J. 1994. "Policing the Ghetto Underclass: The Politics of Law Enforcement." *Social Problems*, 41: 177–194.

Chan, Janet. 1997. *Changing Police Culture: Policing in a Multicultural Society*. New York: Cambridge University Press.

Eck, John E. and W. Spelman. 1987. *Problem Solving: Problem-oriented Policing in Newport News*. Washington, DC: U.S. Department of Justice, National Institute of Justice, Police Executive Research Forum.

Fielding, Nigel. 1995. *Community Policing.* Oxford, England: Clarendon Press.

Fletcher, Connie. 1991. *What Cops Know: Cops Talk About What They Do, How They Do It, and What It Does to Them.* New York: Villard.

Geertz, Clifford. 1973. *The Interpretation of Cultures.* New York: Basic Books.

Geller, William A. and Sgt Guy Swanger. 1995. *Managing Innovation in Policing: The Untapped Potential of the Middle Manager.* Washington, DC: Police Executive Research Forum.

Goldstein, Herman. 1977. *Policing a Free Society.* Cambridge, Mass. Ballinger.

Goldstein, Herman. 1979. "Improving Policing: A Problem-oriented Approach." *Crime and Delinquency,* 25: 236–58.

Goldstein, Herman. 1990. *Problem-Oriented Policing.* Philadelphia: Temple University Press.

Goldstein, Herman. 1993. *The New Policing: Confronting Complexity.* NIJ Research in Brief. Washington, DC: National Institute of Justice, U. S. Department of Justice.

Greene, Jack R. (Ed.). 1982. *Managing Police Work: Issues and Analysis.* Beverly Hills, London, New Delhi: Sage.

Greene, Jack and Stephen D. Mastrofski. (Eds.). 1988. *Community Policing: Rhetoric or Reality.* New York: Praeger.

Herbert, Steve. 1997. *Policing Space: Territoriality and the Los Angeles Police Department.* Minneapolis: University of Minnesota Press.

Herbert, Steve. 1998. "Police Subculture Reconsidered." *Criminology,* 36: 343–369.

Jefferson, Tony. 1990. *The Case Against Paramilitary Policing.* Philadelphia: Open University Press.

Kanter, Rosabeth Moss. 1983. *The Change Masters: Innovation for Productivity in the American Corporation.* New York: Simon & Schuster.

Kanter, Rosabeth Moss, Barry A. Stein, and Todd D. Jick. 1992. *The Challenge of Organizational Change.* New York: Free Press.

Kappeler, Victor E., Richard Sluder, and Geoffrey P. Alpert. 1994. "Breeding Deviant Conformity: Police Ideology and Culture." *Forces of Deviance: The Dark Side of Policing* by V. Kappeler, R. Sluder, and G. Alpert. Prospect Heights, IL: Waveland Press, 97–121.

Kelling, George L. 1974. *The Kansas City Preventive Patrol Experiment: A Summary Report.* Washington, DC: Police Foundation.

Kelling, George L. and Catherine M. Coles. 1996. *Fixing Broken Windows: Restoring Order and Reducing Crime in Our Communities.* New York: Free Press.

Kraska, Peter and Victor Kappeler. 1997. "Militarizing American Police: The Rise and Normalization of Paramilitary Units." *Social Problems,* 44: 1–18.

Langworthy, Robert. 1986. *The Structure of Police Organizations.* New York: Praeger.

Los Angeles Police Department. 2000. *Report of the Board of Inquiry into the Rampart Area Incident.* Los Angeles: Los Angeles Police Department.

Manning, Peter K. 1977. *Police Work: The Social Organization of Policing.* Cambridge, MA: MIT Press.

Martin, Susan E. 1997. "Women Officers on the Move: An Update on Women in Policing." Pp. 363–384 in *Critical Issues in Policing: Contemporary Readings, 3rd Edition,* edited by Roger G. Dunham and Geoffrey P. Alpert. Prospect Heights, IL: Waveland Press.

Mastrofski, Stephen D., Roger B. Parks, Albert J. Reiss, Jr., Robert E. Worden, Christina DeJong, Jeffrey B. Snipes, and William Terrill. 1998. *Systematic Social Observation of Public Police: Applying Field Research Methods to Policy Issues.* Washington, DC: National Institute of Justice.

Miller, Jerome. 1996. *Search and Destroy: African American Males in the US Criminal Justice System.* London: Cambridge University Press.

Moore, Mark H. 1992. "Problem Solving and Community Policing." In Michael Tonry and Norval Morris (Eds.), *Crime and Justice: An Annual Review.* Chicago: University of Chicago Press, 99–158.

Muir, William Ker, Jr. 1977. *Police: Streetcorner Politicians.* Chicago: University of Chicago Press.

National Institute of Justice. 1992. "Community Policing in Seattle: A Model Partnership Between Citizens and Police," Washington, DC: National Institute of Justice *Research in Brief,* August 1992.

National Institute of Justice. 1995. "Community Policing in Chicago: Year Two," Washington, DC: National Institute of Justice *Research Preview,* October 1995.

Reaves, Brian A. 1996. *Local Police Departments, 1993.* (NCJ-148822) Washington DC: Bureau of Justice Statistics.

Reuss-Ianni, E. 1983. *Two Cultures of Policing.* New Brunswick, NJ: Transaction Books.

Sadd, Susan and Randolph M. Grinc. 1996. "Implementation Challenges in Community Policing" *NIJ Research in Brief,* February 1996.

Sampson, Robert J. and Stephen W. Raudenbush. 1999. "Systematic Social Observation of Public Spaces: A New Look at Disorder in Urban Neighborhoods." *American Journal of Sociology,* 105: 603–651.

Schein, Edgar H. 1992. *Organizational Culture and Leadership.* San Francisco: Jossey-Bass Publishers.

Silverman, Eli B. 1999. *NYPD Battles Crime: Innovative Strategies in Policing.* Boston: Northeastern University Press.

Skogan, Wesley. 1990. *Disorder and Decline: Crime and the Spiral of Decay in American Neighborhoods.* New York: Free Press.

Skogan, Wesley G. and Susan M. Hartnett. 1997. *Community Policing, Chicago Style.* New York and Oxford, England: Oxford University Press.

Skogan, Wesley G., Joel F. Knutson, Susan M. Hartnett, Jinha Kim, Jill DuBois, Richard Block, Jennifer T. Comey, Gail Musial, Karla Twedt-Ball, William Toutman, J. Erik Gudell, Emily Keebler, and Justine H. Lovig. 1999. *Community Policing in Chicago, Year Six.* Chicago: Illinois Criminal Justice Information Authority.

Skogan, Wesley G., Arthur J. Lurigio, Susan M. Hartnett, Richard Block, Jill DuBois, Dennis P. Rosenbaum, Justine H. Lovig, Robert Jessen, Marianne Kaiser, Aaron Bicknese, Jennifer T. Comey, Wuyi Wang, Archon Fung, Alexander Young, Jinney Smith, Raj C. Udeshi, and Susan F. Bennett. 1997. *Community Policing in Chicago, Year Four.* Chicago: Illinois Criminal Justice Information Authority.

Skolnick, Jerome. 1966. *Justice Without Trial: Law Enforcement in a Democratic Society.* New York: Macmillan.

Skolnick, Jerome H. and James J. Fyfe. 1994. *Above the Law: Police and the Excessive Use of Force.* New York: Free Press.

Sparrow, Malcolm K., Mark H. Moore, and David M. Kennedy. 1990. *Beyond 911: A New Era for Policing.* New York: Basic Books.

Toch, Hans and Douglas Grant. 1991. *Police as Problem Solvers.* New York: Plenum Press.

Trojanowicz, Robert C., and Michigan State University. School of Criminal Justice. 1982. An evaluation of the Neighborhood Foot Patrol Program in Flint, Michigan. East Lansing: Michigan State University.

U.S. Department of Justice. 1994. *Understanding Community Policing: A Framework for Action.* Bureau of Justice Assistance monograph, August 1994.

Van Maanen, John. 1978. "The Asshole." In Peter Manning and John Van Maanen (Eds.), *Policing: A View From the Street.* Santa Monica, CA: Goodyear, 231–238.

Wambaugh, Joseph. 1975. *The Choirboys.* New York: Dell.

Wilson, James Q. 1989. *Bureaucracy: What Government Agencies Do and Why They Do It*. New York: Basic Books.

Wilson, James Q. 1968. *Varieties of Police Behavior*. Cambridge, MA: Harvard University Press.

Wilson, James, Q. and George L. Kelling. 1982. "Police and Neighborhood Safety: Broken Windows." *The Atlantic Monthly*, March: 29–38.

Wood, Richard L., Amelia Rouse, and Mariah Davis. 1999. *Transitions: Creating a Culture of Community Policing*. Final report to the National Institute of Justice, U.S. Department of Justice.

PART IV

Can It Work?

7

Community Policing
and Problem Solving

NICK TILLEY

Both community policing and problem-oriented policing are widely espoused. They are also often assumed to comprise complementary developments. This chapter tries to spell out clearly and explicitly how the relationship between them should be understood. It addresses two main questions. First, if there is commitment to community policing, what does this mean for the use of problem-oriented policing? Second, if there is commitment to problem-oriented policing, what does this mean for the use of community policing? The chapter begins by looking at ways problem-oriented policing has been drawn into community policing. It goes on to look at ways community policing has been drawn into problem solving. It then considers what has been achieved at the intersection of community and problem-oriented policing, in particular in the United Kingdom. Finally, it argues that potential achievements of problem-oriented policing may have been reduced through its overidentification with community policing.

COMMUNITY POLICING
AND PROBLEM-ORIENTED POLICING

Let us take community policing first, to look at its affinities with problem-oriented policing. A major impetus for advocating community policing in both the United States and Britain was a sense that policing had become detached from the community that it is supposed to serve, most particularly disadvantaged and alienated sections of it (Sherman, 1997; Rosenbaum, 1998). Patrol in motor cars, prioritizing detection and enforcement, and a conception of policing as professional activity in the service of the criminal justice system had all contributed to policing of criminals, rather than policing with and for the community. There had been a retreat from Sir Robert Peel's account of the object of policing as "the prevention of crime" and "preservation of public tranquillity" through work with citizens (cited in Reith, 1956: 135). There had been a growing distance between police and community. In Britain this manifested itself dramatically in Brixton, where the police in effect did battle with the Black community. The police had lost touch, and the Scarman report on the

Brixton riots advocated much greater community consultation and involvement (Scarman, 1981).

The call to community policing is in this sense a modern call to a traditional mission. The police are part of the community and the community is part of the police; the community has responsibilities to help the police as the police have responsibilities to work with the community. There is mutual accountability to address a common, agreed set of goals.

Some of the grounds for community policing have also been more broadly political and ideological. These have had to do with what is considered the proper relationship between bodies with authority and local communities. In a democratic society the idea is that policing should reflect community priorities. There should then be joint efforts to address agreed-on problems, be they to do with disorder or anxieties about safety and security. The police in particular and public authorities more generally are the worse for being distant from those served.

Though community policing has obvious appeal, it is hard to pin down. Notions of community and community policing are notoriously slippery (Eck and Rosenbaum, 1994). The community of community policing can be construed in various ways. Stephen Mastrofski suggests a sociological account where he refers to "a we-ness" derived from shared experience and interaction" (Mastrofski, 1988: 49). George Kelling and Mark Moore refer to communities as much larger entities, where they say that the problem-oriented approach to policing has been tested in several communities: Madison, Wisconsin; Baltimore County, Maryland; and Newport News, Virginia (Kelling and Moore, 1988: 19). In practice, however, the community of community policing appears almost invariably to relate to neighborhood. Indeed, Mastrofski himself refers to neighborhood as the potential community base for community policing, while highlighting difficulties of doing so (Mastrofski, 1988: 49–53). In Britain, community policing is largely the preserve of community beat officers, responsible for community relations in a small, defined geographical patch. This patch will not necessarily fit with Mastrofski's sociological account of community, many having been defined for administrative purposes.

Although the recent stimulus for community policing may have had to do with issues of agency legitimacy, community policing is also expected to yield real outcome benefits. There should be some practical payoffs. More offenders will be caught, people's sense of security will be improved, and there will be less disorder. This explains the affinity of community policing to problem-oriented policing, because problem-oriented policing is about devising responses that have a real impact on problems.

The association of community policing with problem solving is found both in the work of policing scholars and in police agencies. As David Bayley puts it:

> I shall refer to the new crime prevention strategies as CAMPS.
> Consultation, adaptation, mobilization and problem solving are what I
> shall be referring to from now on when I use the phrase "community
> policing." (Bayley, 1994: 105)

As Wesley G. Skogan and Susan Hartnett also say,

> Community policing . . . assumes a commitment to broadly focused problem-oriented policing and requires that police be responsive to citizens' demands when they decide what local problems are and set their priorities. It also implies a commitment to helping neighborhoods solve crime problems on their own, through community organizations and crime prevention programs. (Skogan and Hartnett, 1997: 5).

Many police departments have Web sites where the underlying approach of the agency is described. References to community policing have been commonplace, with problem solving normally described as one of its components. For example, the Web site for the Colonie, New York Police Department (population 80,000, and "a wonderful place to live" according to the site) noted in 2000 that "a subset of Community Policing is called Problem Oriented Policing" (http://www.colonie.org/police/commpolice 2000). Burnsville, Minnesota, went as far to state that "Another name for Community Oriented Policing (COP) is Problem-Oriented Policing (POP)" (*http://www.safenet.org/burnsville/cop* 2000).

When director of the U.S. Department of Justice's COPS Office in 2000, Thomas Frazier (who had also previously been chief of the Baltimore Police Department) tried to spell out what was involved in community policing. He wrote about "a law enforcement department and law abiding citizens work(ing) together (in neighborhoods) to:

1. Arrest offenders
2. Prevent crime
3. Solve ongoing problems, and
4. Improve the overall quality of life" (Frazier, 2000).

With regard to solving ongoing problems, Frazier refers to "police and citizens partnering to implement strategies that provide long term solutions." He adds that "community oriented policing stimulates creative solutions to crime problems—solutions that begin in neighborhoods." He even suggests that "the natural course of community oriented policing will lead to community oriented government . . . bring(ing) together government agencies, neighborhood associations, business communities and value based organizations to ensure safe and productive neighborhoods."

The nature of problem solving in community policing reflects the philosophy of community policing. Its ends, means, actors, and measures are neighborhood based. The local community (or at any rate the law-abiding side of it) identifies the problems, interprets them in terms of neighborhood malfunctions or malpractices, works through a strategy to address those problems, and either implements them directly or applies pressure on those competent to act. The police are partly catalysts to this process, partly collaborators, and partly advisers. Other agencies may be involved routinely or may be drawn in to participate for a particular purpose. It is in these ways that community policing is drawn to problem-oriented policing. Community policing without problem solving would be merely expressive and ideological. Problem solving gives it a purpose with a practical payoff. Problem solving is also a vehicle through which the police may develop a constructive, trusting relationship with citizens.

PROBLEM-ORIENTED POLICING
AND COMMUNITY POLICING

We turn now to problem-oriented policing and its relationship to community policing. As with community policing, problem-oriented policing comes in a variety of shapes and sizes. Its chief architect is, however, Herman Goldstein, and practical developments as well as academic discussion normally begin with his work (Goldstein, 1979, 1990).

Goldstein's complaint about policing was that it had lost sight of what it was there to do: to deal "with the substantive problems that the public looks to the police to handle" (Goldstein 1990: 1). He notes that "our society requires the police to deal with an incredibly broad range of troublesome situations" (p. 1). Goldstein's 1979 article introducing problem-oriented policing begins with a news report of an English bus service, where the driver, in the interests of keeping to his timetable, could not spare the time to pick up customers. The procedural need to keep to time conflicted with the substantive purpose of transporting passengers. The moral for problem-oriented policing is that services need to be provided to meet public needs. Circumstances change and modes of meeting need must adapt. Increasing calls for service had led the police to rush round, like the bus driver, ritually showing up but doing nothing of any use to the members of the public and the difficulties that had led them to make their calls. Response policing, driven by 999 (United Kingdom) or 911 (United States) calls was professional in that what was done accorded with formal requirements, but ineffective and pointless in that the concerns behind the calls were not addressed.

Problem-oriented policing comprises a call to the police to address the substantive problems that lie behind calls for service. It requires the police to look beyond their traditional repertoire of responses—principally, enforcement and use of the criminal justice system—to find more imaginative and effective ways of addressing the source of the calls coming in to them.

There are a number of implications of adopting problem-oriented policing. One is that the police accept that their business includes diverse concerns that the public brings to them, remembering that only a small fraction of calls for service are directly crime related (in Britain the figure stands at 20 percent to 30 percent; see Leigh, Read, and Tilley, 1996; Read et al., 1999). Moreover, accepting that many noncrime issues constitute police business means not only logging them but addressing them too.

A second implication is that police adopt a reflective, analytic approach to the problems faced. To deal with the source of problems, their interconnected-

ness with one another needs to be identified. Moreover, this interconnected-
ness will best be grasped by looking at the conditions generating the problems
with a view to finding one or more points of potential leverage where a practical preventive intervention can be made.

A third implication is that the police will be unable to act entirely in isolation. The police, of course, have some coercive powers granted them
through the criminal justice system, and they use these as their conventional
stock in trade. They also have powers of persuasion that they can use
directly, for example, making requests, giving advice, and issuing instruc-
tions. Where insufficient to motivate change, these may, however, have to be
supplemented through work with third parties to effect interventions leveraging change where the police lack the capacity to implement solutions
directly.

Finally, the criterion of success in problem-oriented policing is effectiveness in (ethically) addressing the issues the public legitimately bring to the
police. That is what policing is deemed to be about (Goldstein, 1977).

How does this fit with community policing? It does so in six ways:

1. Community policing is not restricted to interest in crime so a policing
   approach mandating concerns with noncrime issues appears to fit with it.

2. Problem-oriented policing offers purpose and direction to community
   policing, which has often appeared largely to be more concerned with
   public relations than with having a real impact (see Goldstein, 1990: 23).

3. Many problems manifest themselves most clearly in neighborhoods.
   Indeed, even before the advent of GIS systems, pin maps tended to show
   in which areas crimes and calls for service were concentrated. Problem-
   oriented policing in this sense naturally turns attention to neighborhoods
   and their difficulties.

4. The origins and reproduction of some problems can best be understood
   in relation to local community dynamics (Wilson and Kelling, 1982;
   Skogan, 1990; Sampson, Raudenbush, and Earls, 1997).

5. Members of the community often have an immediate grasp of the nature
   and source of their problems that police officers lack.

6. Some problems may be most realistically addressed through actions with
   or by neighborhood residents.

Note that the connection between problem-oriented and community
policing is a contingent one. Where community policing is already in place, a
problem orientation may give it direction and help it more effectively address
local problems. Moreover, in only some cases will problems most appropriately
be understood and addressed in neighborhood terms. Thus, the introduction of
problem-oriented policing into a police organization may make use of and
inform its community units, if it has them, as well as its other units. In addressing specific problems it may sometimes make sense to interpret what is going
on and to implement measures on a neighborhood basis. Indeed, Goldstein
himself stresses the benefits of "enlisting the citizenry" (Goldstein, 1990: 24),

but he advocates doing so for specific problem-solving purposes rather than for "amorphous efforts" to develop new relationships.

Goldstein (1990) recognizes that the bases of communities vary. Some areas are fractured. In some there is genuine conflict over the use of public space. The local resident population may be poorly placed to address the problems facing them, especially those in areas with chronic and deep-rooted difficulties. The non-law-abiding citizenry may be important in reducing and containing problems as well as the law-abiding citizenry. The neighborhood will often, of course, constitute a context or resource in problem-oriented policing. Problem-oriented policing, however, does not entail community policing in the strong, Frazier sense. It is not, at heart, about redefining the relationship between public service and communities to decrease the distance between the two.

Problem-oriented policing is about addressing more effectively the issues of public concern that the police are asked to deal with. It is also about more efficient use of resources, where ritual attendance to incidents has failed adequately to resolve them, allowing repeats to occur, which create further calls on police time. Problem-oriented policing in this sense is about breaking the vicious circle of increasing demand for response to incidents and diminishing time for preventive attention to them. Ironically, however, though problem-oriented policing addresses issues of effectiveness and efficiency it emphatically does not provide an endorsement for new public management methods of trying to achieve them. The presently modish target setting, monitoring, and comparative performance indicators are anathema because their tendency is to steer the police toward centrally specified activity and objectives rather than problems as they emerge from the various publics served by the police. Performance indicators often introduce those perverse incentives Goldstein mocked at the start of his 1979 paper, in his discussion of British bus services (see Tilley, 1995).

THE CONJUNCTION
OF COMMUNITY POLICING
AND PROBLEM-ORIENTED POLICING

Though they are different in ways outlined so far in this paper, there is some common space between community policing and problem-oriented policing. In Britain, most problem solving took place in this space in one of the few demonstration projects attempting to introduce problem-oriented policing (Leigh, Read, and Tilley, 1996, 1998). It appears also that in the United States a great deal of police agency problem-oriented effort has been made in the context of attempts to implement community policing. In other words much if not most problem-oriented policing on the ground has been developed and delivered in a community policing context.

How has problem orientation fared in practice in its community policing setting? The short answer is "not very well!" Wesley G. Skogan and his colleagues do most in the United States to document problem solving in the context of a massive effort to bring community policing to Chicago (Skogan and Hartnett, 1997). The findings are not all doom and gloom. They do indicate, however, serious weaknesses in what has been delivered. They reveal difficulties in implementation, even where there is clear central commitment to the introduction of community policing with a strong problem-oriented dimension.

Skogan et al. (1999) document the enormous efforts to mobilize, train, and empower police, community and city agencies in the service of beat-based community (crime and noncrime) problem solving. They describe the aspiration to introduce systematic means of problem solving, with steps including problem identification and prioritization, problem analysis, strategy design, implementation, and effectiveness evaluation.

Skogan et al. (1999) find that community problem solving is strongest in communities that have least need of it, that is, in better off, better organized, ethnically homogenous neighborhoods, with better housing, more stable family patterns, and fewer problems. Poorer, more diverse, more divided communities with more problems tend to have a lower capacity for problem solving. There was substantial resistance by the police to involvement in community problem solving. The police were less convinced that the police and citizens could work fruitfully together to solve problems than were members of local communities (Skogan et al., 1999: 121).

Energetic problem solving with the community turned on strong leadership, strong management, and the efforts of exceptional, committed officers (Skogan et al., 2000). In spite of massive implementation efforts, just a quarter of the beats were deemed to be performing very well, whereas another quarter had failed to implement much problem solving. Half were somewhere in between. Skogan et al. concede, furthermore, that the problem solving conducted is unlikely to address the fundamental root causes of community problems and will function at best as a "band aid" (Skogan et al., 1999: 55).

In Britain the most extensively documented (even if not the most elaborate) effort to implement problem-oriented policing attempted to do so through community beat officers, that is, those officers attached permanently to local, geographic areas (see Leigh, Read, and Tilley, 1996, 1998). This attempt to introduce community-based, problem-oriented policing took place in Leicestershire, which was chosen as the site for a demonstration project because it seemed to offer good conditions for it. The force had a history of involvement in innovation.

East Area, where the initiative took place, had reorganized into local policing units. These local policing units were subdivided into smaller beats to make community liaison and problem solving more manageable. East Area also had an energetic commander, Steve Brookes, who was committed to problem-oriented community policing. Brookes had initiated local action groups throughout East Area. These comprised teams of beat officers and members of the community, who were supposed to work together on local problems. The boundaries for the beats and local action groups were drawn around what were deemed natural neighborhood-based communities. Problem-oriented policing was initially introduced to three of the five local policing units in East Area, covering a range of community types: urban and rural, high crime and low crime, and ethnically mixed and predominantly White. The idea was to roll the community-based problem-oriented policing out once the initial implementation hitches had been sorted out.

Beat officers, their supervisors, and senior officers were trained in the SARA process that had been developed in the American Newport News demonstration project introducing problem-oriented policing (Eck and Spelman, 1987). The officers were encouraged to use the problem analysis triangle (PAT) to make sense of problems by looking at significant features of location, offender, and victim in ways that can be associated with routine activities theory (Cohen and Felson, 1979; Felson, 1998). Software was developed (INSIGHT) giving officers the opportunity to analyze calls for service data. Forms were developed that were intended both to help structure problem-solving efforts and to keep a record of what was being implemented and achieved so that lessons could be learned.

The working assumption in the community-based problem-oriented policing in Leicestershire was that among community beat officers and local neighborhood residents there was a good deal of latent talent and goodwill that had only to be released for problem-oriented policing to flourish. Officers would be keen to address problems if given the space and responsibility to do so. Communities would cooperate with the police in identifying, thinking through, and implementing responses to their own problems. Moreover, once areas that had not benefited from the introduction of problem-oriented policing saw what was being achieved they would also be keen to become involved.

In the event there were many disappointments. Although many officers were sympathetic, a large number were cynical. The latter saw problem-oriented policing as faddish nonsense. Only a minority of officers became committed to it in practice. Less than a quarter of the officers involved in the initiative (ten of forty-two) submitted over half (56 percent of 169) of the forms recording problem-solving efforts. Officers resented completing forms describing what they did in problem-solving terms and only filled them in when strong pressure was put on them to do so. When that pressure was applied the supposed problem-oriented efforts reported were often standard police responses dressed up in SARA terms to meet administrative requirements. Just more than two-fifths (42 percent) lacked any indication of the nature of the problem being addressed.

Although the provision of analyzable incident data was welcomed, little constructive use was made of them. Moreover, the traditional policing obsession with recency led to complaints that the data were out of date, if going back more than a few days. Responses tended to fall back on traditional policing methods concerned with enforcement: 60 percent were offender focused, compared with 22 percent and 18 percent, which targeted victims and locations, respectively.

The Leicestershire initiative was followed closely by the introduction of problem-oriented policing in Cleveland, whose progress was also tracked

(Leigh, Read, and Tilley, 1998). In Cleveland problem-oriented policing was considered a whole-force matter from the start, rather than confined to one area. All staff (including civilians as well as officers) were trained in problem-oriented policing, not just the specialist community beat officers where most of the work was initially to be focused. The leadership of the force was enthusiastic and vocal in its support of problem-oriented policing within and outside the service. Their commitment within was made manifest by the fact that they opened 88 percent of the 188 training sessions that were run. As with the Leicester initiative, Cleveland too tried to track and structure problem solving with the use of systematic records.

A review of what was actually delivered in the first 180 completed initiatives across Leicestershire's East Area and throughout Cleveland during their efforts to implement problem-oriented policing found that police-led actions were the most common. Of the problem-solving cases, 40 percent involved patrol, observations, surveillance, warrants, arrests, and warnings. With regard to working with others, the police worked entirely alone in only about a third of cases, but local resident involvement was found in only 13 percent of the initiatives (Leigh, Read, and Tilley, 1998).

Notwithstanding the weaknesses, some sensible but modest problem solving was undertaken, though even this was isolated. One example involved digging ditches around an area suffering a spate of poaching incidents to make life more difficult for the poachers. Another involved the introduction of earlier deliveries to traders in a market town with narrow streets that became seriously congested when large trucks stopped to unload during the rush hour.

The most impressive single piece of work addressed problems in Northfields, a neighborhood of 1,250 houses that had been regularly referred to by the local newspaper as a problem housing estate for at least twenty years. Specific problems included high-crime levels, rapid tenant turnover, intimidation of incoming residents, widespread graffiti, rubbish dumping, large numbers of vacant houses, and drug dealing. Efforts were made to find the sources of these problems; a two-year strategy was developed to address them; and a range of situational, social, and enforcement measures was put in place, involving residents as well as other agencies. In the first year crime overall fell by 29 percent (1,903 to 1,347 incidents), house burglaries by 30 percent (391 to 273), commercial burglaries by 40 percent (283 to 168), and auto-related crime by 47 percent (382 to 201). It is not possible, of course, to be certain what would have happened without the project, but the consistency and scale of these changes suggest that something significant had happened. The initiative was headed by an exceptional police inspector who hand-picked his team to include officers who had the attributes he felt were needed. The inspector devoted enormous energy and personal commitment to the project. He was a local man who spoke the local dialect. This officer has now been promoted. The impetus for maintaining the work in Northfields is ongoing. It is not certain that enough had yet been achieved to make the improvements self-sustaining.

The experience of efforts to introduce problem-oriented policing in Britain in Leicestershire and Cleveland suggest that community-based problem-oriented policing needs more to promote and sustain it than training, data, and the release of existing capacity. Cultural change is needed, too. Some existing officers appeared to be incapable of or fundamentally unsuited to the work (several were eventually moved in Leicestershire for this reason). Moreover, direction was needed by senior officers to focus work. Involving members of the community looked promising, but was rarely achieved in practice. There were examples of systematic, imaginative, well-evidenced work where the police successfully worked with other agencies and the community to overcome problems, but they were patchy and tended to depend on the special attributes of exceptional people. They were not routine and self-sustaining. These findings seem to square well with those from North America.

In practice, in Britain in spite of the difficulties encountered in efforts to implement problem-oriented policing, it has been almost universally endorsed (Read and Tilley, 2000). Her Majesty's Inspectorate of Constabulary (1998), The Audit Commission (1999), the Crime and Disorder Act (1998), and the Crime Reduction Program (1999–2002) all steer toward problem orientation both by the police and by local crime and disorder partnerships, which were put on a statutory footing in the Crime and Disorder Act.

PROBLEM SOLVING BEYOND COMMUNITY POLICING: SOME BRITISH REFLECTIONS

There are criminological, technical, political and organizational, and cognitive reasons for associating problem solving with neighborhoods and therefore with community policing, some of which have already been mentioned. The criminological reasons have to do with the finding that problems concentrate unevenly in space, high-crime-rate areas being associated with low levels of informal social control, significant signs of disorder, the departure of more stable and arrival of less stable residents, and declining investment in the economic infrastructure. The technical reasons have to do with the increasing facility for spatial analysis, with the explosion in use of geographical information systems and the ease with which crime concentrations can be presented dramatically on maps (see Groff and LaVigne, 2002). The political and organizational reasons have to do with the way responsibilities for local government and policing are geographically based. The cognitive reasons have to do with the knowledge people might be expected to have of their local patches, and their potential to act differently there in ways germane to the production and reproduction of problems.

What, then, are the limitations of problem-oriented policing focused on neighborhoods? Following Eck and Rosenbaum's (1994) useful earlier discussion, these can be put under headings of effectiveness, equity, and efficiency.

Effectiveness

There are all sorts of problems in evaluating community policing as a whole. It may be, as Bayley (1994) argues, that "the success of community policing will never be evaluated." It is too fuzzy a concept and too variable in its interpretation and implementation. If community policing is outcome effective in

Table 7.1 Relative Risks of Domestic Burglary by Household Attribute

Household Attribute	Relative Risk
Head of household 16–24	2.71
Home has no security measures	2.71
Home in an area with high levels of physical disorder	2.14
One adult living with children	2.00
Head of household is unemployed	1.80
Respondent resident for less than one year	1.75
Head of household is single	1.73
Home is privately rented	1.73
Head of household is separated	1.63
Household is not insured against theft	1.54
Home in inner city	1.52
Household income is under £5k per year	1.48
Home in a council estate area	1.45
Household has no car	1.38
Head of household is divorced	1.38
Respondent is Afro-Caribbean	1.34
Unoccupied overnight for more than one month in previous year	1.29
Terraced houses	1.18
Home on main road	1.18
Home left empty during weekdays for 5+ hours on average	1.11
All households	1.00

SOURCE: British Crime Survey data, derived from Budd (1999).

what it delivers, that should be revealed in its problem-solving successes. The quality of assessments of what has been achieved though, is generally poor (Rosenbaum, 1998; Read and Tilley, 2000), and results are mixed where evaluations are competent (Skogan, 1994). The argument to be developed here is that pitching problem solving at the neighborhood level misunderstands many problems and communities and risks missing many preventive opportunities. Moreover, much of the most successful problem-oriented work has occurred independently of community policing.

Problems associated with calls to the police are patterned not only by neighborhood. They can be aggregated in other ways and may be so for problem-oriented-policing purposes. Table 7.1, for example, shows relative risk rates for domestic burglary among subgroups in the United Kingdom. Neighborhood is not the only source of variation in risk.

The growing literature on repeat victimization shows that crime problems recur for individuals, households, and businesses (see Farrell, 1995; Farrell and Pease, 1993, 2001; Pease, 1998). Although rates of repeats seem to be highest in high-crime neighborhoods (Trickett et al., 1992), they are also high in low-crime areas. Table 7.2 refers to crime concentrations—number of incidents per victim over a twelve-month period, as measured by the British Crime Survey.

Table 7.2 Levels of Actual and Expected Concentration for Domestic Burglary, Vehicle-Related Crime, and Contact Crime by Residence Type

Incident and Area Type	Expected Concentration	Actual Concentration	Ratio of Actual to Expected Concentration
Domestic Burglary			
Rural	1.02	1.20	1.18
Urban	1.04	1.22	1.17
Inner city	1.07	1.34	1.25
Vehicle-Related Crime			
Rural	1.13	1.60	1.42
Urban	1.15	1.37	1.19
Inner city	1.22	1.58	1.29
Contact Crime			
Rural	1.02	1.50	1.47
Urban	1.05	1.60	1.52
Inner city	1.09	2.35	2.16

SOURCE: Reanalyzed BCS data from Mirrlees-Black (1997).

The expected concentration is the rate that would be expected were one incident not to be associated with heightened risk of another. The ratio of actual to expected concentration shows the rate at which repeats exceed or fall below the expected. It can be seen that across community types and offense types the ratio is higher than expected. Relatively low-crime, rural areas have levels of concentration not markedly lower than urban areas and exceed the expected rate by similar and in some cases higher degrees.

Even within neighborhoods rates of crime vary widely. Table 7.3 shows rates within one small, high-crime area in London (see Curtin et al., 2001). Moreover, here the high-rate enumeration districts tended to be those housing the better off in the area.

Many popular methods of dealing with crime are not effective. There is no reason to expect local residents to be able to judge what will be effective in dealing with their problems. Local residents may have conjectures about crime patterns, but assuming them to be true rather that trying to test them and work on what is empirically substantiated clearly risks the development of initiatives based on false premises. In the London area referred to in Table 7.3, which has been a site for government-funded burglary-reduction efforts, many local conjectures were mistaken. For example, local residents understood the problems to be concentrated in the poorer public housing in the area, but they were not.

Recent Home Office work has identified students as a virtual community experiencing high rates of burglary (in Britain most university students live away from home) (Tilley et al., 1999; Hopkins and Tilley, 2002). There is some, though less robust, evidence that they also suffer high rates of street robbery. Students tend to live in particular areas, not in a single neighborhood. They are also in but normally not of the local community. Their high rates of victimization are not hard to understand. They arrive at university with those lightweight consumer durables preferred by domestic burglars. They live in cheap

Table 7.3 Distribution of Domestic Burglaries and Combined Burglary
Rate by Enumeration District, High Overall Burglary Area in London

Enumeration District	Households	Burglaries	Rate per 1,000 Households over 31 Months
01ACFE01	181	67	370
01ACFE06	205	60	293
01ACFE10	169	41	243
01ACFE04	180	38	211
01ACFE03	228	46	202
01ACFE07	190	29	153
01ACFE12 (part)	188	24	128
01ACFE09	217	23	106
01ACFE02	206	16	78
01ACFE05	220	16	73
01ACFE14 (part)	206	15	73[a]
01ACFE08	186	10	54
01ACFE11	218	5	23
TOTAL	2,594	390	150

[a]Burglaries cover only part of the Enumeration District, the rate is therefore underestimated.

rented accommodation, close to many of those most liable to be involved in crime. Their landlords have little interest in providing secure accommodation. The students lack much security consciousness. The students are also out a lot, carrying small amounts of cash and credit cards, which makes them readily available to street robbers. Students exist as a community at risk but not in terms of common neighborhood residence. They lack common interests and do not associate with other, nonstudent residents in the neighborhoods in which they live.

Neighborhood-based community problem solving will miss students as a relevant community. It may also miss other possible virtual communities: women experiencing domestic violence, isolated members of ethnic minorities experiencing racial harassment, convenience stores experiencing armed robbery, tourists experiencing theft from cars, and so on.

For effective, targeted problem solving, though the neighborhood is far from irrelevant its relevance is a contingent matter. Problems may be better specified for problem-solving purposes using different forms of aggregation.

Much tested problem-oriented work that has been found to be effective in practice seems to have occurred independently of community policing, even where members of the community have played a part in the response. For example, successful efforts to reduce repeat victimization in Britain have involved some mobilization of neighbors to attend specifically to the risk faced by victims, but have not sprung from the neighborhood nor have they been construed as neighborhood problems. This is as true for the work in relation to domestic burglary (Forrester et al, Forrester et al., 1988; 1990; Anderson, Chenery, and Pease, 1995; Chenery, Holt, and Pease, 1997) as it is for the work on domestic violence (Hanmer, Griffiths and Jerwood, 1999). Another example comprises the well-known Boston efforts to reduce gun-related violence through Operation Ceasefire. These may to some degree have worked through social networks, but the networks did not comprise communities as neighborhoods (Braga, Kennedy, and Piehl, 1999). They were certainly not law abiding! The community structure of the gang in Boston was used to communicate more effectively the crackdown responses from agencies that could be expected following shootings. The gang was not engaged in joint problem identification, analysis, or strategy development. A third example comprises work in a district of Charlotte Mecklenburg to reduce theft of kitchen appliances at construction sites. Here, delays in builders' installation of the appliances until resident occupation effected a substantial fall in rates (Clarke and Goldstein, 2002). Neither the builders nor local residents took part in the problem identification, analysis, or strategy development. Effective non-neighborhood-generated problem-oriented work is certainly possible. It is clear too that this involves understanding patterns in more ways than their concentration in particular geographic areas.

There is a growing literature on the successes of situational crime prevention (Clarke, 1995), whose approach is similar to problem-oriented policing, even if concentrating more fully on opportunity-reduction techniques for dealing with problems (Tilley, 1999). Situational crime prevention seldom if ever uses the neighborhood as its unit of analysis. Although neighborhood problem orientation does seem to have had some success, as in Leicester's Northfields, substantial examples do not seem to be numerous. Moreover there are plenty of examples of apparently successful non-neighborhood-focused problem-oriented policing. When it comes to effectiveness the neighborhood is limited as a focus for problem-oriented policing. There are more and different ways of doing problem-oriented work that can be and have been effective.

Equity

Equity refers to fairness or social justice. It has to do with the distribution of resources in relation to need. There are distributive goods and distributive ills. Crime is a distributive ill. Social justice, other things being equal, is improved by reducing the problems of those with more than their fair share.

More needy communities theoretically should receive greater resources than less needy communities, where problem solving is associated with community policing. This would happen if efforts were driven by robust data on problem distribution. In practice, however, better off communities are liable to get more than their fair share of resources because they are more vocal, have greater problem-solving capacities, and are more able to exert leverage.

A "community heal thyself" approach may sound empowering but may not be a realistic route to improved social justice, especially in the most deprived, fractured areas suffering multiple problems. There can also be an element of neighborhood blaming in community problem-oriented policing. It is the neighborhood's problem, and it is for them to solve it, even if in partnership with other agencies. Middle-class communities, when problems do threaten, are able to buy in private solutions (e.g., by installing physical measures or by employing security staff) or to apply pressure on public services to make provisions. It is not clear that they will form those grassroots means of self-management that are often called for in community policing.

Within neighborhoods, many problems are experienced individually or, as shown in Table 7.3, in very small patches rather than by the beat size communities normally dealt with in Britain. Beats vary in size but tend to comprise roughly 2,000 households. Within neighborhood units of that size, there are pockets of high- and low-problem levels. In addition, in low-crime areas there are often high-crime pockets. The phenomenon of repeat victimization shows the concentration of problems on individuals and particular addresses. Neighborhood-focused problem solving, insofar as it addresses need variation, does so at the level of an administratively defined unit of disparity and service delivery. This does violence to the variation of levels of need at more micro levels, ultimately being experienced by individuals and households. It misses some with high need and allocates effort to some with low need.

Lodging problem-oriented policing only as part of community policing will not deliver equitable policing. Problem orientation needs to look beyond the community as a unit of action, analysis, and intervention.

Efficiency

Efficiency has to do with the relative costs of delivering a particular service or achieving a particular outcome (see Roman and Farrell, 2002). Relative outcome efficiency is difficult to measure. It requires robust measurements of the counterfactual (the problem rate in the absence of the intervention), the costs of the problem, and the costs of the intervention. Problems occur in each of these. Establishing the counterfactual is notoriously difficult and contestable even where random allocation is used (see Pawson and Tilley, 1997). Problem costs are tricky to estimate, especially where they are nonfinancial (see Adams, 1995, for a critique of means of attaching sums of money to nonfinancial costs). Initiative costs are probably most simply estimated, but there are contestable conventions in dealing with volunteer inputs, which are often significant in community-based problem solving. The author knows of no fully convincing outcome-focused efficiency measurements for community policing or problem solving in Britain. Discussion of efficiency in problem solving and community policing is therefore speculative and confined here to general principles.

The argument in favor of problem-oriented policing is that grouping incidents and identifying common conditions for them is likely to be more efficient and more effective than dealing with them individually. Confining problem-oriented policing to neighborhoods is apt to shape analysis and intervention only to neighborhoods and their resources. A recent review of problem-oriented policing in Britain (Read and Tilley, 2000) finds that problem solving was indeed generally confined to local neighborhoods, though problems recurred across them. For example, fuel drive-offs and thefts from cars in hotel parking lots were widespread but addressed serially by individual location. Problem-oriented work transcending areas but dealing with a common problem source is presumably more efficient than conducting a series of local problem-solving efforts for each neighborhood. In Britain, for example, it is fairly obvious that the removal of cash prepayment meters for utilities found in council houses to reduce the high burglary rates with which they were associated was more efficient than a series of estate-by-estate efforts (see Laycock and Tilley, 1995a).

CONCLUSION

Both community policing and problem-oriented policing are in difficulty, if not in crisis. Each developed in response to a different problem. Each began with great optimism about what might be achieved. Each seems to have captured the imagination and commitment of significant numbers of police officers and whole police departments. Each has experienced serious implementation obstacles.

Community policing has tended to take off most successfully where least needed—in low-crime, low-disorder areas. It has been slow to deliver measurable benefits overall. British evaluations of the outcome effectiveness of its specific measures, such as neighborhood watch and contact patrols, produce disappointing findings (Bennett, 1990, 1991, 1994; Laycock and Tilley, 1995b). Traditional response policing has few defenders, though it continues to thrive in terms of officer time and effort made.

Problem-oriented policing has been fragile. Its local implementation has turned on exceptional individuals and has not often survived their departure. Most of what has been delivered has been small scale and at the level of the neighborhood, often an extension of response policing rather than a fundamental alternative to it. The evaluation of problem-oriented policing as a whole scarcely makes sense. It is like trying to test whether scientific method works. Moreover, problem-oriented policing is just too disparate to be treated as a single entity. Evaluations of individual problem-oriented policing efforts, even though evaluation is deemed a key component, are thin on the ground and rarely convincing in their findings.

Why the disappointments? Are problem-oriented policing and community policing just too difficult to do? Are they beyond the capacity of individual police officers or police agencies? Are the political environments in which efforts to insert them are made too inhospitable to allow them to thrive? Are the police traditions so well embedded that new methods are continually undermined in practice? Are public expectations of the police inconsistent with moves away from response policing? There may be something in all of these.

The main argument of this chapter, however, is that problem-oriented policing has suffered by being yoked to neighborhood-based community policing. There are, of course, conditions in which local neighborhood dynamics are responsible for problems and where emergent neighborhood organizations can play a significant part in helping to overcome problems. The police can help facilitate or catalyze changes that are needed in these circumstances. Moreover, some problems that might best be addressed by high-level problem solving might also need to be dealt with as effectively as possible in the interim within the neighborhood. But the tendency to frame and respond to all problems roughly in terms of neighborhood dynamics limits what can be achieved. If the police are to move in the direction of greater effectiveness, equity, and efficiency, one way of doing so might be by separating problem-oriented and community policing and making community policing a contingent vehicle for dealing with only some forms of some problems. Community policing might still be needed for its symbolic value in providing conditions for policing by consent, but that does not mean it is most sensibly the organizing principle for all policing. Moreover, even if community policing were there primarily for its symbolic function, it would not of course follow that it is not well advised to help solving real local problems at the same time.

CITATIONS

Adams, John. 1995. *Risk*. London: UCL Press.

Anderson, David, Sylvia Chenery, and Ken Pease. 1995. *Biting Back: Tackling Repeat Burglary and Car Crime*. Crime Detection and Prevention Series Paper 58. London: Home Office.

Audit Commission. 1999. *Safety in Numbers*. London: Audit Commission.

Bayley, David H. 1994. *Police for the Future*. Oxford, England: Oxford University Press.

Bennett, Trevor. 1990. *Evaluating Neighbourhood Watch*. Aldershot, Great Britain: Gower.

Bennett, Trevor. 1991. "The Effectiveness of a Police Initiated Fear Reducing Strategy." *British Journal of Criminology*, 31: 1–14.

Bennett, Trevor. 1994. "Community Policing on the Ground: Developments in Britain." In Dennis P. Rosenbaum (Ed.), *The Challenge of Community Policing*. Thousand Oaks, CA: Sage, 224–246.

Braga, Anthony A., David M. Kennedy, and Anne M. Piehl. 1999. *Problem Oriented Policing and Youth Violence: An Evaluation of the Boston Gun Project*. Final report submitted to the U.S. National Institute of Justice.

Budd, Tracey. 1999. *Burglary of Domestic Dwellings: Findings from the British Crime Survey*. Home Office Statistical Bulletin 4/99. London: Home Office Research and Statistics Directorate.

Chenery, Sylvia, John Holt, and Ken Pease. 1997. *Biting Back II: Reducing Repeat Victimisation in Huddersfield*. Crime Detection and Prevention Series Paper 82. London: Home Office.

Clarke, Ronald V. (Ed.). 1997. *Situational Crime Prevention: Successful Case Studies*. New York: Harrow & Heston.

Clarke, Ronald V. 1995. "Situational Crime Prevention," in Michael Tonry and David P. Farrington (eds.) *Building a Safer Society: Strategic Approaches to Crime Prevention, Crime and Justice* Vol 19. Chicago: University of Chicago Press, 1995, 91–150.

Clarke, Ronald V. and Herman Goldstein. 2002. "Reducing Theft at Construction Sites: Lessons from a Problem-Oriented Project." In Nick Tilley (Ed.), *Analysis for Crime Prevention*. Crime Prevention Studies, Volume 13. Monsey, NY: Criminal Justice Press, 89–130.

Cohen, Lawrence E. and Felson, Marcus. 1979. "Social Change and Crime Rate Trends: A Routine Activity Approach." *American Sociological Review*, 44: 588–608.

Curtin, Liz, Nick Tilley, Mark Owen, and Ken Pease. 2001. *Developing Crime Prevention Plans: Some Examples from the Burglary Reduction Initiative*. Crime Reduction Research Series Paper 7. London: Home Office.

Eck, John and Dennis P. Rosenbaum. 1994. "The New Police Order: Effectiveness, Equity and Efficiency in Community Policing." in Dennis P. Rosenbaum (Ed.), *The Challenge of Community Policing*. Thousand Oaks, CA: Sage, 3–23.

Eck, John and William Spelman. 1987. *Problem-Solving: Problem-Oriented Policing in Newport News*. Washington, DC: Police Executive Research Forum.

Farrell, Graham. 1995. "Preventing Repeat Victimisation." In Michael Tonry and David P. Farrington (Eds.), *Crime and Justice: An Annual Review*, Volume 19. Chicago: University of Chicago Press, 469–534.

Farrell, Graham and Ken Pease. 1993. *Once Bitten, Twice Bitten: Repeat Victimisation and its Implications for Crime Prevention*. Crime Prevention Unit Paper 46. London: Home Office.

Farrell, Graham and Ken Pease. 2001. (Eds.). *Repeat Victimization*. Crime Prevention Studies, Volume 12. Monsey NY: Crime Prevention Studies.

Felson, Marcus. 1998. *Crime and Everyday Life*. Thousand Oaks, CA: Pine Forge Press.

Forrester, David, Mike Chatterton, and Ken Pease, with the assistance of Robin Brown. 1988. *The Kirkholt Burglary Prevention Project*. Crime Prevention Unit Paper 13. London: Home Office.

Forrester, David, Samantha Frenz, Martin O'Connell, and Ken Pease. 1990. *The Kirkholt Burglary Prevention Project: Phase II*. Crime Prevention Unit Paper 23. London: Home Office.

Frazier, Thomas. 2000. A Definition of Community Policing. At http://www.usdoj.gov/cops/news_info/bg_info/bg_definition.htm.

Goldstein, Herman. 1977. *Policing in a Free Society*. Cambridge, Mass: Ballinger Publishing Co.

Goldstein, Herman. 1979. Improving Policing: A Problem-Oriented Approach. *Crime and Delinquency*, 25: 236–258.

Goldstein, Herman. 1990. *Problem-Oriented Policing*. New York: McGraw-Hill.

Groff, Elizabeth R. and Nancy G. LaVigne. 2002. "Forecasting the Future of Predictive Crime Mapping." In Nick Tilley (Ed.), *Analysis for Crime Prevention*. Crime Prevention Studies, Volume 13. Monsey, NY: Criminal Justice Press, 29–57.

Hanmer, Jalna, Sue Griffiths, and David Jerwood. 1999. *Arresting Evidence: Domestic Violence and Repeat Victimisation*. Police Research Series Paper 104. London: Home Office.

Her Majesty's Inspector of Constabulary. 1998. *Beating Crime*. London: Her Majesty's Inspectorate of Constabulary.

Hopkins, Matt and Nick Tilley. 2002. "Crimes Against Students." Summary note to the Home Office of self-completion victimization surveys at four universities in the East Midlands.

Kelling, George L. and Mark H. Moore. 1988. "From Political to Reform to Community: The Evolving Strategy of Police." In Jack R. Greene and Stephen M. Mastrofski (Eds.), *Community Policing: Rhetoric or Reality*. New York: Praeger, 3–26.

Laycock, Gloria and Nick Tilley. 1995a. "Implementing Crime Prevention." In Michael Tonry and David P. Farrington

(Eds.), *Crime and Justice: An Annual Review,* Volume 19. Chicago: University of Chicago Press, 535–584.

Laycock, Gloria and Nick Tilley. 1995b. *Policing and Neighbourhood Watch: Strategic Issues.* Crime Detection and Prevention Series Paper 60. London: Home Office.

Leigh, Adrian, Tim Read, and Nick Tilley. 1996. *Problem-Oriented Policing: Brit Pop.* Crime Prevention and Detection Series Paper 75. London: Home Office.

Leigh, Adrian, Tim Read, and Nick Tilley. 1998. *Brit Pop II: Problem-Oriented Policing in Practice.* Police Research Series Paper 93. London: Home Office.

Mastrofski, Stephen D. 1988 "Community Policing as Reform: A Cautionary Tale." In Jack R. Greene and Stephen M. Mastrofski (Eds.), *Community Policing: Rhetoric or Reality.* New York: Praeger, 47–68.

Mirrlees-Black, Catriona. 1997. *Rural Areas and Crime: Findings from the British Crime Survey.* Research Findings 77. London: Home Office.

Pawson, Ray and Nick Tilley. 1997. *Realistic Evaluation.* London: Sage.

Pease, Ken. 1998. *Repeat Victimisation: Taking Stock.* Crime Detection and Prevention Paper 90. London: Home Office.

Read, Tim and Nick Tilley. 2000. *Not Rocket Science: Problem-Solving and Crime Reduction.* Crime Reduction Research Series Paper 6. London: Home Office.

Read, Tim, Nick Tilley, Jo White, Michelle Wilson, and Adrian Leigh. 1999. "Repeat Calls for Service and Problem Oriented Policing." *Studies on Crime and Crime Prevention,* 8: 265–279.

Reith, Charles. 1956. *A New Study of Police History.* Edinburgh: Oliver and Boyd.

Roman, John and Graham Farrell. 2002. "Cost-Benefit Analysis and Crime Prevention." In Nick Tilley (Ed.), *Evaluation for Crime Prevention.* Crime Prevention Studies, Volume 14. Monsey, NY: Criminal Justice Press, 53–92.

Rosenbaum, Dennis P. 1998. "The Changing Role of the Police: Assessing the Current Transition to Community Policing." In Jean-Paul Brodeur (Ed.), *How to Recognise Good Policing: Problems and Issues.* Thousand Oaks, CA: Sage, 3–29.

Sampson, Robert J., Stephen W. Raudenbush, and Felton Earls. 1997. "Neighborhoods and Violent Crime: A Multilevel Study of Collective Efficacy." *Science,* 277: 918–924.

Scarman, Lord. 1981. *The Scarman Report: The Brixton Disorders.* Cmnd. 8427. London: HMSO.

Sherman, Lawrence W. 1997. "Policing for Crime Prevention." In Lawrence W. Sherman, Denise Gottfredson, Doris MacKenzie, John Eck, Peter Reuter, and Shawn Bushway (Eds.), *Preventing Crime: What Works, What Doesn't, What's Promising.* Washington, DC: U.S. Department of Justice Programs, 1997, 8–58.

Skogan, Wesley G. 1990. *Disorder and Decline: Crime and the Spiral of Decay in American Cities.* New York: Free Press.

Skogan, Wesley G. 1994. "The Impact of Community Policing on Neighborhood Residents: A Cross Site Analysis." In Dennis P. Rosenbaum (Ed.), *The Challenge of Community Policing.* Thousand Oaks, CA: Sage, 167–181.

Skogan, Wesley G. and Susan M. Hartnett. 1997. *Community Policing, Chicago Style.* New York: Oxford University Press.

Skogan, Wesley G., Susan M. Hartnett, Jill DuBois, Jennifer T. Comey, Marianne Kaiser, and Justine H. Lovig. 1999. *On the Beat: Police and Community Problem Solving.* Boulder, CO: Westview.

Skogan, Wesley G., Susan M. Hartnett, Jill DuBois, Jennifer T. Comey, Marianne Kaiser, and Justine H. Lovig. 2000. *Problem Solving in Practice: Implementing Community Policing in Chicago.* Washington, DC: U.S. Department of Justice.

Tilley, Nick. 1995. *Thinking About Crime Prevention Performance Indicators.* Crime Detection and Prevention Series Paper 57. London: Home Office

Tilley, Nick. 1999. "The Relationship Between Crime Prevention and Problem Oriented Policing." In Corina Sole Brito and Tracy Allan (Eds.), *Problem-Oriented Policing: Crime Specific Problems, Critical Issues and Making POP Work.* Washington, DC: Police Executive Research Forum, 253–280.

Tilley, Nick, Ken Pease, Mike Hough, and Rick Brown. 1999. *Burglary Prevention: Early Lessons from the Crime Reduction Programme.* Crime Reduction Research Series Paper 1. London: Home Office.

Trickett, Alan, Denise R. Osborn, Julie Seymour, and Ken Pease. 1992. "What is Different About High Crime Areas?" *British Journal of Criminology,* 32: 81–89.

Wilson, James Q. and George L. Kelling. 1982. "Broken Windows: The Police and Neighborhood Safety." *The Atlantic Monthly,* March: 29–38.

8

Why Don't Problems
Get Solved?

JOHN E. ECK

The problem with problem solving is in the problems. The failure to recognize how little we know about problems, and then to build our knowledge of them, is at the core of the difficulty police have in addressing problems. The failure to take problems seriously is not that of policing alone. Academic police researchers also fail in this regard. Improving problem solving requires much more attention to problems by both police and police researchers.

This chapter examines police problems. It begins with the concept of problem-oriented policing—a fundamental element of any community policing program—and moves through explanations of the limits of police problem-solving capacity to a discussion of how researchers and police can build a greater understanding of the origins of problems and what they can do to reduce them. The argument presented here is divided into three parts. The first section describes the theory of problem-oriented policing and arguments for its superiority over other forms of policing. The second section examines the quality of problem solving, particularly problem analysis, and discusses why we do not know more about how to solve problems. The final section discusses how researchers and police can address these difficulties.

PROBLEM-ORIENTED POLICING

Problem-oriented policing suffers from appearing to be simple. When one tries to explain it to people unfamiliar with policing their reaction is predictable. "Don't the police do that already?" In any large police training session on problem-oriented policing at least one person will say that it is like policing was when they joined the department. Perhaps this is to be expected, for people often adapt to new ideas by attaching them to older concepts. This might explain why some view problem-oriented policing as a simple extension of what currently exists.

Another reason for its superficial simplicity is the use of the term "problem solving." Problem solving is one of those ubiquitous terms. A stroll through the nonfiction section of any bookstore will reveal business books, mathematics books, computer books, psychology books, and many other books with titles using the term. So even without any introduction to police problem solving we think have some idea of what it is about. And the term suggests that for every difficulty there is a solution, perhaps easy, cheap, permanent, and 100 percent effective.

What is often overlooked is that problem-oriented policing is a way of conceptualizing the role of policing in democratic society, whereas problem solving is a process (or more realistically, a group of processes) used to carry out this role (Eck and Spelman, 1987a). Problem solving contains a number of possible objectives:

1. Problem handling—addressing the consequences of problems;
2. Problem management—finding ways of coping with problems;
3. Problem mitigation—reducing the harmful consequences of problems;
4. Problem reduction—reducing the frequency or intensity of problems;
5. Problem elimination—getting rid of problems.

Any one of these is a form of problem solving, but it is safe to say that few people think of all of them when they use the term.

The concept of "problem" is also deceptively simple, leading to superficial understanding and deep confusion. In common parlance, a bank robbery is a problem—so are repeated acts of domestic violence in a single household; so are the behaviors of repeat offenders. Truant school children are problems. Entire neighborhoods get labeled problems. But are these problems? Can one develop a coherent policing strategy around the general notion of "problem"? If "problem" is to provide meaningful guidance to police and an organizing concept for researchers, the term must assume a narrower technical meaning, separate from common use. We repeatedly return to what we mean by the term "problem."

What Is Problem-Oriented Policing?

The public asks the police to do too many different things for us to assert that the function of the police is to do X, or even X, Y, and Z (Goldstein, 1979). This is true if we look across democratic policing in the early twenty-first century, or if we look at police in democratic societies from the early nineteenth century into the foreseeable future. No short list of tasks can capture the diversity of activities. What unites all of these different requests for police service is that something is going wrong for someone somewhere and somebody wants the police to do something about it (Goldstein, 1979). The original works on problem-oriented policing do not attempt to provide a specific definition of a problem. Rather, they appeal to our imagination by giving examples. Nevertheless, we can say that a problem involves repetition. The genesis of problem-oriented policing is the need to give police guidance in handling situations that are commonly brought to their attention (Goldstein, 1967). Therefore, a useful definition of a police problem might be a group of events that are similar in one or more ways, that are harmful to members of the public, and that members of the public expect the police to handle.

Problem-oriented policing is about paying attention to problems, putting problems first in all police decision making rather than dwelling prematurely on the police organization. Goldstein's (1979) concern with the "means over ends syndrome"—that the police are far more concerned with how they are organized, appear, and act than what they accomplish with their organization, appearances, and actions—diagnoses the malady that focusing on problems is designed to overcome. If addressing problems comes first, anything that does not directly address problems must come later. In short, the middle term of "problem-oriented policing" gets too little attention. Problems are often policed, even if the most backward police agency, but that does not mean police are oriented toward problems—pay close attention to them, study them, and make them the center around which all other police activities revolve.

Problem-oriented policing is often connected with community policing. They share some characteristics, including an overriding emphasis on responsiveness to the public. The fundamental difference between them is that in problem-oriented policing working with communities is a means—perhaps one of the most important means—to address problems, where as in much that is called community policing, working with communities is an end in itself, a means for enhancing police legitimacy and public support, a means for improving other police services (e.g., investigating crimes), or a means for improving community functioning (Eck and Rosenbaum, 1994; Eck and Spelman, 1987b; Goldstein, 1990). Clearly, forms of community policing and problem-oriented policing are compatible, but that does not make them one and the same, nor can one be sure that if a police department does one it will get the other, perhaps as a bonus.

Neither is problem-oriented policing the routine application of the SARA process. SARA, developed by the Newport News Police Department and the Police Executive Research Forum (Eck and Spelman, 1987a) is a process that enjoys widespread popularity and is used by police throughout North America and Great Britain. Though the SARA process captures the most salient features of problem-oriented policing—an attention to a problem, an empirical examination of the nature and causes of the problem, a search for ways of addressing the problem, and an inquiry into whether the problem changed as a result of these efforts—it does not necessarily foster quality problem solving. This is because the SARA process focuses on individual problems and does not help link one problem-solving experience to other problem-solving experiences. Also, the SARA process is just one way of operationalizing problem solving for police; there are other means for addressing problems and some may be superior (Read and Tilley, 2000).

Is Problem-Oriented Policing Effective?

We are interested in problem-oriented policing because it promises a more effective approach to handling chronic public concerns. Therefore, it is relevant to ask whether it delivers on this promise. Though the question is important, there is no simple answer. From one perspective, the question cannot be answered. From another, the answer is so obviously "yes" that it one is tempted to pay no attention to evidence. And from a third perspective, there is an increasing body of evidence supporting claims of its effectiveness. Let's look at each perspective in turn.

In some ways problem-oriented policing is untestable. The claim that policing is about addressing problems is essentially normative. Goldstein (1990) moves from a claim that is empirically testable—that the public asks the police to do a lot of different things and these things can be grouped into meaningful categories called problems—to an assertion that the police should focus on these problems. One either accepts this prescription or doesn't, but no amount of empirical testing can prove Goldstein correct or incorrect. One could logically assert that problems occur for a variety of reasons, but it is the role of others to address them. The police role is merely to provide temporary bandages until this is done. Such a position would be equally unassailable by empirical evidence.

Given that one accepts that police should focus on problems, the notion that police should seek ways to prevent chronic problems through careful analysis and a broad search for effective responses is unassailable. No evidence for its superior performance is needed. It is an application of the scientific method to police work. What is the alternative for police? Police should react in an uninformed manner to crises as they appear? Police should spend the public's money without understanding what one is doing or trying to achieve? Police should use coercive force carelessly, thereby risking public support for the police? Police should act on only hunches and unexamined experience, and ignore information? Surely not. Thus, one can legitimately claim that any analysis of problems is superior to the absence of analysis, and any attempt to find improved solutions to problems must be superior to no such attempt. From this perspective, the answer is obvious. The question is not whether problem-oriented policing is better than the forms of policing it seeks to replace, but whether there are even better ways to implement problem-oriented policing than those currently in use.

Nevertheless, one still would like to see evidence that problems do get solved and that police acting in accordance with a problem-oriented approach achieve better results than police who do not. It might be the case that problems are either (1) so simple that even the most rudimentary and cursory examination is as good as a problem-oriented approach, or (2) so complex that they are beyond the capacity of the police to address even when the most sophisticated problem analysis is applied, so the police might as well address them in a simple manner. In either situation, problem-oriented policing is not superior to the forms of policing it is designed to replace. To the extent that we agree that the police should focus on problems we must ask, "Does problem-oriented policing deliver better results than other forms of policing?"

Sherman and Eck (2002) review problem-oriented policing evaluation findings and methods, including recent rigorous evaluations of problem-oriented policing efforts (Braga et al., 1999; Mazerolle et al., 2000). The evidence to date suggests that problem-oriented policing consistently shows effectiveness at preventing crime relative to common alternatives. In the same volume, Eck (2002) points to a body of evaluations of place-based prevention schemes implemented by police agencies that also provide evidence for the effectiveness of problem-oriented policing. Thus, there is a growing body of empirical evidence supporting the assertion that problem-oriented policing can deliver what it promises.

In summary, if one accepts the proposition that the business of the police is to address a wide variety of problems nominated by the public, the logic of problem-oriented policing is virtually unassailable. How could the police address these problems without undertaking a scientific empirical analysis designed to yield a fitting response? Evaluations of problem-oriented policing indicate that this approach can result in solutions to problems (though not in every instance) and that problem-oriented policing, on average, results in more prevented crime and disorder than do non-problem-oriented approaches with which it has been compared.

WHAT'S THE PROBLEM
WITH PROBLEM SOLVING?

Many of the basic ideas of problem-oriented policing have spread throughout policing in North America and Great Britain. In part this is due to the incorporation of problem solving within community policing. The COPS Office, part of the U.S. Department of Justice, promotes problem solving as part of its mission (e.g., see Office of Community Oriented Policing Services, 1998; Police Executive Research Forum, 2000). In both Great Britain and the United States, an annual award is given for excellence in problem solving. In the United States, the Police Executive Research Forum, a nonprofit police organization, sponsors the award. In Great Britain, the Home Office, a department of central government, sponsors it. It is probably safe to say that in the United States, Great Britain, and Canada, few police agencies of any size are without some form of formally endorsed problem solving and few executives of larger agencies would disagree with the notion that an important function of the police is to get to the root of persistent problems and find ways to get rid of them.

Nevertheless, it is obvious from reviewing problem-solving efforts in these countries that few police agencies go beyond a shallow exploration of problems to examine creative methods for addressing them. Much of problem solving is a simple examination of police data coupled with the officer's experience with the problem. This is not a new observation. From the beginning, concern has been raised about the difficulties of engaging police in deep examination of problems (Goldstein and Susmilch, 1982). Several researchers point to the limited scope of analysis, the narrow range of responses, and police difficulties in conducting problem solving (Eck and Spelman, 1987a; Buerger, 1994; Capowich and Roehl, 1994; Skogan et al., 1999; Read and Tilley, 2000; Scott and Clarke, 2000). It is safe to say that the problem solving practiced in policing today is but a shadow of the original concept (Scott, 2000).

It is progress that police are increasingly conscious of problems. It is progress that the police use data to investigate problems. Given the evidence of effectiveness, perhaps not much else is required. Maybe most problems do not require much beyond pausing to think more carefully about what to do. Yet, working with police officials it becomes obvious that they often feel ineffective and stymied by slow or lack of progress in their problem-solving efforts. Furthermore, there is some evidence that the greater the range of data used to examine problems, the more likely officers are to select innovative responses (Eck and Spelman, 1987a). This suggests that the practice of problem-oriented policing is less effective than it should be and that if problem analysis were improved, so would police effectiveness.

Why Is So Much Problem Solving Mediocre?

There are several explanations for the difficulties police face in conducting in-depth problem-solving efforts (Goldstein and Susmilch, 1982; Eck and Spelman, 1987a; Buerger, 1994; Capowich and Roehl, 1994; Skogan and Hartnett, 1997; Leigh, Read, and Tilley, 1998; Clarke, 1998; Read and Tilley, 2000). Most of these explanations put the focus on police officers, police organizations, or other groups. It's worth looking at them briefly to see why most of these explanations are inadequate, even if each has some validity. The first four explanations place the cause within the police organization. The next three focus on external support. And the last three draw attention to the methods of problem solving.

Police Officers Do Not Have the Analytical Skills Required to Analyze Problems This type of explanation focuses on the skills of people hired to become police officers and the training they receive once hired. It is certainly true that police officers are not hired based on their abilities to investigate problems, and if they receive training in problem solving it is usually eight hours or less. Of course, we have little evidence that this is the cause. If this is the principle cause of the difficulty, the solution is to hire people on the basis of their analytical skills and provide them with sufficient training. This assumes that we know what such skills are and that we can select for them. It also assumes that we know how to train police in problem solving. There is no evidence supporting any of these assumptions.

To date, little attention has been paid to how to guide police officials in problem analysis. Eck and Spelman (1987a) propose an analysis guide that is largely unworkable. More recently, routine activity theory has been expanded (Eck, 1994; Felson, 1995) and adapted to assist in problem solving (Office of Community Oriented Policing Services, 1998), but this guidance is not very detailed nor is it clear how it would vary across problem types.

Police Managers and Supervisors Do Not Know How to Foster Problem Solving This is probably true. But like insufficient training, it is not clear what sort of things one could recommend to managers and supervisors that goes beyond generic exhortations to reward good behavior and sanction bad behavior. Can supervisors discriminate between quality problem solving and superficial problem solving? Is there a body of empirical evidence that could be used to help supervisors make such distinctions? The answer in both cases is "no."

Police Agencies Resist Change This explanation has been used to explain the slow progress or failures of all attempts to change police practices, yet it is unclear whether the police are any more resistant to change than any other public or private institution. Are police organizations any more resistant to change than other organizations, say, universities? Despite a large literature on police organizations, particularly with regard to community policing, there is little practical advice that research can provide police executives. In fact, resistance to new approaches is to be expected if we cannot provide practical guidance to how to act in accordance with the new approach.

Police Workloads Prevent Anything but Superficial Analysis Though some police use such arguments, other police claim that there is sufficient time to address problems thoroughly, except in extreme circumstances. One thing is clear—problem solving unfolds on a different time scale than responding to calls. Call handling is measured in seconds, minutes, and hours. Problem solving is measured in hours, days, weeks, and even months. It is more likely that the difficulty with time is not how much is available, but how much time police are willing to take.

There Is Too Little Involvement of Communities, and Communities Often Do Not Cooperate There is merit to both of these explanations, but both explanations assume that in most, if not all, circumstances members of communities have some important contribution to the solution of problems. Sometimes some community members do have something to contribute. We need to take into account the geographic scale of neighborhoods and problems. Neighborhoods usually cover much larger areas than most problems, and as a consequence most neighborhood members have little direct experience with any specific problem. But it is not always that even the most proximate community is aware of the problem or agrees what should be done about it. Community members as a group may have little information or insight into the problem or may disagree intensely about the problem. In some circumstances they may have a vested interest in maintaining the problem (Walker and Mills, 1999). Furthermore, community members are usually more in the dark about how to systematically analyze problems than police are.

This is not to say that the police should routinely ignore community members' concerns or impose onerous "solutions" on them. Nevertheless, it is likely that community partnerships are not absolutely essential for addressing all problems. Without knowledge about problems and how to systematically analyze them, police-community partnerships become situations in which the blind lead the blind.

Local Government Agencies Provide Too Little Support Like the community explanation, there is some truth to this. If a police officer wants to close a drug house through the use of nuisance abatement, for example, and the city attorney is unwilling to take the case to civil court, there is little the officer can do. As with communities, police officials addressing problems have an easier time of it when they have the cooperation of other local government agencies. Nevertheless, in the absence of a thorough analysis of problems it is hard to make a convincing case for cooperation from other agencies. If our understanding of problems were greater perhaps we would see greater cooperation.

Little Is Known about What Works under What Circumstances This is certainly the case. There are two ways to address this concern, though neither is entirely satisfactory. One approach is to systematically experiment with prevention interventions (Sherman et al., 2002). This is a slow process, particularly if high standards of evidence are required. But because most experimentation pays closer attention to internal validity than to external validity, it is likely that the results will not be generalizable enough for police to use without changing the nature of the intervention. Another approach is to systematically record and organize problem-solving experiences and share them among police. However, few problem-solving efforts result in a formal evaluation. Though evaluations would allow more useful sharing of ideas among problem solvers, the lack of internal validity to most such efforts coupled with unknown external validity make such information problematic. Both approaches should be taken, but they are unlikely to have much short-term payoff.

The Problem-Solving Process Used Is Linear, but Most Problem Solving Is Nonlinear Such criticisms are usually addressed to the SARA process, which suggests a sequential four-step approach moving from problem identification (scanning), to analysis, to implementing a solution (response), to an evaluation (assessment). If the problem has not been resolved in a satisfactory manner, the problem solver is to go back to an earlier step and begin again. Officers do move back and forth among the steps, particularly if a problem is acute and immediate prophylactic action is required. Nevertheless, it is not clear that developing an "organic" problem-solving process would help officers do a better job. One reason they may jump among problem-solving steps is that they are attempting to solve the problem through trial and error when a more systematic approach would be more productive. Problem solving is similar to research and to criminal investigations, but in neither case do we advocate research or investigative practices that jump back and forth. Instead, training and supervision strongly encourage flexible adherence to linear analytical processes.

We Do Not Know How to Solve Problems Because We Do Not Know Much about the Problems This explanation goes to the heart of the matter. Even if we were able to correct each of the deficiencies described by the previous nine explanations, police would not make much greater progress against problems unless they also knew more about problems. Rather than being causes of mediocre problem solving, the difficulties enumerated previously are consequences of a lack of understanding of problems. Knowing how problems arise and under what circumstances is essential for addressing each of the previously mentioned deficiencies. An understanding of problems would greatly aid police administrators in developing training and improving supervision. It would enable more effective collaboration with community members and agencies of government. Such knowledge would help direct experimentation and evaluations, and it would be useful for developing more efficient problem-solving processes.

Why Don't We Know More
about How to Solve Problems?

It is interesting that in the process of adopting elements of a problem-oriented approach the police and their advisors have fallen victim to the very malady a problem-oriented approach was designed to address: the means over ends syndrome. Much attention has been placed on the design of the police agencies and police relations with community members. Practitioners, and their academic allies, place a great deal of emphasis on the decentralization of decision making, restructuring workloads, officer deployment, information technology, and police-community relations. Most training involves a day or less presentation of the SARA process, perhaps coupled with other skills training (public speaking, or how to run a meeting, for example). All of this has been done under the "field of dreams" assumption: if we create the right police agency environment, police officers will address problems. Of course, no one states it so bluntly, but this assumption becomes apparent when one asks police executives what they have done to develop a problem-oriented approach in their agency. These executives will inevitably point to the organizational developments they have made, or community partnerships they have forged.

Almost never do they describe how much more they know about their problems. They do not mention efforts to learn about problems and problem solving apart from a few individual problem-solving projects. Thus, for example, a department may have addressed a large number of problems involving drug houses, but no one will have assembled the lessons of these efforts. Police agencies do not systematically inquire into what makes problems arise and why they persist. There is little emphasis on evaluating problem-solving outcomes, so it is difficult to know what worked. And this makes it difficult to build useful knowledge.

It may be too much to ask police agencies to undertake these efforts. In medicine most practicing physicians do not engage in research, neither do most practicing civil engineers, practicing lawyers, or practitioners of other professions. What these professions have, that the police do not, are many people who spend considerable effort on applied problem research. A quick review of any academic journal that routinely publishes articles on policing will reveal that few articles deal with police problems or ways of analyzing them. These issues are far out of the mainstream of police research. Even within criminology most research deals with issues that are distal to police problems. Most criminological research focuses on why some people become persistent offenders (Felson and Clarke, 1998). By the time problems come to police attention, the question of why people offend has little relevance. Rather, the most pressing concerns are why they are offending here (and not somewhere else), why they are selecting these targets (and not some other target), why are the events occurring at these times (and not some other times), and what one can do to prevent such offending. These are not questions most criminologists study or care about. Some progress has been made with the surge in interest in crime mapping, but there are many nongeographical issues that are seldom touched, and much police mapping is used to reinforce standard forms of policing rather than to analyze problems.

THE RETURN OF THE PROBLEM SOLVER

What would we do if we were serious about problem-oriented policing? The first thing we would do is to admit our ignorance about problems. We do not know what types of problems exist. We know little about specific problems, even those that have received research attention. We have only the beginnings of theories of problems. We have only the most rudimentary protocols for investigating problems. And we have only hunches as to how information about problems is supposed to lead police to effective responses. Given this level of ignorance it is surprising that police agencies engage in problem solving and are effective at it.

What Types of Problems Exist?

The most obvious starting place for improving problem-solving quality is with the problems themselves. And the two most basic questions are: What do we mean by "problem?" What sort of things are they?

The term "problem" is extraordinarily general, even if we restrict ourselves to problems that can be defined as "reoccurring events, harmful to members of the community, that have something in common, and members of the public expect the local police to address." Such a definition eliminates from consideration difficulties internal to police agency and single events. It also eliminates many problems that would be of direct concern to the FBI and state police agencies but are seldom reported to local police agencies (e.g., stock fraud). Nevertheless, we need to understand problems with greater precision and in greater detail. This requires a problem classification scheme.

Given the rich diversity of concerns citizens bring to local police it may be impossible to create a scheme that can classify all problems, but it is possible to develop a problem classification scheme that sorts out most problems faced by local police agencies. A test of such a system is whether most problems can be fitted into the system and whether those problems that do not fit are rare and peculiar.

An initial attempt at problem classification has been made (Eck and Clarke, Forthcoming). Because the purpose of creating such a classification system is to improve police handling of problems, the scheme is organized around simple categories that police can easily recognize. The Eck-Clarke Common Problem Classification Scheme avoids quasi-legal terminology that structures much crime classification. The scheme includes problems that are not typically thought of as crimes or disorders. Furthermore, the classification scheme reflects problems as they might be rather than as they are initially perceived (much as the classification of a disease is based on a full examination rather than the initial symptoms presented by the patient). As a start, the Eck-Clarke Common Problem Classification Scheme uses a two dimensional typology: environment and behavior.

The environment dimension is an exhaustive list of locations where problems can occur. The foundation of the behavior dimension is Felson's (1987) typology. Felson's categories were substantially modified to account for problems the police handle but are not criminal. The behavior categories incorporate notions of intent, harm, and offender-target (victim) relationship. Absent any one of these items, the concerns are not central police problems. These categories are not based on outcomes. Death, for example, could be the result of any of several behaviors (see the Appendix).

Table 8.1 summarizes the scheme. Each cell in the table is the intersection of an environment and a behavior and constitutes a distinct type of problem. Definitions of the column and row headings are in the Appendix. The Eck-Clarke scheme contains sisty-six types of problems (six categories of behaviors by eleven categories of environments). Each behavior and each environment category is broad, containing a variety of potential subbehaviors or subenvironments. Therefore, each column or row can be subdivided further, creating many additional meaningful categories (e.g., if each column and row in Table 8.1 can be divided into five subtypes this would yield $30 \times 55 = 1,650$ problem types). Adding other dimensions would create another exponential increase in the number of categories. Even at these early stages of developing a classification scheme, it is apparent that there are many types of problems, most of which we know little about.

Any useful classification system will impose its own discipline on people who use it (Bowker and Star, 2000). The Eck-Clarke scheme implies that unless a problem is environmentally and behaviorally defined it has not been specified enough to permit a problem-oriented approach. This means that some concerns that are often listed as problems are eliminated. Consider truancy. It is a common issue that involves the police. However, absent any other information, truancy is not a problem in the technical way defined by the Eck-Clarke scheme: there are no environmental or behavioral foci. Truancy is usually brought to police attention because the truants are either causing trouble for others or are endangering themselves. If we use the scheme to probe the

Table 8.1 The Eck-Clarke Common Problem Classification Scheme

	BEHAVIORS					
ENVIRONMENTS	Predatory	Consensual	Conflicts	Incivilities	Endangerment	Misuse of Police
Residential						
Recreational						
Offices						
Retail						
Industrial						
Agricultural						
Educational						
Human service						
Public ways						
Transport						
Open/Transitional						

concern with truancy we begin to see the value of the classification criteria. If the concern is "residential burglaries committed by young people who should be in school," we have a predatory-residential problem. If the concern is "students absent from school and hanging out and annoying retail shoppers and merchants," we have an incivility-retail problem. These are two different problems. Though they may share some solutions, there are many solutions they might not share.

The fact that the police are constantly asked to address concerns such as "bored youth in housing projects" does not mean that we need to consider it a problem. This is an environmentally focused concern. It is repetitive, but it violates the behavioral conditions of requirement for intent, harm, and offender-victim relationship. If the concern is "bored youth in housing projects annoying people using the sidewalk," the (incivilities-residential) problem is defined in a way that begins to allow it to be addressed.

It is worth noting that in both of the preceding examples, the poorly defined problem was couched in terms of the people who seem to cause the concern. In both of these examples, the concern seems to be more the status of the people involved than their behavior. In the first case, the students are not where they should be (in school) and in the second the kids have a particular mental disposition (boredom). This suggests that whenever a concern is framed in terms of people's status, the concern needs to be redefined in terms of behavior and where that behavior occurs. Furthermore, if the police cannot identify the behavioral and environmental elements required, other organizations might best address the issue.

This classification scheme also helps police avoid another pitfall, confounding neighborhoods with problems. Some neighborhoods have many troublesome events and it is common for an entire neighborhood to become the subject of a problem-solving project. Though no one has examined this issue systematically, it is likely that few such projects succeed in solving their problems. If police examine specific problems within the neighborhoods they will probably be far more effective and responsive to neighborhood residents than if they attempt to address the community at large. This is a special case of Weick's (1984) point that addressing social issues on the small scale is often more helpful than addressing large-scale issues.

How Should One Analyze Problems?

Given the diversity of problems—a diversity that exists independently of the classification system used—what guidance can be given about how to analyze and resolve problems? There are two answers to this question, and both are useful.

The first approach is to systematically assemble research and experience on specific problems. The classification scheme described earlier is an offshoot of such an approach. The COPS Office has published nineteen problem-specific guides, including such problems as fights and assaults in bars and taverns (Scott, 2001a), street prostitution (Scott, 2001b), street drug dealing (Sampson, 2001), commercial burglaries (Clarke, 2002), and graffiti (Weisel, 2002). These guides provide problem solvers with summaries of research and experience that suggest useful ways to tackle problems and describe unproductive approaches that should be avoided.

For problems that have been studied and police have a great deal of documented experience, problem-specific guides are helpful. But many problems have little or no research or documented police experience. Even for the most thoroughly explored problems there are large gaps in knowledge, contradictory findings, and many weakly supported assertions. In addition to problem-specific guides, there is a need to provide police guidance for exploring problems in general, even in the absence of systematic information.

The second approach is to develop generic analysis protocols. The PAT, based on routine activity theory, is an example (Eck, Forthcoming-b). Such protocols need to be grounded in theories of behaviors rather than based solely on general principles of rigorous inquiry. Criminological theories are an obvious starting point, but most police problems do not neatly fall within the area of criminology (e.g., endangerment-public ways problems, a.k.a. traffic problems). Even for problems in which criminologists are interested, most criminological theories are of little use for problem solving. Most theories of crime are theories about why some people engage in crime and others do not. These theories typically address conditions that are beyond the capability of most problem-solving efforts to address. Theories that deal with opportunities for crime and how offenders, potential victims, and others make decisions based on perceived opportunities have great potential utility for guiding problem solving (Clarke, 1998; Felson and Clarke, 1998).

Both theoretic generic guidance and problem-specific guidance are useful. Each has its own strengths and weaknesses. Problem-specific guides can provide a great deal of useful, detailed insights that generic guidance lacks. But generic guidance can offer insightful questions for examining new problems. In both cases, the greatest help for problem solvers will come from questions rather than from specific answers (Eck, Forthcoming-b). Studies are often weak on generalizability; therefore, acting on the specific findings of a single or a few studies is highly problematic. These findings are useful for sensitizing police to things they should look into. Generic guidance about data sources is less useful to police than are questions they should ask about problems. This is because police agencies vary considerably with regard to data availability and data-collection capability. Some agencies can launch community surveys, for example, but for others this source of data is out of the question. Rather than point police to particular data sources and methods, guides should recognize that most questions are answerable using a variety of data.

How Do You Link Analysis to Response?

There is a well-known cartoon showing a scientist finishing a complex equation on a blackboard. In the middle of the equation are the words "a miracle occurs here." We expect miracles when we advocate problem analysis. Somehow insights will appear in the heads of problem solvers and they will have solutions. Such miracles do occur, on occasion, for a few police officers. But for many police problem solvers there is no flash of insight; they find the data overwhelming and do not know how to use it to find an effective solution. The result is that their actions are remarkably like what they probably would have done about the problem in the absence of analysis—enforcement.

Focusing on analysis questions rather than data sources can help by reducing the amount of useless information collected (Eck, Forthcoming-b). These questions, however, need to link the characteristics of the problem to possible solutions so that the answer to a question points to a possible solution option. For example, a guide on drive-by shootings might ask a question such as, "Do shooters select targets based in part on the ease of escape following the shooting?" A generic guide might ask if speed or ease of escape is an important consideration for offenders. Such questions draw attention to street patterns and traffic flow. When the answer to the question is "yes," the attention of problem solvers should be drawn to a possible option, changing street and traffic patterns. When the answer is "no," problem solvers should look to other potential options.

There are potential solutions in the minds of most problem solvers, even before they look into a problem. Often, the people who nominate problems package them with suggested solutions. There are also published lists of possible solutions. Clarke's typology of situational crime prevention measures is a useful example (Clarke and Homel, 1997). Selecting among solutions is often more difficult than coming up with a solution. Problem-solving guides need to tell police what conditions are necessary for classes of solutions to be effective. As important, a fundamental role of any guide should be to help problem solvers eliminate solutions. The published guides identify potential solutions that do not seem to work well.

What Is the Role of Evaluation?

There is a need for more and better evaluations of police interventions. It is hard to argue against more and better information, but it is worth thinking about what this information will be used for. Evaluators distinguish between internal and external validity. Internal validity pertains to the confidence that we have that the findings are correct for the subjects studied. External validity pertains to our confidence that these findings will hold for subjects who were not studied. Professional evaluators pay far more attention to internal validity than external validity. Practitioners care about both but would probably emphasize external validity because they want to know if the results apply to their agency. If practitioners are looking for a generic solution to a widespread concern—say, domestic violence—they want justification for believing that a study is both internally valid and applicable to their setting. They may even willing to relax standards of internal validity if this gains them some external validity because an internally valid study that is not locally applicable is less useful than a highly applicable study that is weak on internal validity but hints at a useful application. The willingness of police administrators to adopt well-publicized interventions that have little or no scientific evidence of effectiveness speaks to policy makers' interest in external validity over internal validity.

Practitioner emphasis on external validity is rational and is not something that can be lightly pushed aside. This can be illustrated with a simple thought experiment. Imagine a randomized experiment, conducted using volunteer officers with tight controls on their actions under a restricted time frame imposed by an external funding source. The results may have high internal validity—the findings are highly credible for the subjects studied and the circumstances examined. When these results are put into routine practice in other agencies (or even the same agency after the experiment) the tight controls will be absent, the officers will not be volunteers, there will be no experimental deadlines, and no funding agency representatives and researchers will be present. One can expect a great deal of slippage in performance between the experiment and the real-world implementation. Not knowing whether the experimental findings are applicable to everyday application might make a police administrator hesitant to adopt findings from a randomized trial.

On the other hand, imagine a pre-post experiment (no randomization or control group) resulting from a problem-solving process. The results may have low internal validity, but because the setting is closer to the everyday world of policing, the results may be more generalizable—applicable to a wide range of everyday policing circumstances. Police administrators might well choose to base their decisions on the weaker study, even if they had limited confidence in the exact magnitude of the findings.

Statements about validity are statements about our confidence in research findings and their applicability to people, places, and circumstances not studied. Because zero confidence is rare and 100 percent confidence is unachievable, all statements about internal and external validity are matters of degree. At one extreme we know with great confidence about outcomes that cannot be reproduced in everyday practical circumstances. At the other extreme we have little confidence in widely applicable results. Clearly, something between these extremes is required. Achieving a useful balance requires trading off internal validity and external validity.

Evaluations in problem-oriented policing serve three functions (Eck, Forthcoming-a). The first is to offer some level of accountability. One would like to know that the publicly funded police in a democratic society are achieving what they claim. The second function is to provide feedback to the problem solvers so they can make necessary changes in their response to a problem. These are the two most important reasons for evaluating problem-solving efforts. If one does not evaluate, one does not know whether the problem has diminished. External validity is of less concern for these two functions. The third function of evaluation is to draw attention to increase the *a priori* probability that a possible solution will work if applied. Though this is an important function, difficulties with assessing the external validity of evaluations make empirically based claims for future success of solutions only marginally superior to claims based on thorough analysis. In short, the greatest stumbling block to using evaluations to pick solutions is external validity.

It is important to keep in mind the task of problem solvers. They are trying to find solutions that fit specific problems. Consequently, evaluation information, regardless of the number and rigor of evaluations, is helpful for narrowing the field of options suggested by the analysis. Like most selection processes with more candidates than openings, it is easier to reject the unfit than to select the best. In this context, what would be most helpful to police is not a list of what works but a list of interventions organized by the circumstances under which they do not work. The reason for this is that most interventions work in some circumstances. The question is, is this one of those circumstances or is it some other circumstance?

WHAT ARE POLICE RESEARCHERS TO DO?

Throughout this discussion I have made a distinction between police and researchers of police. After more than a third of a century of work, researchers—academic and nonacademic—are part of the institution of policing in the United States. No longer is improving policing just in the hands of the police and police policy makers. Researchers have a major role in influencing policy. Consequently, the failures of the police to make progress are in part due to the failures of researchers. Researchers who prefer to remain aloof should ask themselves three questions. Has any important publication on police not made recommendations for improving policing? Would they prefer that police policy makers ignore what they write? Is it possible to conduct any insightful research on policing without engaging the police in a dialogue about improvements? The answer to each of these questions is "no". In short, questions about police reforms are about police research and vice versa.

If researchers are serious about changing the way police do business, their research agenda needs to focus on police problems. Police opinion about what would be useful research may not be any more useful than the general public's opinion of what would constitute useful health research. Police officials may want research on police organizations (e.g., the decentralization of detectives) or community relations, but we must ask ourselves which form of research is likely to lead to the greatest improvement in policing.

If researchers are interested in having the police do a better job at identifying and reducing harmful concerns the public brings to their attention, their most pressing concern should be the development of a criminology of problems. Of far less use are studies of police leadership and management, police organizational structure, and police deployment. Even the role of community involvement is less important than problems. If the internal and external workings of police agencies—the means—cannot be strongly linked to problem-solving ends, they are not interesting topics. Linking the practice of policing to problem-solving outcomes means that researchers and police will have to be far more oriented to the substantive community problems that lie between the means and the ends.

CITATIONS

Bowker, Geoffrey C. and Susan Leigh Star. 2000. *Sorting Things Out: Classification and Its Consequences.* Cambridge, MA: MIT Press.

Braga, Anthony A., David L. Weisburd, Elin J. Waring, Lorraine G. Mazerolle, William Spelman, and Frank Gajewski. 1999. "Problem-Oriented Policing in Violent Crime Places: A Randomized Controlled Experiment." *Criminology,* 37: 541–580.

Buerger, Michael E. 1994. "The Problems of Problem-Solving: Resistance, Interdependencies, and Conflicting Interests." *American Journal of Police,* 13: 1–36.

Capowich, George E. and Jan E. Roehl. 1994. "Problem-Oriented Policing: Actions and Effectiveness in San Diego." In Dennis Rosenbaum (Ed.), *The Challenges of Community Policing:*

Testing the Promises. Newbury Park, CA: Sage, 127–146.

Clarke, Ronald V. 1998. "Defining Police Strategies: Problem Solving, Problem-Oriented Policing and Community-Oriented Policing." In Tara O'Connor Shelley and Anne C. Grant (Eds.), *Problem-Oriented Policing: Crime Specific Problems, Critical Issues and Making POP Work.* Washington, DC: Police Executive Research Forum, 315–330.

Clarke, Ronald V. 2002. *Burglaries of Retail Establishments.* Problem-Oriented Guides for Police Series, Volume 15. Washington, DC: Office of Community Oriented Policing Services.

Clarke, Ronald V. and Ross Homel. 1997. "A Revised Classification of Situational Crime Prevention Techniques." In Stephen P. Lab (Ed.),

Crime Prevention at the Crossroads.
Cincinnati, OH: Anderson, 17–30.

Eck, John E. 1994. "Drug Markets and
Drug Places: A Case-Control Study of
the Spatial Structure of Illicit Drug
Dealing." Unpublished Ph.D.
dissertation, University of Maryland,
College Park.

Eck, John E. 2002. "Preventing Crime at
Places." In Lawrence W. Sherman,
David Farrington, Brandon Welsh, and
Denise Gottfredson (Eds.), *Evidence-
Based Crime Prevention.* New York:
Routledge, 241–294.

Eck, John E. Forthcoming-a. "Learning
from Experience in Problem-
Oriented Policing and Situational
Prevention: The Positive Functions of
Weak Evaluations and the Negative
Functions of Strong Ones." In Nick
Tilley (Ed.), *Evaluation in Crime
Prevention.* Crime Prevention Studies,
Volume 14. Monsey, NY: Criminal
Justice Press.

Eck, John E. Forthcoming-b. "Police
Problems: The Complexity of Problem
Theory, Research and Evaluation." In
Johannes Knutsson (Ed.), *Problem-
Oriented Policing and Crime Prevention.*
Crime Prevention Studies, Volume 15.
Monsey, NY: Criminal Justice Press.

Eck, John E. and Ronald V. Clarke.
Forthcoming. "Classifying Common
Police Problems: A Routine Activity
Approach." In Martha Smith and
Derek Cornish (Eds.), *Theory for
Practice in Situational Crime Prevention.*
Crime Prevention Studies, Volume 16.
Monsey, NY: Criminal Justice Press.

Eck, John E. and Dennis Rosenbaum.
1994. "The New Police Order:
Effectiveness, Equity and Efficiency in
Community Policing." In Dennis P.
Rosenbaum (Ed.), *The Challenges of
Community Policing: Testing the Promises.*
Newbury Park, CA: Sage, 3–26.

Eck, John E. and William Spelman. 1987a.
*Problem Solving: Problem Oriented Policing
in Newport News.* Washington, DC:
Police Executive Research Forum.

Eck, John E. and William Spelman. 1987b.
"Who Ya Gonna Call?" *Crime and
Delinquency,* 33: 31–52.

Felson, Marcus. 1987. "Routine Activities
and Crime Prevention in the
Developing Metropolis." *Criminology*
25: 911–931.

Felson, Marcus. 1995. "Those Who
Discourage Crime." In John E. Eck
and David Weisburd (Eds.), *Crime and
Place.* Crime Prevention Studies,
Volume 4. Monsey, NY: Criminal
Justice Press, 53–66.

Felson, Marcus and Ronald V. Clarke. 1998.
*Opportunity Makes the Thief: Practical
Theory for Crime Prevention.* Crime
Prevention and Detection Series Paper
98. London: Home Office.

Goldstein, Herman. 1967. "Police Policy
Formulation: A Proposal for
Improving Police Performance."
Michigan Law Review, 65: 1123–1146.

Goldstein, Herman. 1979. "Improving
Policing: A Problem-Oriented
Approach." *Crime and Delinquency,* 25:
236–258.

Goldstein, Herman. 1990. *Problem-Oriented
Policing.* New York: McGraw-Hill.

Goldstein, Herman and Charles E.
Susmilch. 1982. *Experimenting with the
Problem-Oriented Approach to Improving
Police Service: A Report and Some
Reflections on Two Case Studies*
(Photocopy Vol. 4 of the Project on
Development of a Problem-Oriented
Approach to Improving Police
Service). Madison: University of
Wisconsin Law School.

Leigh, Adrian, Tim Read, and Nick Tilley.
1998. *Brit Pop II: Problem-Oriented
Policing in Practice.* Crime Prevention
and Detection Series Paper 93.
London: Home Office.

Mazerolle, Lorraine G., Justin Ready,
William Terrill, and Elin Waring. 2000.
"Problem-Oriented Policing in Public
Housing: The Jersey City Evaluation."
Justice Quarterly, 17: 129–158.

Office of Community Oriented Policing
Services. 1998. *Problem-Solving Tips: A
Guide to Reducing Crime and Disorder
Through Problem-Solving Partnerships.*
Washington, DC: U.S. Department of
Justice, Office of Community
Oriented Policing Services.

Police Executive Research Forum. 2000. *National Evaluation of the Problem-Solving Partnerships (PSP) Project for the Office of Community Oriented Policing Services (COPS), U.S. Department of Justice.* Washington, DC: Police Executive Research Forum.

Read, Tim and Nick Tilley. 2000. *Not Rocket Science? Problem-Solving and Crime Reduction.* Crime Reduction Research Series Paper 6. London: Home Office.

Sampson, Rana. 2001. *Drug Dealing in Privately Owned Apartment Complexes.* Problem-Oriented Guides for Police Series, Volume 4. Washington, DC: Office of Community Oriented Policing Services.

Scott, Michael. 2000. *Problem-Oriented Policing: Reflections on the First 20 Years.* Washington, DC: U.S. Department of Justice, Office of Community Oriented Policing Services.

Scott, Michael S. 2001a. *Assaults in and Around Bars.* Problem-Oriented Guides for Police Series, Volume 9. Washington, DC: Office of Community Oriented Policing Services.

Scott, Michael S. 2001b. *Street Prostitution.* Problem-Oriented Guides for Police Series, Volume 9. Washington, DC: Office of Community Oriented Policing Services.

Scott, Michael and Ronald V. Clarke. 2000. "A Review of Submissions of the Herman Goldstein Award for Excellence in Problem-Oriented Policing." In Corina S. Brito and Eugenia E. Gratto (Eds.), *Problem-Oriented Policing: Crime-Specific Problems, Critical Issues and Making POP Work,* Volume 3. Washington,

DC: Police Executive Research Forum, 213–230.

Sherman, Lawrence W. and John E. Eck. 2002. "Policing for Crime Prevention." In Lawrence W. Sherman, David Farrington, Brandon Welsh, and Denise Gottfredson (Eds.), *Evidence-Based Crime Prevention.* New York: Routledge. 295–329.

Sherman, Lawrence W., David Farrington, Brandon Welsh, and Denise Gottfredson. (Eds.) 2002. *Evidence-Based Crime Prevention.* New York: Routledge.

Skogan, Wesley G. and Susan M. Hartnett. 1997. *Community Policing, Chicago Style.* New York: Oxford University Press.

Skogan, Wesley G., Susan M. Hartnett, Jill DuBois, Jennifer T. Comey, Marianne Kaiser, and Justine H. Lovig. 1999. *On the Beat: Police and Community Problem Solving.* Boulder, CO: Westview Press.

Walker, Samuel and Andy Mills. 1999. "Citizens in the POP Process: How Much is Too Much?" In Corina S. Brito and Tracy Allan (Eds.), *Problem-Oriented Policing: Crime Specific Problems, Critical Issues, and Making POP Work,* Volume 2. Washington, DC: Police Executive Research Forum, 177–194.

Weick, Karl E. 1984. "Small Wins: Redefining the Scale of Social Problems." *American Psychologist,* 39: 40–49.

Weisel, Deborah Lamm. 2002. *Graffiti.* Problem-Oriented Guides for Police Series, Volume 9. Washington, DC: Office of Community Oriented Policing Services.

APPENDIX

The Eck-Clarke Problem Classification Scheme

Described here is each of the categories of the two dimensions in the Eck-Clarke Common Problem Classification Scheme. More detailed information about this scheme and its development can be found in Eck and Clarke (Forthcoming).

ENVIRONMENTS

Environments are distinguished from each other based on their primary functions and the uses to which they are put. The vast majority of local police problems can be put into eleven possible types of environments.

1. Residential—houses, apartments, motels, etc.
2. Recreational—bars, restaurants, public parks, amusement parks, nightclubs, etc.
3. Offices—office buildings, government buildings, etc.
4. Retail—retail shops, post offices, banks (front office), etc.
5. Industrial—manufacturing and wholesale.
6. Agricultural—farmland, pastures, fish farms, etc.
7. Education—colleges, schools, libraries, etc.
8. Human Services—hospitals, soup kitchens, drug treatment facilities, jails, courts, police stations, etc.
9. Public Ways—paths, streets, highways, parking facilities, etc.
10. Transport—buses, trains, ships, planes, etc.
11. Open/Transitional—vacant property, construction sites, ravines, rivers, fields, etc.

Residential environments are locations where people dwell. They vary from single-family homes and estates, apartments, to summer cottages, hotels and motels, and homeless shelters. Though most are in fixed locations, a few are mobile, such as recreational vehicles.

Recreational environments are places where people go to have a good time. Some cater to adults only—such as bars, nightclubs, and adult movies—whereas others cater to children—such as playgrounds. Many serve a diverse clientele—such as campgrounds and movie theaters. Some of these environments are open to the public for free, whereas others charge admission or have some other restriction on access (e.g., membership).

Offices are locations of white-collar work where there is little face-to-face interaction between the workers and the general public. These environments involve the processing of information. There is typically restricted access (formally through guards and entry code requirements, informally by the relative absence of signage directing passersby to the location, or by virtue of the fact that most people have no interest in the location). Many government and corporate buildings fall into this category.

In contrast to offices, retail locations are designed to deal with walk-in or drive-up customer traffic. They also involve monetary transactions. A branch bank with clerks, loan officers, and other people who serve the public falls into this category, but the bank headquarters where the public is not encouraged to come falls into the office category. Similarly, a post office branch is a retail location, though a mail-sorting facility is an industrial location, and the post office headquarters building in Washington, D.C., is an office environment.

Industrial locations involve the processing of things. That is why a mail-sorting or package-sorting facility is in this category. Factories and warehouses all belong in this category. They are similar to offices in that the public is not usually invited in (except in a restricted manner, such as tour groups) and that cash transactions are not a large part of the function of the environment.

Agricultural locations include farmland used to raise crops and animals but also include aquaculture sites, such as commercial fish farms and mussel beds.

Education environments are places of learning. They range from day care centers and elementary schools to colleges and universities. Libraries are in this category because their principal function incorporates some form of study. But the exact classification of libraries is difficult because it depends on how libraries are used. Thus, even this relatively specific place might need to be divided into subcategories: college libraries, public branch libraries, corporate libraries, and so on.

Human service environments are similar to retail environments except that the clientele typically comes in when something is wrong, and monetary transactions are less frequent. In many of these environments members of the public are compelled to be present, such as courts, jails, prisons, and some drug treatment centers. Many are public facilities though they are often private. The public areas of medical facilities (hospitals, doctors and dentists offices, etc.) are in this category. However, a medical laboratory building is an industrial location and an annex used for hospital administration is an office environment. A department of motor vehicles office that issues drivers licenses should be classified as a retail environment rather than a health/welfare/human service environment because it has a high volume of monetary transactions and it sells a service—permission to drive a vehicle.

Public ways connect all other environments. The most common are roads and highways, but footpaths and bike trails also are in this group. Parking facilities are included here because they are intimately connected with roads. These ways can be both private and public. A private drive into a walled community is included in this category, as is a parking lot on a corporate office campus or a parking garage next to a hospital.

Transport environments involve the mass movement of people. They include the terminals and stations as well as the conveyances. Buses, bus stations, and bus stops are included in this category, as are airplanes and airports, trains and train stations (as well as tracks), ferries and ferry terminals, and ocean liners and piers.

Open/transitional environments are areas without consistent or regular designated uses. Abandoned properties, for example, had a specific function but have not received a new function to replace it. Construction sites are also transitional. They are moving from one function to another. Some open areas have not be set aside for a specific use, and there are no current plans to do so, often because the terrain is unsuitable for most human functions or because it has been set aside for environmental reasons. Steep hillsides and ravines, rivers, lakes, forests, and meadows can all fall into these categories. They differ from parks (recreation and leisure) in that most open areas have not been set aside for recreational purposes, though people may unofficially use them for this purpose.

BEHAVIORS

Behaviors incorporate notions of intent, harm, and offender-target (victim) relationship. They do not necessarily correspond to commonly used crime categories. A problem involving assaults, for example, could be either a type of predatory problem or a type of conflict problem.

1. Predatory—burglary, robbery, rape, child abuse, etc.
2. Consensual—drug sales, prostitution, illegal gun sales, stolen property sales, etc.
3. Conflicts—fights, assaults, etc.
4. Incivilities—drinking in public, panhandling, skateboarding, etc.
5. Endangerment—things leading to accidents and suicide, etc.
6. Misuse of Police—false reporting, etc.

Predatory problems involve many of what people commonly refer to as crime. The offender is clearly distinct from the victim and acts in a way the victim objects to.

Consensual problems do not have clearly defined victims and offenders; rather, the parties involved knowingly and willingly interact for their own purposes. This typically involves some form of transaction.

Conflicts involve people who interact in a violent manner. These problems have characteristics similar to the first two types of problems. Like consensual problems, conflict problems often involve people who have some pre-existing relationship. Like consensual problem, interpersonal conflict problems often involve people who are roughly coequals (even though one party may instigate the dispute, the other party has the opportunity to defend himself or herself or leave). Like predatory problems, however, interpersonal conflict problems arise when one party objects to the actions of the other.

Incivility problems have clear offenders, but the victims are often diffuse—spread over several individuals. Many concerns that are annoying, unsightly, noisy, or disturbing but do not involve serious property damage or injury fall into this category. This category should be subdivided into more meaningful categories.

Endangerment problems are created when the offender and the victim are the same person or when the offender had no intent to harm the victim, as in the case of accidents. They can either be intentional acts (suicide attempts) or by-products of other acts (vehicle accidents or drug overdoses). Sometimes it may be difficult to tell the difference.

The final category is misuse of police. This category is reserved for demands on police service that should not be directed to the police. False reporting of crimes, repeated calling about issues citizens can handle themselves (and are not in the previous categories)—for example, reports of flooded basements following storms—or repeated calls about fictitious events should be placed in this group. As a rule, misuse of police should be a category of last resort, used only when none of the earlier categories fit and when the sole harm stemming from the behavior is the expenditure of police resources.

9

Community Policing and Quality of Life[1]

MICHAEL D. REISIG AND
ROGER B. PARKS

Does community policing work? Is it the neighborhoods that are home to poor people or the neighborhoods that are home to the better off that do better because of community policing? Community policing advocates claim that various reforms, such as partnering with residents and taking officers out of their cars and putting them in closer contact with residents, can produce positive outcomes. This chapter provides evidence to support these claims. Residents of neighborhoods who believe that police work with them and that their neighbors work with the police report an enhanced quality of neighborhood life. So, too, do residents of neighborhoods where the police engage in alternative patrol strategies, not simply relying on motor patrols. Of particular note, our results suggest that community policing can have positive results even in disadvantaged neighborhoods.

A DIFFERENT WAY TO POLICE
NEIGHBORHOODS

Critics of traditional police practices charge that the professional model places too much emphasis on reactive responses to 911 calls and is linked to a number of undesirable outcomes, including a breakdown in police relations with the community and a failure to address the correlates of crime. In response to these concerns, many changes in policing have taken place in the last decade. One fundamental shift has been the expanded scope of policing—departments around the country have broadened their mission beyond simply fighting crime and now place greater emphasis on addressing citizen quality-of-life issues. Toward this end, various strategic reforms have been adopted and alternative tactics

[1]Preparation of this chapter was supported by Grant No. 95-IJ-CX-0071 by the National Institute of Justice, Office of Justice Programs, U.S. Department of Justice. Data collection was supported by the National Institute of Justice and by the Indianapolis Department of Public Safety. Points of view in this document are those of the authors and do not necessarily represent the official position or policies of the U.S. Department of Justice nor the Indianapolis Department of Public Safety.

implemented. For example, police patrol boundaries have been realigned to match existing neighborhood lines, and officers who work there are expected to build partnerships with the communities they serve (Cordner, 1999). The success of these initiatives is contingent on several factors, including a sound understanding of the dynamics associated with citizens' quality-of-life assessments.

Much of the research into what influences citizens' quality of life is guided by the "incivilities thesis." Included under this general heading is a group of theories linking evidence of uncivil or disorderly behavior (e.g., aggressive panhandling and public drinking) and of physical decay (e.g., abandoned cars and burned out buildings) to citizens' quality-of-life assessments, especially fear of crime. Although the levels of explanation differ (i.e., individual and neighborhood) and processes vary (i.e., psychological and ecological), each of these theories provides guidance for police reformers.

In this chapter we model relationships between community policing and quality of life at two levels. We document how neighborhood residents' perceptions of police partnerships with citizens are related to their assessments of their own quality of life—a relationship we characterize as psychological and social psychological in nature (Taylor, 1997). We also examine ecological or contextual relationships, seeking to learn whether variation in police patrol activity along the lines recommended by community policing advocates is related to neighborhood variation in mean quality-of-life assessments. In short, we seek to determine whether community policing works in the eyes of the public.

To examine these issues, we use the findings of interviews with nearly 6,000 neighborhood residents, in conjunction with Census and crime data from the sixty-two areas where they lived. The neighborhoods are located in two cities, Indianapolis, Indiana, and St. Petersburg, Florida. They are the same areas examined in Chapter 5 by William Terrill and Stephen Mastrofski.

QUALITY OF LIFE AND
COMMUNITY POLICING

Scholars examine quality-of-life issues at the individual level, probing psychological and social psychological relationships, and at the neighborhood level, tracking community ecology. In this section we review research in both traditions to illustrate that it is necessary to take both individual- and neighborhood-level processes into account.

Residents and Community Policing

Early research investigating citizens' quality of life—frequently indexed by fear of crime—adopted a psychological orientation. Researchers assumed that the interpretive processes of situational dynamics are internal to individuals (Taylor, 1999: 71). In other words, citizens' emotional reactions and judgments regarding their local surroundings are a product of their values and prior experiences (Reiss, 1973: 392). The differential distribution of these factors across social grouping explains, at least partially, why those who are least likely to be victimized (i.e., elderly, White females) express the greatest concern, and vice versa (Bureau of Justice Statistics, 1993; Miethe, 1995; Warr, 1984). James Garofalo and John Laub (1978) posit that residents' concern for their community, which is reflected in attitudes toward neighborhood change; perceptions of neighbors' and visitors' behavior; and environmental features such as the presence of litter and trash is intimately connected to "urban unease." Residents who perceive their immediate physical surroundings as deteriorating and view neighborhood inhabitants as unruly will experience higher levels of anxiety and mistrust, which may ultimately lead to social withdrawal and seeking refuge indoors. Put another way, physical decay and social disorder are viewed by many area residents as problematic and, perhaps, even threatening. In his review of the neighborhood research literature, Ralph Taylor (1999: 74) concludes that the psychological approach to understanding the link between incivilities and fear has been consistently supported (e.g., see McGarrell, Giacomazzi, and Thurman, 1997).

What can the police do to quell residents' reactions to disruptions of their quality of life? The simple answer would be for police to rid communities of what local residents define as inappropriate public behavior. This proposition is, more often than not, easier said than done. Nevertheless, research indicates that some efforts toward this end have been successful. Antony Pate's (1986) study in Newark reveals that foot patrol coverage during the evening hours over a one-year period significantly improved residents' perceptions of disorder problems, safety, and crime problems. Similarly, Wesley Skogan's (1990) assessment of Houston's "citizen contact patrol" initiative, which was designed to increase informal contacts between the police and citizens, reveals that citizens in study beats reported lower levels of perceived social and physical disorder, and higher levels of area satisfaction after the program had been up and running for nearly one year. As these results suggest, the police can do things to enhance citizens' quality of life; however, such efforts do not always produce the desired effect.

One of the key philosophical elements of community policing is the careful consideration of citizen input "when making policies and decisions that affect the community" (Cordner, 1999: 138). Police agencies throughout the United States have developed a number of different mechanisms for collecting citizen input, including community surveys and neighborhood meetings. Citizen input can help ensure that police activities are consistent with local values and needs. It also increases police accountability and responsiveness, and helps police officers maintain legitimacy in the community. For police initiatives to be successful at alleviating the adverse effects associated with perceived incivilities, it is imperative that citizen input be as representative as possible, especially in diverse communities.

Research demonstrates that the exclusion (accidental or otherwise) of certain segments of the community can result in undesired outcomes. For example, Skogan (1990: 107) finds that the positive effects of the community policing initiatives in Houston were reserved for home owners and Whites. Upon further analysis, Skogan discovers that those at the bottom rungs of the social ladder were underrepresented in terms of program awareness and frequency of nonemergency contacts with police. He warns that community policing activities may not be appropriate in socially fragmented neighborhoods because "some residents can easily become *targets* of the programs, and they are not likely to be happy about that" (p. 109, emphasis in original). In their evaluation of a community policing program in public housing projects in Philadelphia, a program intended to improve police relations with the local community, Alex Piquero and colleagues (2000) find that citizens' quality-of-life assessments in the experimental sites remained largely unchanged following program implementation. What is more, these residents also rated the police less favorably than did residents of matched comparison areas. The authors conclude that the views of residents of the targeted areas may have felt a "sense of intrusion" resulting from proactive police work in their community (p. 112). It has been documented for some time that adverse perceptions of the police are linked to low quality-of-life assessments among citizens (Block, 1971; see also Cao, Frank, and Cullen, 1996; Reisig and Parks, 2000).

The message of this research is that community policing initiatives will be most effective at addressing the negative affects associated with perceived incivilities if the police are able to establish meaningful working partnerships with a representative cross-section of the community. Only then can the police be assured that their actions are aligned with local values and needs, and then can they reduce the risk of annoying traditionally disenfranchised segments of the community.

Neighborhoods and Community Policing

The incivilities thesis is also investigated at the level of geographic units such as neighborhoods, police beats, Census tracts, and face blocks. This body of literature rests on the proposition that the psychological processes that precede fear of crime and related quality-of-life outcome measures are embedded in local community contexts. Residents of neighborhoods characterized by high levels of incivilities often reside as well in areas experiencing high crime rates. This observation leads some to conclude that crime and incivilities share common structural origins (Hunter, 1978, cited in Taylor, 1999: 67–68). This conjecture finds support in the research literature (Sampson and Raudenbush, 1999; Skogan, 1990: 75).

Most of the aggregate-level research on crime, delinquency, and more recently, incivilities is inspired by the classic work of Clifford Shaw and Henry McKay (1942). Shaw and McKay posit that neighborhood structural characteristics, such as economic status, residential mobility, and ethnic heterogeneity weakened community social organization. Disorganized neighborhoods are structurally deficient because they lack the ability to maintain effective regulative controls and are socially weak in that they are unable to realize common values (Kornhauser, 1978: 120). Local communities that lack social organization, Shaw and McKay hypothesize, would experience higher rates of crime and delinquency.

Of course the macrostructural dynamics influencing neighborhood life today are different from those of yesteryear. William Julius Wilson (1987) argues that processes such as deindustrialization and the out-migration of working and middle-class minority residents from the inner city have produced serious structural constraints for residents of some neighborhoods, including a lack of employment opportunities, low-quality public education, and few conventional role models. These conditions are concentrated in largely African-American, inner-city neighborhoods. What results are homogeneously impoverished communities, plagued by high rates of joblessness and welfare dependency, inhabited by disadvantaged, underclass citizens.

Disadvantaged, disorganized communities lack the social controls necessary to regulate the behavior of residents and visitors. Albert Hunter (1985) identifies three social orders that provide regulative control: private—family and close friends, parochial—neighbors and neighborhood associations, and public—formal governmental bureaucracies. Research shows that the density of friendship networks, frequency of neighboring activities (informal gatherings with fellow residents), informal surveillance (keeping an eye on each others' property), and supervision of neighborhood youths are all associated with lower rates of crime (Bellair, 1997, 2000; Sampson and Groves, 1989). The ecological processes associated with public controls, however, are less well understood.

Neighborhoods with high levels of public social controls are successful in securing "public goods and services that are allocated by agencies located outside the neighborhood" (Bursik and Grasmick, 1993: 17). Public resources include such things as external funding to community organizations and a close working relationship with local police departments. In a recently published study, Maria Velez (2001) reports that public social controls (a perceptual measure reflecting ties to local government and the police) reduced the risks of household and personal victimization, even in structurally disadvantaged neighborhoods. For our purposes it is important to note that Velez's (p. 345) public social control measure included survey questions concerning the police, including: "Do you think the police department tries to provide the kind of services that people in your neighborhood want?" and "How would you rate the overall quality of police services in your neighborhood?" The extent of public social control was judged to be higher in neighborhoods where citizens believed the police provided needed services and where citizens were happy with the service they received.

What can we infer from these research findings with regards to police policy and practice? First, aggressive patrol tactics may be viewed by some as intrusive and inconsistent with community needs, thus further alienating residents in disadvantaged neighborhoods who already report high levels of disaffection with police (Reisig and Parks, 2000; Sampson and Jeglum-Bartusch, 1998; see also Anderson, 1990: 190–206). We might also conclude that such tactics, although perhaps appealing politically, will ultimately prove ineffective at reducing crime and incivilities because they fail to support private and parochial social orders (Hunter, 1985: 239; Sampson and Raudenbush, 1999: 638). Put differently, formal social controls that aim to efficiently catch criminals fail to take into account the fact that all three orders—private, parochial, and public—are highly interdependent (Hunter, 1985: 240). In short, police attempts to address neighborhood ills will be most effective if they successfully unite friends and neighbors to work with police toward a common goal: improve neighborhood quality of life by improving regulative abilities, reducing incivilities and fear of crime, and increasing levels of neighborhood satisfaction. Although sparse, existing evaluation research suggests that such attempts can be successful.

Wesley Skogan and Susan Hartnett's (1997) evaluation of the CAPS program provides one of the most complete neighborhood-level assessments conducted to date. The CAPS program involved numerous community policing initiatives, including permanent assignment of patrol officers to fixed beats, training officers in problem-solving strategies, and the creation of citizen advisory committees and regular neighborhood meetings between residents and police. CAPS was implemented in five experimental police districts that varied in terms of race and income, and differed with regards to the nature of the problems confronting neighborhood residents. In the most disadvantaged experimental district, Englewood, Skogan and Hartnett (pp. 223–224) report that the community's biggest problems declined following the implementation of CAPS. In particular, the percentage of citizens ranking drug selling on the streets as a "big problem" declined from 63 percent in 1993 to only 49 percent in 1994, and concerns regarding "abandoned-building problems" also decreased (from 43 percent to 27 percent). Similar observations were recorded for a second distressed neighborhood, Austin. In the two experimental beats on the opposite end of the socioeconomic spectrum, which were predominately White, the results were less clear. For example, although Rogers Park residents reported marked improvements in street crime, declines in disorder-related problems were modest and similar to the reductions in the comparison area. Skogan and Hartnett (p. 225) note that the measurable reductions in burglary, auto theft, and gang violence in Morgan Park, another affluent area, were not attributable to CAPS.

The ability of police to effectively include citizen input when making decisions regarding policy and practice and to build meaningful, collaborative partnerships with the community has important implications regarding their performance. Using the individual-level orientation of the incivilities thesis as a point of departure, we hypothesize that individuals' evaluations of the ability of the police to establish collaborative partnerships with the community will significantly influence quality-of-life assessments. From our reading of the neighborhood-level literature, we hypothesize that community policing strategies will have a greater chance of success if officials seek the formal and informal cooperation of friends and neighbors. Stated a bit differently, formal social control efforts should seek to integrate parochial and private social orders. One way of doing so is for police to focus on areas where "social worlds collide" (Hunter, 1985: 235–236), such as streets and sidewalks. At the neighborhood level, we hypothesize that neighborhoods where a greater proportion of citizens see police officers out of their cars and either on foot or bike will also evaluate their local surroundings more favorably, reporting higher levels of safety and greater overall satisfaction with their neighborhood.

DATA AND METHODS

Indiana University's Center for Survey Research conducted telephone interviews with 6,125 residents of Indianapolis and St. Petersburg in the summer months of 1996 and 1997. These sites were selected because both cities were implementing community policing (albeit in different ways); both were diverse in social, economic, and demographic terms; and both were receptive to hosting a large research program—the POPN. The sample for the interviews in each city was stratified by boundaries of primary police assignment areas: patrol beats in Indianapolis and community policing areas in St. Petersburg. Each city's assignment areas were drawn to closely match existing neighborhood boundaries given available patrol resources; hereafter, these geographical units are referred to as neighborhoods.

All of the fifty neighborhoods that fall under the jurisdiction of the Indianapolis Police Department were selected for Indianapolis, which also includes some areas with independent police forces that preexisted the creation of metropolitan government in the region. Twelve neighborhoods were included from St. Petersburg, a subset of that city's forty-eight community policing areas. The neighborhood areas included in the overall study ranged from one-fourth mile to nearly five square miles in size, and between 1,169 and 19,808 in population. The survey plan called for completion of 100 interviews in each neighborhood, and 90 or more completions were obtained in fifty-six of the sixty-two neighborhoods. Households were selected randomly from residences with listed telephone numbers. Interviews were completed by telephone with a household respondent selected randomly from among residents eighteen years of age and older. Because of missing information, the original sample size was reduced to 5,938 residents. In the analysis presented here, the number of interviews available within each neighborhood ranged from 56 to 117 (the average was 96).

To determine the distribution of different racial and ethnic groups across neighborhoods in terms of economic well-being, we trichotomized a measure of socioeconomic status into low, medium, and high categories. The original measure was a weighted factor score of three 1990 Census measures: percent high income (exceeding $74,999), percent professional and managerial positions, and percent college degree. We found that predominantly White (greater than 75 percent) neighborhoods were distributed fairly evenly across the socioeconomic status spectrum. Predominantly Black (greater than 75 percent) neighborhoods were found in the low and medium socioeconomic status categories. Mixed neighborhoods (those greater than 30 percent White and greater than 30 percent Black) were in the high socioeconomic status category. Although no set of neighborhoods can be said to typify conditions across America's cities, the neighborhoods included in the analysis capture a wide range of variation in racial composition and socioeconomic status.

Measuring Quality of Life

Quality of life as perceived by neighborhood residents was measured in three ways: by their assessment of incivility problems in the neighborhood, by their perception of how safe they were when walking in their neighborhood at night, and by their assessment of the neighborhood as a place to live. Each of these factors reflects people's judgments about their local surroundings.

To measure incivilities, citizens were asked to judge the current state of six neighborhood problems: litter and trash, loitering, vandalism, gangs, abandoned buildings, and drug dealing. Each of these problems was assessed using a three-point scale ranging from "no problem" to "a major problem." A measure of *perceived incivility* was created by first summing responses across the six items. The alpha reliability for this scale was 0.79. Because it was highly skewed, the measure of perceived incivility was logarithmically transformed. We also computed a *neighborhood incivilities* measure (see Taylor, 1999: 73), by aggregating responses to the six problem questions to the neighborhood level, summing the results (alpha = 0.90), and using the natural log of the index because it also was skewed.

The validity of aggregated perceptual measures of incivilities has become an issue in recent years. To address this concern, researchers assess the convergent validity of multimethod measures of incivilities, such as community surveys and on-site assessments. Although some researchers report that the link between perceptual and on-site assessments is (at best) weak (Piquero, 1999; Taylor, 1999), the most convincing available evidence suggests perceptions of social disorder are highly correlated ($r = 0.71$) with systematic observations of social disorder (Raudenbush and Sampson, 1999: 31). The latter finding lends support to using aggregate citizens' perceptions in neighborhood-level models.

Perceived safety was measured by responses to a single question, "How safe would you feel walking alone in your neighborhood after dark?" There were four response categories, ranging from "very unsafe" to "very safe." This question has been used extensively as a measure of fear of crime, and much of the psychologically oriented research investigating the link between incivilities and fear of crime, as well as community policing evaluation research, relies on it (e.g., McGarrell, Giacomazzi, and Thurman, 1997; Skogan and Maxfield, 1981; Skogan and Hartnett, 1997). Some argue it "more accurately measures the risk to self" and reflects a person's "judgment about the likelihood of criminal victimization" (Ferraro and LaGrange, 1987: 76), but joining this debate is well beyond the scope of this chapter. Because even its critics concede the measure taps personal judgments about inappropriate neighborhood behaviors (criminal or otherwise), the variable seems well suited for an analysis of citizens' quality of life assessments.

Another key measure, *neighborhood rating*, was gauged using responses to the question: "In general, how do you rate your neighborhood as a place to live?" This item included four response categories, ranging from "poor" to "excellent." Similar measures are used by evaluators examining the impact of community policing programs (e.g., see Skogan, 1990: 104).

Measuring Community Policing

We measured two aspects of community policing: the extent to which police and residents worked together on local problems and the use by police of alternatives to motor patrol. We labeled the first aspect *police partnerships* and measured it using responses to two survey items that evaluate citizen and police efforts to form meaningful working relationships. One item asked citizens how many of their neighbors were "willing to cooperate with the police." Five response categories were used, ranging from "almost no one" to "just about everyone." The second question asked citizens to rate the job the police were doing in terms of "working with people in your neighborhood to solve local problems." There were four response categories, ranging from "a poor job" to "an excellent job." The correlation between the two survey items was +0.32. Because the two questions featured a different metric, the items were combined by creating a weighted factor score. This scale reflects citizens' assessments of the two-sided nature of community policing (i.e., the contributions of both citizens and the police).

Our second measure of community policing focused on whether patrol strategies recommended by community policing advocates—foot patrols and bike patrols—were visible in the study neighborhoods. Survey respondents were asked whether they had observed a police officer (1) walking in their neighborhood (i.e., foot patrol) or (2) riding a bicycle (i.e., bike patrol) within the past month. The combination of foot and bike patrol was observed relatively infrequently by citizens, ranging from 0 percent to 27 percent across neighborhoods. Our neighborhood-level community policing factor, *alternative patrol,* was measured by first calculating the percentage of neighborhood respondents who had either seen an officer on foot or bike within the past month. Next, we selected those neighborhoods that scored 1 standard deviation or more above the mean. A measure was then created that identified neighborhoods ($n = 6$) that, comparatively speaking, were the recipients of higher levels of foot and bike patrol.

We rely on self-reports of foot and bike patrol only because we were unable to obtain official police records for patrol deployments. There is evidence to suggest, however, that area residents are well tuned in to alternative patrol practices (see Pate, 1986: 150). Nevertheless, our investigation was carried out after foot and bike patrols were already deployed (and we had no control over deployments), so we have to be concerned with whether alternative patrols were used primarily in neighborhoods without too many "problems." The evidence suggests otherwise. The six neighborhoods designated as receiving higher levels of foot and bike patrol were located throughout the socioeconomic status spectrum. Using the trichotomized neighborhood socioeconomic status measure developed earlier, we found that two were low-socioeconomic status neighborhoods, three were high-socioeconomic-status neighborhoods, and the remaining neighborhood was a medium-socioeconomic-status neighborhood. Thus, alternative patrol activities were found in neighborhoods characterized by different levels of socioeconomic status.

We hypothesize that alternative patrol should improve citizens' quality-of-life assessments because foot and bike patrols put officers in close proximity to the public and thereby increase the likelihood that officers can act in anticipation of neighborhood problems as opposed to merely responding to calls for service. Nevertheless, officers who are on foot and bike also contribute to police presence and, along with their fellow officers in patrol cars, may also deter criminal behavior. Accordingly, we considered including self-reports of car patrols in the measure but found a healthy negative correlation between car patrol and the alternative patrol measure ($r = -0.59$) at the neighborhood level. This finding indicates that citizens' living in residential areas where alternative patrols were more prevalent were less likely to report seeing officers in their cars as compared with citizens residing in other neighborhoods. This issue is revisited when our findings are discussed later in the chapter.

Measuring Neighborhood Context

Neighborhood socioeconomic structure and crime all provide context for the implementation of community policing. To assess the association between quality of life and community policing initiatives requires accounting for the effects of these varying contexts.

We used information from the 1990 Census to account for structural disadvantage and its uneven distribution across urban neighborhoods described by Wilson (1987). We created a measure of *concentrated disadvantage* using a factor score summarizing four 1990 Census figures: percent poor, percent labor force unemployed, percent female-headed families, and percent Black. Each of these items had a relatively large factor loading.

We used the second neighborhood variable to capture neighborhood variations in crime. A *violent crime rate* was calculated using reported incidents of homicide, robbery, aggravated assault, and forcible rape culled from 1995 police records. To better approximate a normal distribution, we analyzed the natural log of violent crime rate per 1,000 neighborhood residents.

Individual Characteristics

There is little doubt that the quality-of-life outcomes used in this analysis are affected by factors other than the community policing variables examined here. To partially adjust for such factors, we included several individual-level features of each respondent in the analysis: gender, race (African-American and other minority), age, education, and home ownership.

ANALYSIS AND FINDINGS

The primary objective of this chapter is to determine whether community policing has positive effects for neighborhood residents. Those effects might be psychological, affecting residents of a given neighborhood in different ways, as well as ecological, affecting all residents in the same way. To test for these effects, we use hierarchical linear modeling (HLM) techniques that allow us to simultaneously estimate the effects of individual- and neighborhood-level independent variables on the outcome measures. The models presented next were estimated using HLM Version 5.04 following modeling procedures outlined by Bryk and Raudenbush (1992: 60–80).

Past research indicates that a salient component of quality of life is neighborhood incivility. Accordingly, we conducted a rigorous test of the effects of community policing by including measures of the extent of perceived incivility at both the citizen and neighborhood levels. We included a host of other measures that may also covary with quality-of-life outcomes, to guard against potential spuriousness. If the effect of variables of interest to our research— police partnership and alternative patrol—remain strong even after controlling for incivilities, individual factors, and other controls, we will conclude that community policing has an effect. Where we observe significant effects in the hypothesized direction, we discuss the magnitude of these effects relative to other factors.

Methodological Issues

A common challenge to ecological research is dealing with typically strong associations among variables measured at the neighborhood level. For example, in our data we observed strong relationships between concentrated disadvantage and violent crime ($r = 0.69$) and the extent of neighborhood incivility ($r = 0.67$). A relationship of similar magnitude was also observed between violent crime rate and neighborhood incivilities ($r = 0.70$). On the one hand, these results support the notion that neighborhood crime and incivilities share common origins. On the other, multicollinearity (those strong correlations among all of the presumably causal factors) creates difficulties when estimating multivariate models.

To investigate the multicollinearity matter, we regressed perceived safety (aggregated to the neighborhood level) on our four neighborhood variables: alternative patrol, violent crime rate, concentrated disadvantage, and neighborhood incivilities. We then calculated conditioning indices to measure the dependency of one variable on the others and variance proportions for each independent variable. We found that all conditioning indices exceeded 0.30 and that none of the independent variables had more than one variance proportion greater than 0.50. These results indicate that, in general, multicollinearity is not a problem in this research (Tabachnick and Fidell, 2001: 98).

To further test whether multicollinearity would bias our findings, we inspected changes in the standard errors of the regression coefficients. To do this we first estimated four single-variable regression models, one model per independent variable. Next, we compared the standard errors for each neighborhood-level independent variable in the single-variable model against the standard error from the full model that included all four variables. If multicollinearity exists, we should see substantially smaller standard errors in the trimmed, single-variable models (Bachman and Paternoster,

1997: 493). When comparing the full model against the trimmed models, the largest change in the standard error was observed for two variables: violent crime rate (from 0.50 to 0.37) and neighborhood incivilities (from 0.25 to 0.18). Overall, these changes do not appear to be substantial. These findings also suggest that multicollinearity among the neighborhood variables is not an issue. At the individual level, bivariate relationships were also examined, and only modest to weak correlations were observed ($r < 0.30$) among them. Finally, we regressed individual's perceived safety on the full set of independent variables: perceived incivilities, police partnership, and individual characteristics. The resulting conditioning indices and variance proportion estimates indicated that multicollinearity was not an issue for individual-level analysis.

Analyses Using HLM

Reliability of Neighborhood Mean Estimates We began the HLM process by assessing whether the variable means computed for each neighborhood were reliable estimates of the true neighborhood means for perceived safety and neighborhood rating (Bryk and Raudenbush, 1992: 63). To do so, reliabilities were averaged across the set of sixty-two neighborhoods. The reliability estimate for each perceived safety was 0.87 and for neighborhood rating it was 0.96. These estimates indicated that the sample means were indeed reliable measures of the true neighborhood means for the quality-of-life measures. This, in turn, provided confidence that neighborhood differences in the outcome measures could be detected with a high degree of precision.

Within- and Between-Neighborhood Variance Components We next determined how much of the variance in the quality-of-life outcome measures was found between neighborhoods, and how much was the result of differences in responses within neighborhoods and of measurement error (see Bryk and Raudenbush, 1992). The intraclass correlation coefficient, Δ, measures the proportion of the total variance in outcomes that is ecological, or between neighborhoods. For perceived safety the value of Δ is 0.07, meaning that 7 percent of the total variance in this outcome lies between neighborhoods and 93 percent is attributable to differences within neighborhoods and to measurement error. For neighborhood rating, the value of Δ is 0.19. The chi-square values for between-neighborhood variance for perceived safety ($\Pi^2 = 480.02$, $p < 0.01$) and neighborhood rating ($\Pi^2 = 1479.41$, $p < 0.01$) reveal sufficient of variation in these outcomes to model each as a function of neighborhood-level factors. These variance component results are consistent with prior research using similar measures (e.g., see Taylor, 1997: 68). Duncan and Raudenbush (1999: 33) note that a relatively small variance between neighborhoods may still admit of a medium to large effect size in the program evaluation sense. Overall, the initial tests and descriptive statistics indicate that the data are appropriate for estimating HLM.

Individual-Level Fixed Effects We next estimated fixed-effects HLM for perceived safety and neighborhood rating. Fixed-effects models assume that each citizen-level variable has the same effect in each neighborhood (i.e., that the value of each regression coefficient does not vary from neighborhood to neighborhood; see Rountree, Land, and Miethe, 1994: 398–403). Because we have clear expectations regarding the relationships between the key variables, we use one-tailed tests of statistical significance ($p < 0.05$).

We begin by focusing on the individual-level effects in both the perceived safety and neighborhood rating models. As expected, perceived incivility was correlated with perceived safety and with neighborhood rating. Not surprising, residents who perceive high levels of social disorder and physical decay are more likely to report they have concerns about their safety and are less satisfied with their neighborhood. These findings are consistent with those of others who examine effects of incivilities on fear (McGarrell, Giacomazzi, and Thurman, 1997; Skogan, 1990; Taylor, 2001: 219–224).

We also find significant community policing effects at the individual level in both models. First, residents who evaluate police partnerships in favorable terms also perceive their neighborhood as more safe. They were also more likely to express higher levels of satisfaction with their neighborhood. It should be noted that the individual-level effects were observed after adjusting for six individual characteristics (e.g., race, age, and education) and neighborhood contextual features. Each individual-level model accounted for more than 25 percent of the within-neighborhood variance in the outcome measures (29 percent for perceived safety and 27 percent for neighborhood rating).

At this point in the analysis we know that perceived incivilities and police partnership significantly influence citizens' quality-of-life assessments. What we do not know, however, is which factor weighs heavier in the minds of the public. To estimate this we calculated standardized regression coefficients (β) for both perceived incivilities and police partnership in each model. In the perceived safety model, perceived incivility was more strongly related to individual safety judgments ($\beta = -0.35$) than was the police partnership variable ($\beta = 0.21$). Similar effects were observed with regards to neighborhood rating: perceived incivilities ($\beta = -0.36$) and police partnership ($\beta = 0.28$). On average, the relationship of perceived incivilities to citizens' quality-of-life assessments was nearly 45 percent stronger in magnitude than was their perception of police partnership. These results, which are expressed in absolute values to emphasize the magnitude of the effect as opposed to the direction, are displayed in Figure 9.1.

Neighborhood-Level Fixed Effects We now turn our attention to the neighborhood-level models. Not surprising, perceptions of safety are significantly lower in racially segregated, impoverished neighborhoods and in neighborhoods plagued with social disorder and physical decay. Violent crime was not related to perceptions of safety after adjustment for concentrated disadvantage and incivilities.

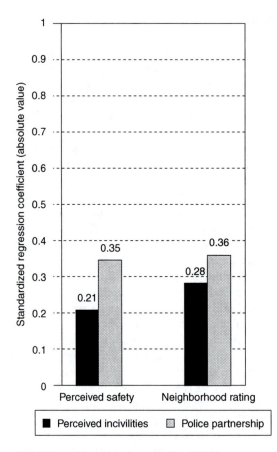

FIGURE 9.1 Citizen-level results (*N* = 5,938).

Similar patterns emerged in the neighborhood rating model. First, a significant relationship was observed between perceived incivilities and neighborhood rating, whereas violent crime rate failed to achieve statistical significance. In the neighborhood rating model, however, concentrated disadvantage was not a significant predictor.

In both models we find some evidence of a community policing effect. Visible police foot and bike patrols were associated with higher perceptions of safety and higher neighborhood ratings. The six neighborhoods where a higher proportion of citizens reported having seen an officer on bike or foot within the past month were also neighborhoods that, net of disadvantage, crime, and incivilities, had higher mean scores for perceived safety and satisfaction with their neighborhood. Both neighborhood-level models explained more than 75 percent of the between-neighborhood variance (80 percent for perceived safety and 76 percent for neighborhood rating, respectively).

In terms of relative importance, the standardized coefficients show that neighborhood incivilities was the strongest neighborhood-level covariate ($\beta =$ −0.54 for perceived safety and −0.75 for neighborhood rating). In comparative

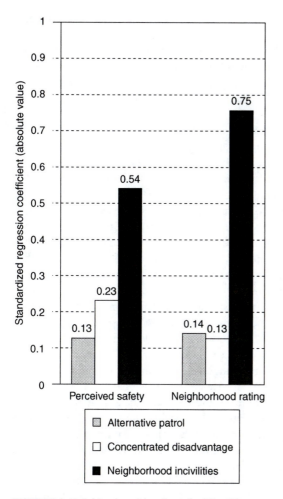

FIGURE 9.2 Neighborhood-level results (N = 62).

terms, the magnitude of the effects of alternative patrol and concentrated disadvantage were weak (see Figure 9.2 for absolute values). Two points should be
emphasized here. First, these findings support the hypothesis that neighborhood-
level community policing initiatives are associated with positive outcomes related
to quality of life. Second, the findings suggest that the neighborhood-level effects
are relatively weak.

Further Tests

In the estimation process discussed previously, the slope estimate for police
partnership in the HLM was constrained so as not to vary across neighborhoods. Doing so requires the assumption that the effect of police partnership
is not a function of neighborhood context. The soundness of this assumption

is questionable. To explore this issue, we reestimated each model discussed previously but this time allowed the slope for police partnership to vary from neighborhood to neighborhood. If between-neighborhood variation was found to exist, we would next test whether this variation was a function of concentrated disadvantage, to learn whether community policing might be, as some suggest, less effective in more distressed neighborhoods (Wilson and Kelling, 1982).

The results (not shown) for the perceived safety model reveal that the slope for police partnership did not vary across neighborhoods. Accordingly, we conclude that police partnership had positive effects on levels of perceived safety even in seriously disadvantaged neighborhoods. In the neighborhood rating model, however, we find evidence that the police partnership slope did vary significantly across neighborhoods. Accordingly, we modeled the slope as a function of concentrated disadvantage. The results reveal that the significance of police partnership persisted. In contrast, concentrated disadvantage did not reach statistical significance. It appears, then, that the positive effects of police partnership on neighborhood rating transcend neighborhood disadvantage. In other words, citizens who rate their partnerships with the police in healthy terms also express greater levels of satisfaction with their immediate surrounding irrespective of the level of structural disadvantage facing them.

Just because we do not find evidence of a multilevel interaction does not mean, however, that evaluations of police partnerships with the community are consistent across different social groupings. To examine this, we regressed police partnership on respondents' individual characteristics: race, gender, age, education, and home ownership. The results from the ordinary least squares model shows that Blacks and other racial minorities, youths, the poorly educated, and renters rated police partnerships in less positive terms. Although statistically significant, the magnitude of these effects is relatively modest (standardized coefficients range from -0.18 to 0.19). Nevertheless, from these results it appears that police partnerships are not perceived equally across ethnic and social groups in the two cities.

Finally, we turn to the issue of police patrol at the neighborhood level. We hypothesized that alternative patrols, such as officers on foot and bike, put officers in closer proximity to citizens—perhaps enabling them to anticipate neighborhood problems and putting them in a better position to enlist the cooperation of other—thus melding the public, private, and parochial social orders. Others, however, contend that foot and bike patrols are effective because they contribute to police presence. If this is the case, the visibility of car patrols may also be associated with higher quality-of-life assessments at the neighborhood level. To test this hypothesis, we constructed a neighborhood-level police patrol car measure by identifying survey respondents who reported they had seen an officer patrolling by automobile in their neighborhood within the past month, and we aggregated these scores to the neighborhood level. This measure of *car patrol* is the proportion of respondents who reported seeing a patrol car in their neighborhood. Next, we entered car patrol into a means as outcomes regression model (see Bryk and Raudenbush, 1992: 18–20), which also included concentrated disadvantage, violent crime rate, and neighborhood incivilities. The analysis revealed that visible car patrol had no effect on neighborhood quality of life. In light of the lack of evidence to the contrary, we maintain that alternative patrols were effective in the eyes of the citizens, not because this practice contributed to perceived police presence but because such activities provide police with more opportunities to communicate with local citizens in a meaningful way.

DISCUSSION

We began this chapter by outlining two versions of the incivilities thesis—one focused on individual reactions, and the second on neighborhoods. We then considered potential benefits of community policing in each context. At the citizen level, we measured community policing using respondents' assessments of police partnerships with area residents. Community policing at the neighborhood level was measured using the proportion of respondents who reported seeing police officers on bicycle patrols or walking around. The relationships of these community policing measures with indicators of citizens' quality of life were assessed at both citizen and neighborhood levels using cross-sectional data and multilevel modeling techniques.

We find that visible community policing was positively related to quality of life at both individual and neighborhood levels. Respondents who believe that a healthy level of collaborative relations between citizens and the police exist to address neighborhood problems feel safer and express greater satisfaction with their local surroundings. We find no evidence to suggest that these positive effects of police partnerships are less pronounced in neighborhoods characterized by structural disadvantage. Put differently, individual perceptions of collaborative partnerships were related positively to feelings of safety and higher neighborhood ratings whether a person resided in a more affluent neighborhood where community policing might be easy to implement or in an impoverished neighborhood where its successful implementation might be questioned. In light of these findings, we conclude that community policing can have a positive impact on the psychological processes responsible for citizens' quality-of-life judgments.

Comparing community policing across neighborhoods, we find alternative patrol strategies advocated by community policing reformers (e.g., Trojanowicz et al., 1998: 6) to be associated with higher levels of perceived safety and more positive feelings regarding neighborhood surroundings. Similar to Sampson and Raudenbush (1999: 638) and others working in the social disorganization tradition (Bursik and Grasmick, 1993: 173–175; Hunter, 1985; Velez, 2001), we observe that community policing initiatives can have positive neighborhood-level effects. Our findings show these effects were weak relative to those of neighborhood conditions, but statistically significant. Our findings, therefore, are consistent with Taylor's (1997: 69) contention that a large portion of the variation between citizens in their perceived quality of life is linked to differential police activities among neighborhoods (cf. Duncan and Raudenbush, 1999: 33).

There are some important limitations regarding our analyses. First, the results reported were derived from data gathered at one point in time. Accordingly, we claim only to have observed associations between community policing activities and citizen quality of life. We cannot demonstrate, for example, that alternative patrol strategies caused higher mean levels of perceived safety. To make such claims, we would have had to employ a quasi-experimental design with neighborhoods matched according to important structural features, implementation of community policing initiatives carried out with systematic variation, and pre- and post-testing of measurable effects. We note, however, that our findings are consistent with others reporting positive community policing effects using similar methods, although they study fewer neighborhoods (e.g., see Skogan, 1990).

Because of the one-point-in-time nature of our research, we must consider two competing hypotheses. The first, mentioned previously, is that alternative patrols were implemented in neighborhoods where citizens already experienced comparatively higher levels of quality of life. The evidence showed that this was not the case. The second, rival hypothesis is that citizens' quality-of-life assessments influenced their evaluations of police partnerships. Unfortunately, the research design employed here does not allow us to rule out this possibility.

Another concern is the use of citizens' perceptions and self-reports to construct community policing measures. Our measure, police citizen collaboration, is itself an outcome measure—an evaluation made by neighborhood residents of the efforts of police and citizens to work together to address local problems. It is uncertain the extent to which these survey-based assessments would closely match administrative records and other, independent measures of the extent and effectiveness of community policing efforts.

One instance in which we can compare resident's perceptions with an alternative measure of community policing effectiveness involves responses to our survey of police officers. Police officers who worked in the study neighborhoods were also surveyed, and they were asked questions similar to those posed to citizens regarding collaborative, working partnerships. Officers were asked: "How many citizens are willing to work with police" and "How many citizens would provide information to police?" At the neighborhood level, which is the common level of measurement, the correlation between citizen reports and officer reports is $+0.61$. Although there is concern about our citizen-based measure of police citizen collaboration, we gain additional confidence in it from this level of agreement. Of course, other alternative measures of the relationship between police and citizens, if available, could have been used to further test the validity of the citizen survey measure. Examples include assessments made by community leaders (see Scott, 2002) and observations made by trained observers at neighborhood meetings (see Skogan and Hartnett, 1997). Future assessments investigating the matter should combine measures from a variety of perspectives.

Our results support the use of informal modes of policing that seek to strengthen ties between community members and the police. We find that such initiatives are associated with positive outcomes not only in affluent residential settings. They may also improve the quality of life in disadvantaged neighborhoods. In the eyes of the public, community policing appears to hold promise.

CITATIONS

Anderson, Elijah. 1990. *Streetwise: Race, Class, and Change in an Urban Community.* Chicago: University of Chicago Press.

Bachman, Ronet and Raymond Paternoster. 1997. *Statistical Methods for Criminology and Criminal Justice.* New York: McGraw-Hill.

Bellair, Paul E. 1997. "Social Interaction and Community Crime: Examining the Importance of Neighbor Networks." *Criminology,* 35: 677–704.

Bellair, Paul E. 2000. "Informal Surveillance and Street Crime: A Complex Relationship." *Criminology,* 38: 137–169.

Block, Richard L. 1971. "Fear of Crime and Fear of the Police." *Social Problems,* 19: 91–101.

Bryk, Anthony S. and Stephen W. Raudenbush. 1992. *Hierarchical Linear Models: Applications and Data Analysis Methods.* Newbury Park, CA: Sage.

Bureau of Justice Statistics. 1993. *Highlights from Twenty Years of Surveying Crime Victims.* Washington, DC: U.S. Department of Justice.

Bursik, Robert J., Jr. and Harold G. Grasmick. 1993. *Neighborhoods and Crime.* Lanham, MD: Lexington.

Cao, Liqun, James Frank, and Francis T. Cullen. 1996. "Race, Community Context and Confidence in the Police." *American Journal of Police,* 15: 3–22.

Cordner, Gary W. 1999. "Elements of Community Policing." In Larry K. Gaines and Gary W. Cordner (Eds.), *Policing Perspectives: An Anthology.* Los Angeles: Roxbury, 137–149.

Duncan, Greg J. and Stephen W. Raudenbush. 1999. "Assessing the Effects of Context in Studies of Child and Youth Development." *Educational Psychologist,* 34: 29–41.

Ferraro, Kenneth F. and Randy LaGrange. 1987. "The Measurement of Fear of Crime." *Sociological Inquiry,* 57: 70–101.

Garofalo, James and John Laub. 1978. "The Fear of Crime: Broadening Our Perspective." *Victimology,* 3: 242–253.

Hunter, Albert. 1985. "Private, Parochial, and Public Social Orders: The Problem of Crime and Incivility in Urban Communities." In Gerald D. Suttles and Mayer N. Zald (Eds.), *The Challenge of Social Control: Citizenship and Institution Building in Modern Society.* Norwood, NJ: Ablex, 230–242.

Kornhauser, Ruth Rosner. 1978. *Social Sources of Delinquency: An Appraisal of Analytic Models.* Chicago: University of Chicago Press.

McGarrell, Edmund F., Andrew L. Giacomazzi, and Quint C. Thurman. 1997. "Neighborhood Disorder, Integration, and the Fear of Crime." *Justice Quarterly,* 14: 479–500.

Miethe, Terance D. 1995. "Fear and Withdrawal from Urban Life." *Annals of the American Academy of Political and Social Sciences,* 539: 14–27.

Pate, Anthony M. 1986. "Experimenting with Foot Patrol: The Newark Experience." In Dennis Rosenbaum (Ed.), *Community Crime Prevention: Does It Work?* Beverly Hills, CA: Sage, 137–156.

Piquero, Alex. 1999. "The Validity of Incivility Measures in Public Housing." *Justice Quarterly,* 16: 793–818.

Piquero, Alex, Jack Greene, James Fyfe, Robert J. Kane, and Patricia Collins. 2000. "Implementing Community Policing in Public Housing Developments in Philadelphia: Some Early Results." In Geoffrey P. Alpert and Alex R. Piquero (Eds.), *Community Policing: Contemporary Readings,* 2nd edition. Prospect Heights, IL: Waveland, 95–122.

Raudenbush, Stephen W. and Robert J. Sampson. 1999. "Ecometrics: Toward a Science of Assessing Ecological Settings, with Application to the Systematic Social Observation of Neighborhoods." *Sociological Methodology,* 29: 1–41.

Reisig, Michael D. and Roger B. Parks. 2000. "Experience, Quality of Life, and Neighborhood Context: A Hierarchical Analysis of Satisfaction with Police." *Justice Quarterly,* 17: 607–630.

Reiss, Albert J, Jr. 1973. "Monitoring the Quality of Criminal Justice Systems." In Angus Campbell and Philip Converse (Eds.), *The Human Meaning of Social Change.* New York: Sage, 388–403.

Rountree, Pamela Wilcox, Kenneth C. Land, and Terance D. Miethe. 1994. "Macro-Micro Integration in the Study of Victimization: A Hierarchical Logistic Model Analysis Across Seattle Neighborhoods." *Criminology,* 32: 387–414.

Sampson, Robert J. and W. Byron Groves. 1989. "Community Structure and Crime: Testing Social-Disorganization Theory." *American Journal of Sociology,* 94: 774–802.

Sampson, Robert J. and Dawn Jeglum-Bartusch. 1998. "Legal Cynicism and Subcultural Tolerance of Deviance: The Neighborhood Context of Racial Differences." *Law and Society Review,* 32: 777–804.

Sampson, Robert J. and Stephen W. Raudenbush. 1999. "Systematic Social Observation of Public Spaces: A New Look at Disorder in Urban Neighborhoods." *American Journal of Sociology,* 105: 603–651.

Sampson, Robert J., Stephen W. Raudenbush, and Felton Earls. 1997. "Neighborhoods and Violent Crime: A Multilevel Study of Collective Efficacy." *Science,* 277: 918–924.

Scott, Jason D. 2002. "Assessing the Relationship Between Police-Community Coproduction and Neighborhood-Level Social Capital." *Journal of Contemporary Criminal Justice,* 18: 147–166.

Shaw, Clifford R. and Henry D. McKay. 1942. *Juvenile Delinquency and Urban Areas.* Chicago: University of Chicago Press.

Skogan, Wesley G. 1990. *Disorder and Decline: Crime and the Spiral of Decay in American Neighborhoods.* Berkeley, CA: University of California Press.

Skogan, Wesley G. and Susan M. Hartnett. 1997. *Community Policing, Chicago Style.* New York and London: Oxford University Press.

Skogan, Wesley G. and Michael G. Maxfield. 1981. *Coping with Crime.* Beverly Hills, CA: Sage.

Tabachnick, Barbara G. and Linda S. Fidell. 2001. *Using Multivariate Statistics,* 4th edition. Boston, MA: Allyn and Bacon.

Taylor, Ralph B. 1997. "Crime, Grime, and Responses to Crime: Relative Impacts of Neighborhood Structure, Crime, and Physical Deterioration on Residents and Business Personnel in the Twin Cities." In Steven P. Lab (Ed.), *Crime Prevention at the Crossroads.* Cincinnati, OH: Anderson, 63–75.

Taylor, Ralph B. 1999. *The Incivilities Thesis: Theory, Measurement, and Policy,* in *Measuring What Matters.* Washington, DC: U.S. Department of Justice.

Taylor, Ralph B. 2001. *Breaking Away from Broken Windows.* Boulder, CO: Westview.

Trojanowicz, Robert, Victor E. Kappeler, Larry K. Gaines, and Bonnie Bucqueroux. 1998. *Community Policing: A Contemporary Perspective.* 2nd edition. Cincinnati, OH: Anderson.

Velez, Maria B. 2001. "The Role of Public Social Control in Urban Neighborhoods: A Multi-Level Analysis of Victimization Risk." *Criminology,* 39: 837–864.

Warr, Mark. 1984. "Fear of Victimization: Why are Women and the Elderly More Afraid?" *Social Science Quarterly,* 65: 681–702.

Wilson, James Q. and George L. Kelling. 1982. "Broken Windows: The Police and Neighborhood Safety." *The Atlantic Monthly,* 127: 29–38.

Wilson, William Julius. 1987. *The Truly Disadvantaged.* Chicago: University of Chicago Press.

Index

administrative policing, 31
administrative subculture, 145–46, 151
advisory committees, 10
alternative patrol, 215
analytic process of reform, 153
area-based strategy, 14
The Audit Commission (1999), 174
Aurora, Illinois, 82–104
autonomy, 140

battered women's programs, 16
beat boundaries, 21
beat meetings, 58–60
    attendants of, 60–63
    neighborhood impact of, 69–73
    observations and participant survey,
        74–75
    police concerns and, 66–69
    representation of neighborhood
        concerns and, 63–66
behavior dimension, 195
Britain, community policing in, 165–81
broken windows model, 15, 154
    coercion and, 129, 112–13
    in Indianapolis, 117
    vs. partnership model, 115–17
Brookes, Steve, 171
bureaucratic process of reform, 153

CAMPS, 166
CAPS, 63, 66, 68–71, 212
car patrol, 222–23
centralization, 30, 43–45
change(s)
    in dimensions of work, 92
    management and supervisory, 91–92
    receptivity to, 92
    theories of, 80–83
Chicago, community policing and, 58–74
"choir practice," 140
civilian subculture, 146–49, 152
closed systems, 39–41
code enforcement, 16
coercion, 110
    community policing and, 111–15
    definition of, 122
    effects of community policing on,
        125–30
    encounter characteristics and, 124–25
    influences on, 123–25
    measuring, 119–23
    officer characteristics and, 123–24
    study on, 115–19
    suspect characteristics and, 124
    training and, 128
collaboration of partnerships, 10
community partnerships, 9–10

Community Policing Consortium, 3
community policing
    adoption trends in, 3
    arrests and, 114
    attitudes regarding, 107
    community of, 166
    cultural challenges to, 151–53
    defining, 4–6
    explanation of, 45–46
    impact of environment on, 41–42
    impediments to adopting, 42
    information requirements for, 46
    measuring, 123, 215–16
    objectives of, 4
    philosophy of, 31
    residents and, 208–10
    risks and, 23–24
    shape of, 25–26
    special units in, 81–82
    street-level, 96–98
community-oriented activities, 95–96
community representation, 57–74
complexity, in organizations, 42–43
computerization, 47
concentrated disadvantage, 216
confidential hotlines, 16
consolidation, 153–57
cooperative truancy reduction programs, 16
coordination of partnerships, 10
COPS Office. See Office of Community
    Oriented Policing Services
cosmopolitanism, 25
Crime Act. See Violent Crime Control and
    Law Enforcement Act
Crime and Disorder Act (1998), 174
crime control, 37
crime prevention, 15–18, 38
Crime Prevention through Environmental
    Design (CPTED), 15
Crime Reduction Program
    (1999–2002), 174
cultural process of reform, 153
customer-based approach, 32

data analysis strategy, 90–91
decision making, 44
differentiation, 43
disorderly behavior, 208

Eck-Clarke Common Problem
    Classification Scheme, 195–96,
    203–6
ecological research, 217
effectiveness of problem-oriented policing,
    174–78

efficiency of problem-oriented policing,
    179–80
empty-holster cops, 151
encounter characteristics, coercion and,
    124–25
enforcement, 13
environment dimension, 195
environments, police organizations and,
    39–42
equity of problem-oriented policing,
    178–79
evaluation design, 87–88
evaluations of police interventions, 199–200
expert COP subculture, 149–50

fixed effects models, 219–21
formalism, 30
formalization, 43–44
fragmentation, 153–57
Frazier, Thomas, 167

geo-deployment, 21
geographic accountability, 85
Geographic Information System (GIS)
    software, 11
Goldstein, Herman, 10, 31, 168

Her Majesty's Inspectorate of
    Constabulary (1998), 174
hierarchical linear modeling (HLM),
    217, 218–21
horizontal differentiation, 43

impact coercion, 122
incivilities thesis, 208, 210–23
Indiana University's Center for Survey
    Research, 213
Indianapolis, Indiana, 117–32, 208–25
individual-level effects, 219
individual-level orientation, 212
industrial model, 33–34
information sharing, 9–10
in-person officer interviews, 118, 119
institutional shifts, vs. organizational
    change, 36–39
intelligence, policing and, 46
internal consistency, 7
iterative process of reform, 153

job dimensions, 106
job enrichment theory/model, 80–81, 82
job satisfaction, 93–94, 107
Joliet, Illinois, 82–104

King, Rodney, 112

Law Enforcement Assistance
Administration, 15
local theory of change, 81–83

management changes, 91–92
management policies, implementation of,
106–7
mediation, 16
methods of program implementation,
87–91
military model, 33–34
mission statements, 23
model of innovation, 25
multicollinearity, 217–18

National Institute of Justice, 22
National Institute of Law Enforcement
and Criminal Justice, 15
Neighborhood Area Resource
Coordinator (NARC), 14
Neighborhood Enhancement Teams
(NETs), 9
neighborhood incivilities, 214
neighborhood-level models, 219–21
Neighborhood-Oriented Policing (NOP)
units, 82–85, 92, 102
neighborhood rating, 214
neighborhoods, 207–8
community policing and, 210–13
HLM analysis of, 218–21
impact of beat meetings on, 69–73
NOP units. *See* Neighborhood-Oriented
Policing units

Office of Community Oriented Policing
Services (COPS Office), 3–6, 79, 189
officer characteristics, coercion and 123–24
officer friendly approach, 16, 112
officer survey measures, 106–8
open systems, 39, 40, 41
opportunistic subculture, 143–44, 152
organization change(s), 18–24, 30–50
vs. industrial shifts, 36–39
from traditional to community, 33–36
organizational complexity, 42–43
organizational model, 34
organizational reform, 79–91
methods for, 87–91
results of, 91–98
organizations, environments and, 39–42

paramilitary subculture, 141–43, 151–52, 156
partnership model, 113, 118
vs. broken windows model, 115–17
partnerships, 6–10, 42

patrol observations, 118–19
Peel, Sir Robert, 165
peer emulation, 25
perceived incivility, 214
perceived safety, 214
perceived safety models, 222
performance criteria, 22
phantom subculture, 150–51
physical coercion, 122
physical decay, 208
police
beat meetings and, 66–69
distrust of, 35
police agencies, as control-centered
bureaucracies, 35
police culture, 136–37
challenges to community policing,
151–53
development of, 155
fragmentation of. *See* police subcultures
traditional, 137–38, 140–41
Police Executive Research Forum
(PERF), 13, 85, 189
police partnerships, 215
police researchers, 200–201
police roles, community views and, 94–95
police subcultures, 139
administrative, 145–46, 151
civilian, 146–49, 152
expert COP, 149–50
future of, 153–57
opportunistic, 143–44, 152
paramilitary, 141–43, 151–52, 156
remnants of traditional culture, 140–41
weak community-oriented, 150–51
police survey measure, 88
police work, changing the nature of, 45–48
policing
alternatives to, 155–57
customer-based approach, 32
history of, 30–31
industrial model, 33–34
institutional change in, 36–39
institutional premise of, 49
intelligence and, 46
military model, 33–34
organizational model, 34
shifts in, 36–48
traditional, 45
from traditional to community, 33–36
policing process of reform, 153
POPN. *See* Project on Policing
Neighborhoods
prevention, 15–18, 38
preventive problem solving, 14

primary intervention, 46
problem classification scheme, 194–97
problem solving, 10–15, 96, 154
  difficulties in, 190–93
  information sources for, 98
  intelligence and, 46
  knowledge and behaviors of, 107–8
  preventive, 14
  problems of, 189–94
  variation in, 47
problem-oriented policing, 185–86
  community policing and, 165–81, 187
  defining, 186–87
  effectiveness of, 187–89
  limitations of, 174–80
  researchers and, 200–201
  solving problems, 194–200
problems
  analysis of, 197–99
  defining, 194
problem-solving partnerships, 9, 42
professional policing, 154
professionalism, 34
program implementation, 87
Project on Policing Neighborhoods
  (POPN), 117, 213
public resources, 211

quality of life, 207
  community policing and, 208–13
  measuring, 214
quality-of-life policing, 154

reform, processes of, 153
reliability, 218
researchers, 200–201
resident involvement, 57–58
  community policing and, 208–10
  concerns about neighborhood
    conditions, 63–66
  concerns about police, 66–69
  in Chicago, 58–60
  neighborhood impact of, 69–73
  resident representation, 60–63

results of program implementation, 91
risk mediation, 25

SARA model, 11
secondary intervention, 46
single-variable regression models, 217–18
spatial dispersion, 43
special units, 23–24, 81–82
specialization, 30
split-force model, 47, 49
St. Petersburg, Florida, 117–32, 208–25
stop-and-frisk reports, 113–14
street-level community policing, 96–98
subcultures. *See* police subcultures
Sunbelt City Police Department
  (SCPD), 137
supervisory changes, 91–92
suspect characteristics, coercion and, 124
systems, open vs. closed, 39–41

Taylor, Fredrick, 80
traditional police culture, 137–38,
  140–41
traditional policing, 45
traditional subculture, 152
training, coercion and, 128

uncivil behavior, 208
urban unease, 209
us-versus-them view, 140–41

value statements, 23
variance components, 218
verbal coercion, 122
vertical differentiation, 43
victim assistance, 16
Violent Crime Control and Law
  Enforcement Act (1994), 3
violent crime rate, 216

weak community-oriented subculture,
  150–51

zero tolerance, 14, 37